Child Development in Practice

Child Development in Practice

Edited by

Ioanna Palaiologou
& Cathryn Knight

3rd Floor
HYLO
103–105 Bunhill Row
London, EC1Y 8LZ
UK

2455 Teller Road
Thousand Oaks
California 91320

10th Floor, Emaar Capital Tower
2 MG Road, Sikanderpur, Sector 26
Gurugram, Haryana – 122002
India

8 Marina View Suite 43-053
Asia Square Tower 1
Singapore 018960

Editor: James Clark
Assistant editor: Harry Dixon
Production editor: Nicola Marshall
Copyeditor: Sarah Bury
Marketing manager: Lorna Patkai
Cover design: Wendy Scot
Typeset by: C&M Digitals (P) Ltd, Chennai, India
Printed in the UK

Library of Congress Control Number: 2025950630

British Library Cataloguing in Publication data

A catalogue record for this book is available from the British Library

ISBN 978-1-0362-1576-7
ISBN 978-1-0362-1575-0 (pbk)

Contents

Acknowledgements

In this journey of creating this book, we would like to express our deepest gratitude to the team at Sage Publishing for their unwavering support and commitment to this project. A heartfelt thank you also goes to all the contributing authors, whose enthusiasm and dedication have been instrumental in bringing this book to life.

We are especially grateful to our husbands for their patience, encouragement and support throughout the process. Their understanding during long hours of writing and editing has meant the world to us.

About the editors

Ioanna Palaiologou

Ioanna Palaiologou is an Associate Professor at the School of Education (Psychology in Education), University of Bristol. She is also a Chartered Psychologist with the British Psychological Society with specialism in child development and learning theories. Her research interests focus on ethics, child development, the role of digital technologies and implications on pedagogy.

Cathryn Knight

Cathryn Knight is an Associate Professor at the School of Education (Psychology in Education), University of Bristol. Her research focuses on inclusive education and special educational needs. She is committed to advancing equity and inclusion in educational policy and practice.

About the contributors

Shazza Ali

Shazza Ali is a Lecturer in Psychology in Education at the University of Bristol. Her research interests include positive psychology, positive emotions and prosocial behaviours in children and young people, the arts and creativity, intergroup relations and group processes.

Monica Cheng

Monica Cheng is a postgraduate researcher in Education at the University of Bristol, whose research explores children and adolescents' development and wellbeing. She is also the founder and director of a child development centre in Hong Kong, where she has pioneered innovative practices to support children's holistic development. Her research focuses on student wellbeing, educational leadership and policy, and the integration of wellbeing initiatives into mainstream education.

Olga Fotakopoulou

Olga Fotakopoulou is an Associate Professor of Developmental Psychology at Birmingham City University's College of Psychology. She is also a Chartered Psychologist with the British Psychological Society with specialism in the development of children and young people. Her research focuses on the social and emotional development of children, as well as their interactions with new technologies and the subsequent impact on their development.

Carolina Gordillo-Bravo

Dr Carolina Gordillo-Bravo is a Lecturer (Psychology in Education) in the School of Education, University of Bristol. She researches neuroscience and the science of learning, with a focus on educational design and game-based learning. Her work explores how games enhance declarative memory and learning outcomes.

Elena Hoicka

Elena Hoicka is a Professor at the School of Education (Psychology in Education) at the University of Bristol. Her research focuses on the early years, including humour, creativity, pretend play, social cognition and parent–child interaction.

Philippa L. Howard

Philippa Howard is a Senior Lecturer in Psychology in Education at the University of Bristol. Her research explores language processing differences associated with autism, focusing on reading comprehension. She aims to uncover why autistic individuals often face challenges in understanding written text in order to inform inclusive education practices.

Emma Jenks

Emma Jenks is a Lecturer in Psychology in Education at the University of Bristol. Her research interests include lived experiences of neurodiversity, participatory approaches and inclusive higher education.

Fidelia Law

Fidelia Law is a Lecturer at the University of Bristol, teaching Psychology of Education. Her research addresses educational inequality and promotes inclusion in STEM. She collaborates with community organisations and informal learning sites to empower youth as change agents for a more equitable, sustainable future.

Felicity Sedgewick

Felicity Sedgewick is an Associate Professor in Neurodiversity in Education in the School of Education, University of Bristol. Her work focuses on the relationships and mental health of neurodivergent people, particularly women, non-binary people and university students, and ways to support positive life experiences for these groups. She is committed to participatory practices and research which reflects community priorities.

Esmé Sung

Esmé Sung is a Lecturer in Psychology of Education at School of Education, University of Bristol and a Chartered Psychologist. Her research explores resilience, positive psychology, student engagement, emotional expression and regulation, wellbeing, personal growth and career development.

Maria Tsapali

Maria Tsapali is a Senior Lecturer in Psychology in Education in the School of Education at the University of Bristol. She is a Chartered Psychologist of the British Psychological Society specialising in cognitive development and learning sciences. Her research focuses on the use of cognitive science to design effective learning environments.

Preface

Child development is a vital area of study for professionals across education, psychology, social work and health care. In the 21st century, understanding how children grow, learn and interact with their environments is more important than ever. Rapid technological change, shifting social structures, global migration, and increasing awareness of mental health and neurodiversity have all contributed to a more complex developmental landscape in which children develop. As such, the study of child development must evolve to reflect these realities.

This book introduces critical topics of child development through a multidisciplinary lens. Written by psychologists and researchers with extensive experience, it offers both foundational knowledge and contemporary insights. It is designed to support students in developing a nuanced understanding of child development and to serve as a valuable resource for lecturers and practitioners working with children, particularly in the area of education.

The chapters cover key theories and concepts that have shaped the field, while also encouraging critical engagement with dominant paradigms, particularly those rooted in Western, Educated, Industrialised, Rich, Democratic (WEIRD) contexts. By challenging these assumptions, the book invites readers to consider how child development, and its surrounding theory and research, is influenced by cultural, environmental and socio-political factors that extend beyond traditional psychological frameworks.

Although the book is organised into chapters that explore each aspect of development separately, it is essential to emphasise that child development is holistic. Each domain – cognitive, emotional, social and physical – interacts dynamically, influencing and shaping one another. As the chapters will demonstrate, no area of development occurs in isolation. Moreover, factors such as culture, environment, socio-economic conditions and political contexts play a central role in shaping developmental trajectories. Understanding these interconnections is key to supporting children effectively and ethically in diverse settings.

Beginning with Chapter 1 Understanding Development, the book lays the groundwork for conceptualising development in childhood. Chapter 2 continues with Key Debates in Child Development, highlighting the complexities and evolving nature of the field.

Chapter 3 discusses the methodologies and ethical considerations in Researching Child Development, while Chapter 4 examines the Influential Factors that shape developmental trajectories.

Neurodivergence is thoughtfully explored in Chapter 5, and in Chapter 6 The Role of Neuroscience is discussed as a key way of understanding developmental processes.

Physical and emotional development are addressed in Chapters 7 and 8. Chapter 9, focuses on Attachment and Adverse Childhood Experiences, a vital area for professionals working with vulnerable children.

Social development is the focus of Chapter 10 while Chapter 11 explores Memory, Attention and Perception. Chapter 12 provides insights into Language Development, a cornerstone of cognitive and social growth.

Finally, Chapter 13 brings a unique lens to Play and Humour, highlighting their importance in children's emotional and social lives.

This book does not merely present child development as a static body of knowledge, it encourages readers to think critically, reflect deeply and engage with the diverse realities of children's lives. It is a guide for students and a companion for educators, aiming to foster inclusive, culturally responsive and evidence-informed practices in the study and support of child development.

How to study this book

Studying child development is not just about memorising theories – it is about understanding the complex, interconnected ways children grow, learn and experience the world. *Child Development in Practice* is designed to guide you through this journey, one chapter at a time, helping you to build a deep and reflective understanding of the subject.

The book is structured into 13 chapters, each focusing on a different aspect of development, but before diving into the specific domains like memory, language or social development, it's essential to begin with the foundations.

Start with **Chapters 1, 2 and 3**. These chapters are your compass. They introduce the core concepts of development, the key debates that shape the field and the research methods used to study children. As you read, take time to pause at the reflection points. These are not just questions – they are invitations to think critically, to connect theory with your own experiences or observations and to begin forming your own perspective on what development means.

Once you have built that foundation, move on to **Chapter 4**, which explores the powerful influence of culture, environment, socio-economic status and political contexts. These are not background details – they are central to how children develop. Understanding these factors will help you to see development not as a universal path but as a journey shaped by context.

From there, the book takes you into the heart of contemporary child development. **Chapter 5** challenges traditional deficit-based views of neurodivergence, encouraging you to think inclusively and respectfully about difference. **Chapter 6** introduces the role of neuroscience, showing how biology and brain science underpin many aspects of development.

The next set of chapters – **7 to 12** – delve into the specific domains of physical, emotional, social and cognitive development. You will explore how children form attachments, how they regulate emotions, how they interact socially, and how they develop memory, attention and language. These chapters are rich with examples, research and reflection points. As you read, look for connections. For example, how does emotional development influence memory? How does language shape social interaction?

Finally, **Chapter 13** brings everything together through the lens of play and humour. It is an insightful chapter that reminds us that development is not just about milestones – it is about meaning, creativity and connection.

Throughout the book, you will find questions to consider and reflection points to guide your thinking.

1

Understanding child development

Ioanna Palaiologou and Cathryn Knight

Chapter objectives

By the end of the chapter, you will gain:

- A comprehensive overview on development.
- An understanding of the origins and evolution of developmental psychology.
- An introduction to key developmental theories from across the world.
- A critical examination of theories.

Overview of the chapter

This chapter will cover human development from a historical perspective, the origins of the science of development and current perspectives in the 21st century, including the consideration of the advantages of technology. Key theories relevant to the study of development, such as cognitive, social and biological neuroscience psychology, will be introduced. The chapter will discuss how development has a holistic nature. It will also offer criticism on some of the key theories covered, including the emphasis on Western, Educated, Industrialised, Rich and Democratic (WEIRD) research and review the ethics employed in some studies of development.

Why should you read this chapter?

By reading this chapter, you will not only gain a broad understanding of development, but also appreciate the complexities and nuances that come with studying human growth and behaviour. It will equip you with the critical thinking skills necessary to evaluate and apply developmental theories and practices effectively.

What is development?

The field of human development has been the subject of interest by many disciplines across the centuries. Sociology, for example, examines how social structures, relationships and cultural contexts impact human development. Meanwhile, education focuses on creating learning environments that can support development and anthropology provides cultural and evolutionary perspectives. This chapter focuses on the psychological perspective of development, viewing it as the systematic continuities and changes in the individual that occur across the lifespan, including biological, physical, cognitive, social and emotional growth.

In psychology, particularly developmental psychology, human development refers to the scientific study of the psychological changes that occur in humans as they grow. As will be shown in Chapter 2, however, the study of human development is dominated by many debates and diverse views. This field examines various stages and aspects of development, including cognitive, emotional and behavioural changes, as well as the influence of genetics, neuroscience (see Chapter 6) and the environment on these processes (see Chapter 4). All these topics will be explored in detail in the following chapters in the book.

Child development is the process through which children undergo biological, physical, cognitive, emotional and social changes from birth to adolescence. It involves the progression of skills and abilities such as motor skills, language, problem-solving and social interactions. According to Baltes et al. (1980), three goals of developmental psychology are to describe, explain and optimise development.

Key focuses in child psychology are, first, *maturation*, which refers to the natural developmental process driven by genetics that leads to physical, behavioural and psychological growth independent of learning or experience (Singh, 2024). Second, the study of child development focuses on both patterns of change, known as *normative development* (Bickhard, 2006), and individual variations in patterns of change, known as *ideographic development* (Jiwen, 2024). In developmental psychology, the focus is on understanding the important ways that developing children resemble each other and how they are likely to differ as they proceed through life (more on this in Chapter 5).

Historical perspective on human development

The study of human development has a rich and multifaceted history that dates back to ancient times, yet its formal scientific origins began to take shape in the late 19th and early 20th centuries. The ancient Greek philosophers, such as Socrates, Plato and Aristotle, were among the earliest thinkers to ponder profound questions about the mind, behaviour and human nature. Similarly, the earliest history of the study of human development can be traced in China, Persia and India. In the 17th century, French philosopher René Descartes proposed the concept of dualism, which posited that the mind and body are distinct entities that interact to shape the human experience

(Miller, 2022). Their philosophical inquiries delved into the essence of **human existence,** the nature of knowledge and the principles governing human behaviour. As psychology evolved into a distinct scientific discipline, it gradually separated from its philosophical roots, embracing empirical and experimental methods to study human development more rigorously. This historical progression highlights the enduring influence of ancient philosophical thought on modern psychological theories and practices, demonstrating the importance of understanding the historical context in which the field has developed (see also Chapter 2).

Psychology emerged as separate and distinct discipline in the mid-1800s, where a German psychologist Wilhelm Wundt (1832–1920), who is often regarded as the father of experimental psychology, established the first psychology laboratory at the University of Leipzig in Germany in 1879. This event is considered the formal birth of psychology as an experimental and scientific discipline. Wundt's approach emphasised introspection and the systematic study of conscious experience (Arduini-Van Hoose, 2021). He regarded psychology as an exploration of human consciousness and attempted to investigate mental processes through experimental approaches. Although the technique of introspection that he employed is now largely dismissed as lacking scientific rigour, his contributions provided an important groundwork for the development of modern research methods (see Chapter 3 on research methods).

Structuralism and functionalism: Psychology's first schools of thought

Edward Titchener (1867–1927): A prominent student of Wilhelm Wundt, Edward Titchener played a crucial role in bringing Wundt's ideas to the United States. He developed the school of structuralism, which aimed to understand the structure of the mind by breaking it down into its most basic components. Structuralists believed that by analysing the individual elements of consciousness, such as sensations, feelings and images, they could gain a better understanding of the overall structure of the mind (Spielman et al., 2021). Titchener's work laid the foundation for experimental psychology in the USA, emphasising introspection as a method to explore the inner workings of the mind.

Functionalism: Emerging as a reaction to structuralism, functionalism was influenced by thinkers such as William James and John Dewey (see Chapter 2). Unlike structuralism, which focused on the components of the mind, functionalism emphasised the functions and purposes of mental processes and behaviour (Beck & Grayot, 2021). This approach was concerned with how mental activities helped an organism to adapt to its environment. Functionalists believed that understanding the practical applications of mental processes was more important than merely analysing their structure. They studied individual differences and the ways in which mental processes operated to aid survival and adaptation (Ormerod, 2019). Functionalists employed various methods, including direct observation and experimentation, to study the human mind and behaviour in real-world contexts.

William James (1842–1910): A key figure in the development of functionalism, William James was a highly influential psychologist and philosopher in the United States. His seminal work, '*The Principles of Psychology*' ([1890] 1983), is considered one of the most important texts in the history of psychology. James's approach to psychology was pragmatic, focusing on how mental processes function to help individuals adapt to their environments. He emphasised the importance of studying the purpose of behaviour and mental activities, rather than just their structure. James's ideas laid the foundations for the functionalist approach, which would go on to influence various areas of psychology, including educational psychology, developmental psychology and applied psychology.

The rise of psychoanalysis

Psychoanalysis emerged in the late 19th and early 20th centuries, primarily through the work of Sigmund Freud, who sought to understand the underlying causes of psychological distress and mental disorders (see also Chapter 13). His observations and clinical experiences led him to propose that unconscious processes significantly influence human behaviour and emotions.

Freud's early work with patients suffering from hysteria and other neuroses revealed that many symptoms lacked a clear physiological basis. This realisation prompted him to explore the mind's hidden depths, leading to the development of key concepts such as the unconscious, repression and the significance of early childhood experiences. Freud's method of free association, where patients were encouraged to verbalise their thoughts without censorship, became a cornerstone of psychoanalytic therapy.

The publication of his seminal work, '*The Interpretation of Dreams*' (Freud, 1900), marked a pivotal moment in the establishment of psychoanalysis. In this book, Freud introduced the idea that dreams are a window into the unconscious mind, revealing repressed desires and unresolved conflicts. Over time, psychoanalysis evolved to encompass a comprehensive theory of personality development, psychopathology and therapeutic techniques.

Freud's ideas were both revolutionary and controversial, sparking debates and further research within the psychological community. Despite criticism and modifications by subsequent theorists, the core principles of psychoanalysis have had a lasting impact on psychology, psychiatry and the broader understanding of human behaviour.

The rise of behaviourism

Behaviourism emerged as a dominant force in psychology during the early 20th century, largely in response to the introspective methods of psychoanalysis and structuralism. Pioneered by John B. Watson, behaviourism emphasised the study of observable behaviour over the analysis of the mind. Watson argued that psychology should be an objective science, focusing on measurable and quantifiable behaviours rather than subjective mental states. This approach was further developed by B.F. Skinner, who introduced the concept of operant conditioning, demonstrating how behaviour could be shaped by reinforcement and punishment. Behaviourism's emphasis on empirical research and its practical applications in areas such as education, therapy and behaviour modification contributed to its widespread acceptance and influence. By prioritising observable phenomena, behaviourism provided a clear, scientific framework for understanding and predicting human behaviour, setting the stage for later developments in cognitive psychology and other fields. Behaviourism is often criticised, however, for its limited scope in explaining complex behaviours and higher cognitive functions (Munsey Mapel, 1977). For example, it struggles to account for phenomena such as language acquisition and creativity, which involve intricate mental processes.

The rise of cognitive psychology

In the 1950s and 1960s, the cognitive revolution emerged in psychology, leading to a shift in focus from psychoanalysis and behaviourism to cognitive psychology. While psychologists continued to study observable behaviours, they also became increasingly interested in understanding the processes occurring within the mind. The cognitive revolution marked a shift away from behaviourism towards a focus on mental processes such as memory, perception and problem-solving. This period saw the emergence of influential figures, such as Jean Piaget (1896–1980), who contributed to the development of cognitive psychology, and cognitive development theory, which shifted the focus from behaviour to mental processes, exploring how children's thinking evolves through stages (see Chapters 2 and 13).

The rise of developmental psychology

Developmental psychology emerged as a distinct field in the late 19th and early 20th centuries, driven by the need to understand the psychological changes that occur throughout the human lifespan. Early pioneers, such as John Locke, Jean-Jacques Rousseau and Charles Darwin (see Chapter 2), laid the groundwork with their theories on human behaviour and development (Daum & Manfredi, 2022). The field initially focused on child and adolescent development but gradually expanded to include adult development and ageing, recognising the continuous nature of psychological growth. Influential figures such as G. Stanley Hall and Arnold Gesell contributed to the establishment of developmental psychology as a scientific discipline, emphasising the importance of systematic observation and longitudinal studies. Today, developmental psychology encompasses a wide range of topics, including cognitive, emotional and social development, and employs diverse methodologies to explore the complex interplay of genetic, environmental and cultural factors in shaping human development.

The rise of humanism

Humanism in psychology emerged as a significant movement in the mid-20th century, primarily as a reaction to the limitations of behaviourism and psychoanalysis. Behaviourism, with its focus on observable behaviour and reinforcement, and psychoanalysis, with its emphasis on unconscious processes, were seen by humanistic psychologists as overly deterministic and dehumanising (McLeod, 2025). Humanistic psychology, which is often referred to as the 'third force' in psychology, was championed by figures such as Carl Rogers (1951, 1961) and Abraham Maslow (1943). This approach emphasises personal growth, self-actualisation and the inherent goodness of individuals. It focuses on the whole person and their subjective experiences, advocating for the study of individuals rather than groups. Humanistic psychology introduced new methods of inquiry, such as qualitative research and case studies, and offered a broader range of effective therapeutic practices. It has faced criticism, however, for its perceived lack of scientific rigour and its reliance on subjective experiences, which some argue can be difficult to measure and validate (Fassin, 2019; Jakelić, 2021). Despite these criticisms, humanism has had a lasting impact on psychology, promoting a more holistic and optimistic view of human nature.

Developmental psychology in the 21st century: An overview

Developmental psychology in the 21st century has evolved to encompass a broader and more nuanced understanding of human growth and change across the lifespan. This field now integrates diverse methodologies and interdisciplinary approaches to study the complex interplay of genetic, environmental and cultural factors influencing development. Advances in technology, such as neuroimaging and computational modelling, have provided deeper insights into cognitive and emotional development. Researchers have increasingly focused on the impact of social contexts, including family dynamics, education systems and societal changes, on developmental trajectories (Fivush, 2022; Gauvain, 2022). Additionally, there is a growing emphasis on understanding developmental processes in diverse populations, recognising the importance of cultural and individual differences.

Key aspects emerging in the 21st century include:

- Positive psychology: Moving away from deficit language, this approach emphasises positive experiences that facilitate wellbeing (Seligman & Csikszentmihalyi, 2000).
- Technological advances: Technology, including neuroimaging and artificial intelligence (AI), has significantly influenced modern perspectives on development.

- Media literacy: This perspective focuses on teaching children critical thinking skills to navigate and evaluate media content, promoting healthy media consumption habits.
- Interdisciplinary approaches: These approaches highlight the integration of various disciplines, such as genetics, sociology and anthropology.
- Global perspectives: Global perspectives consider the influence of cross-cultural studies and global research collaborations, emphasising the decolonisation of developmental psychology.

In the 21st century, child development theories have evolved to incorporate new insights from various fields, including neuroscience, genetics and cultural studies. Some prominent theories and perspectives that have gained traction in recent years are:

- Integration of domains: Development is a holistic process that integrates cognitive, social, emotional and physical domains (see also Chapter 2).
- Contextual influences: Environmental, cultural and contextual factors significantly impact development (see Chapter 4).

Overview of schools of thought in psychology

Table 1.1 offers an overview of the school of thought and key theorists who have influenced the field of developmental psychology in 21st century, most of whom will be explored in this book.

Table 1.1 Overview of schools of thought in psychology

School of thought	Key figures	Key concepts	Region of origin
Structuralism	Edward Titchener	Analysing the structure of the mind: Structuralism aims to break down mental processes into their most basic components, such as sensations, feelings and images, to understand the structure of the mind	USA
Functionalism	William James, John Dewey	Functions and purposes of mental processes: Functionalism focuses on how mental activities help an organism to adapt to its environment, emphasising practical applications and the study of individual differences	USA
Psychoanalysis	Sigmund Freud, Carl Jung, Anna Freud, Melanie Klein	Unconscious mind and defence mechanisms: Psychoanalysis explores the influence of the unconscious mind on behaviour, including concepts such as repression, projection and the psychosexual stages of development. Jung added the idea of the collective unconscious and archetypes	Austria, Switzerland, UK, USA

(Continued)

Table 1.1   (Continued)

School of thought	Key figures	Key concepts	Region of origin
Behaviourism	John B. Watson, B.F. Skinner	Observable behaviour and conditioning: Behaviourism studies behaviour through observable actions and conditioning processes, such as classical and operant conditioning, reinforcement and punishment	USA
Humanistic Psychology	Carl Rogers, Abraham Maslow	Self-actualisation and free will: Humanistic psychology emphasises personal growth, self-actualisation and the importance of free will and self-determination. Maslow's hierarchy of needs outlines the stages of human motivation	USA
Cognitive Psychology	Jean Piaget, Ulric Neisser	Mental processes and information processing: Cognitive psychology investigates internal mental processes such as perception, memory, problem-solving and cognitive development. Piaget's stages of cognitive development describe how children's thinking evolves	Switzerland, USA
Islamic Psychology	Malik Badri, Rasjid Skinner	Holistic understanding of the self: Islamic psychology integrates spiritual and psychological perspectives, focusing on the heart and soul, and the connection to God. It emphasises the importance of spiritual wellbeing alongside mental health	Global (Islamic World)
Liberation Psychology	Ignacio Martín-Baró	Social justice and empowerment: Liberation psychology addresses social injustice and aims to empower marginalised communities through community-based approaches and participatory action	Latin America
African Psychology	Nwoye Augustine, Wade Nobles	Indigenous knowledge systems: African psychology incorporates indigenous knowledge systems, cultural context and communal values, emphasising the importance of community and collective wellbeing	Africa
Asian Psychology	Durganand Sinha, Kuo-Shu Yang	Cultural sensitivity and integration: Asian psychology integrates traditional and modern psychological practices, focusing on cultural sensitivity and the unique psychological needs of Asian populations	Asia
Developmental Psychology	Jean Piaget, Lev Vygotsky	Stages of cognitive and social development: Developmental psychology studies the progression of cognitive and social development across the lifespan, including Piaget's stages of cognitive development and Vygotsky's Zone of Proximal Development	Switzerland, Russia

School of thought	Key figures	Key concepts	Region of origin
Social Psychology	Kurt Lewin, Henri Tajfel	Group dynamics and social identity: Social psychology examines how individuals' thoughts, feelings and behaviours are influenced by social interactions, including concepts like group dynamics, Social Identity Theory and field theory	Germany, UK
Positive Psychology	Martin Seligman, Mihaly Csikszentmihalyi	Strengths and wellbeing: Positive psychology focuses on the study of strengths, wellbeing and happiness, including concepts like flow, resilience and the factors that contribute to a fulfilling life	USA, Hungary
Evolutionary Psychology	Leda Cosmides, John Tooby	Adaptive functions of psychological traits: Evolutionary psychology explores how psychological traits and behaviours have evolved to solve adaptive problems, emphasising the evolutionary basis of behaviour	USA
Educational Psychology	Jerome Bruner, Lev Vygotsky	Constructivist theory and scaffolding: Educational psychology studies how people learn, including theories like constructivism, scaffolding and social learning, which emphasise the role of interaction and support in learning	USA, Russia
Clinical Psychology	Aaron Beck, Albert Ellis	Cognitive therapy and rational emotive behaviour therapy: Clinical psychology focuses on diagnosing and treating mental disorders, including approaches like cognitive therapy, which addresses cognitive distortions, and rational emotive behaviour therapy, which challenges irrational beliefs	USA
Neuro-psychology	Brenda Milner, Oliver Sacks	Brain–behaviour relationships: Neuropsychology studies the relationship between brain function and behaviour, including the impact of neurological disorders on cognitive and emotional processes, often through detailed case studies	Canada, UK
Attachment Theory	John Bowlby, Mary Ainsworth	Emotional bonds and attachment styles: Attachment Theory explores the formation of emotional bonds between children and their caregivers, identifying different attachment styles such as secure, avoidant, ambivalent and disorganised	UK, USA
Ecological Systems Theory	Urie Bronfenbrenner	Environmental systems and development: Bronfenbrenner's Ecological Systems Theory posits that an individual's development is influenced by a series of interconnected environmental systems, ranging from immediate surroundings (microsystem) to broader societal structures (macrosystem)	USA

Although Western ideas of developmental psychology tend to dominate the study of human development, psychology has become a subject of study in other continents that are not well known in Western countries. When considering theories of development, it is important to examine their origins and the context in which they were formulated as this can provide valuable insights into the assumptions, biases and perspectives that underpin the theory. Table 1.2 highlights the key differences between Western psychology, African psychology, Islamic psychology and Asian psychology:

Table 1.2 A comparison of different schools of thought in psychology across the world

Aspect	Western psychology	African psychology	Islamic psychology	Asian psychology
Foundations	Empirical and scientific methods, rooted in European and North American traditions	Indigenous knowledge systems, cultural traditions and communal values	Islamic teachings, Quran, Hadith and classical Islamic scholars	Cultural beliefs and traditions, influenced by ancient texts and philosophies
Philosophical underpinnings	Individualism, scientific study of mind and behaviour, measurable phenomena	Holistic worldview, interconnectedness with community and environment	Integration of spiritual and psychological perspectives, holistic view of self	Collectivism, harmony and balance within oneself and with the environment
Key concepts	Unconscious mind, conditioning, self-actualisation, cognitive processes	Ubuntu (interconnectedness), communalism, spirituality	Qalb (heart), Nafs (self), Ruh (spirit), Aql (intellect)	Harmony, non-attachment, the Middle Path, moral development
Focus	Observable behaviours, mental processes, biological underpinnings	Collective wellbeing, community relationships, spiritual practices	Spiritual wellbeing, connection to God, holistic health	Social harmony, holistic mind–body connection, cultural context
Methods	Experimental research, psychotherapy, cognitive-behavioural therapy (CBT)	Traditional healing practices, community-based approaches, participatory action	Spiritual practices (prayer, dhikr), traditional healing, integration with modern therapy	Meditation, mindfulness, traditional healing practices, integration with modern therapy

Aspect	Western psychology	African psychology	Islamic psychology	Asian psychology
Cultural sensitivity	Rooted in Western value systems, adaptations needed for non-Western cultures	Culturally sensitive, aligned with African values and traditions	Culturally and spiritually aligned with Muslim communities	Emphasises cultural context, sensitive to diverse Asian populations
Holistic vs reductionist	Often reductionist, breaking down mental processes into components	Holistic, considering spiritual, emotional, and physical aspects	Holistic, integrating spiritual and psychological health	Holistic, viewing mental and physical health as interconnected

Child development versus human development: Understanding the key differences

The field of child development specifically focuses on the physical, cognitive, social, emotional and moral development of children from infancy to adolescence. It examines how children grow and change during these formative years, including milestones such as language acquisition, motor skills, social interactions and emotional regulation. The field of human development is broader, however, and encompasses the entire lifespan, from infancy to old age. It includes child development but also studies the developmental changes that occur in adulthood and ageing.

Researchers in child development often focus on specific stages of childhood, such as infancy, early childhood, middle childhood and adolescence. Each stage has distinct characteristics and developmental milestones. Piaget's stages of cognitive development describe, for example, how children's thinking evolves from sensorimotor to formal operational stages (see Chapter 2). While human development includes the stages of childhood, it also extends to adult development, including young adulthood, middle adulthood and late adulthood. Erikson's psychosocial stages of development, for instance, cover the entire lifespan, addressing challenges and growth opportunities at each stage. As will be shown in Chapter 3, research methods often involve observing children in natural settings, conducting experiments, and using developmental assessments to understand how children learn, grow and interact. Applications include educational practices, parenting strategies and interventions to support healthy development. In human development, research methods are more varied and can include longitudinal studies, cross-sectional studies and case studies that track individuals over time. Applications extend to areas such as career development, ageing and mental health interventions across different life stages.

Key theories in child development (see Table 1.1) focus on understanding the unique aspects of childhood growth and learning. These theories provide a comprehensive view of development across the lifespan, integrating physical, psychological and social dimensions.

In summary, while child development is a crucial part of human development, it is distinct in its focus on the early years of life and the specific challenges and milestones associated with childhood. Human development, on the other hand, provides a broader perspective that includes the entire lifespan, offering insights into how individuals grow and change from infancy to old age.

Critique of key developmental theories

Developmental psychology has provided valuable insights into human growth and change, but it is not without its criticisms. This section discusses some of the key critiques of developmental studies.

Ethnocentrism and WEIRD bias

One of the most significant critiques is the ethnocentric bias in developmental research. Many foundational studies have been conducted on WEIRD (Western, Educated, Industrialised, Rich and Democratic) populations, which represent only a small fraction of the global population (see also Chapter 2). This bias raises questions about the generalisability of developmental theories to non-WEIRD contexts. Attachment Theory, for example, developed by John Bowlby and Mary Ainsworth, emphasises the importance of secure attachment in early childhood (see also Chapter 9). Cross-cultural studies (e.g., Sagi-Schwart, 2008) have shown, however, that attachment behaviours and parenting practices can vary across different cultures and have found that while secure attachment is common across cultures, the prevalence of different attachment styles varies. For instance, avoidant attachment was more prevalent in Western European countries, whereas ambivalent attachment was more frequent in Israel and Japan. It suggests that developmental theories may not fully capture the diversity of human development across different cultural settings.

Consider this 1.1

- Why is it important to understand and care about non-WEIRD societies, and what can we gain from learning about them?

Deterministic models

Developmental theories often present deterministic models that outline fixed stages of development. Jean Piaget's theory of cognitive development, for instance, describes a series of stages that children supposedly progress through in a linear fashion. However, critics (e.g., Cherry, 2023; Gauvain, 2022) argue that this stage-based approach oversimplifies the complexities of human development and fails to account for individual variations and the influence of environmental factors. Such models may not adequately reflect the dynamic and non-linear nature of development.

Consider this 1.2

- In what ways do stage-based theories of development, such as Piaget's cognitive development theory, oversimplify the complexities of human growth?

Overemphasis on nature versus nurture

While developmental psychology has made strides in understanding the interplay between genetics (nature) and environment (nurture), some theories have been criticised for overemphasising one aspect over the other. For example, early theories often focused heavily on genetic determinism, neglecting the significant impact of environmental and cultural factors (see Chapter 2). This nature-centric view can overlook the significant impact of environmental factors, such as socio-economic status, education and cultural practices, and the importance of social interactions and cultural tools in cognitive development (see Chapter 4).

The use of deficit language

The use of deficit language in developmental psychology has been increasingly critiqued for its potentially harmful implications. Deficit language, which focuses on what individuals lack or cannot do, can inadvertently reinforce negative stereotypes and stigmatise those with developmental disorders (see Chapter 5). This approach often overlooks the strengths and potential of individuals, leading to a narrow and sometimes biased understanding of their capabilities. For instance, labelling children with developmental language disorder (DLD) primarily by their deficits can overshadow their unique abilities and resilience (see Chapter 12). A shift towards more inclusive and strength-based language is advocated to foster a more supportive and empowering environment for individuals with developmental challenges.

The shift to positive psychology represents a significant transformation in the field. Traditionally, psychology focused primarily on diagnosing and treating mental health issues, emphasising deficits and problems. However, in the late 1990s, psychologists like Martin Seligman and Mihaly Csikszentmihalyi pioneered the positive psychology movement, which focuses on enhancing wellbeing and fostering positive qualities such as happiness, resilience and strengths (Seligman & Csikszentmihalyi, 2000). Positive psychology (see Chapter 8) aims to understand and promote factors that allow individuals and communities to thrive.

Ethical concerns

Ethical considerations in psychological studies on child development have evolved significantly over the past century. Early 20th-century experiments, such as John B. Watson's 'Little Albert' experiment, would be deemed highly unethical by today's standards. Watson and Rayner (1920) conditioned a young child to fear a white rat by pairing it with a loud, frightening noise. This experiment caused significant emotional distress to the child, and there was no effort to decondition the fear response or ensure the child's long-term wellbeing. Such practices would violate contemporary ethical principles, including nonmaleficence and beneficence, which prioritise the avoidance of harm and the promotion of wellbeing (Banks et al., 2022). Modern ethical standards, as outlined by the American Psychological Association (APA) or the British Psychological Society (BPS), emphasise the importance of informed consent, the right to withdraw and the minimisation of harm (see Chapter 3).

These historical examples highlight the necessity of rigorous ethical guidelines to protect vulnerable populations in psychological research. Contemporary frameworks ensure that studies are designed to respect the dignity and rights of participants, particularly children, who are especially susceptible to harm.

Methodological limitations

The reliance on quantitative methods in developmental research has also been criticised. While these methods provide valuable data, they can sometimes fail to capture the richness and complexity of human experiences. Qualitative approaches, such as case studies and ethnographic research, are now on the rise and can offer deeper insights into the lived experiences of individuals and the contextual factors that shape their development (see Chapter 3).

Case study 1.1: Navigating the challenges of disrupted development

Martin

Martin is a 4-year-old boy who, along with his family, fled their home country due to conflict and sought asylum in the UK. The family faced traumatic experiences during their journey, including exposure to violence and unstable living conditions.

Arriving in UK unable to speak English, Martin found it difficult to communicate and, due to significant trauma caused by witnessing violence, found it difficult to trust the staff in the setting he was attending. The different custom, food and social norms made it a struggle to settle in the early childhood setting.

Examples of the impact on development

- *Trauma and stress*: The experiences of fleeing from conflict and living in refugee camps can lead to increased stress and trauma, affecting Martin's emotional regulation, mental health and education. Chronic stress and trauma can affect attention, memory and learning abilities.

- *Language barriers*: Limited exposure to the English language can create challenges in communication and social integration with peers and adults in the UK.
- *Cultural differences*: Navigating a new cultural environment may lead to feelings of isolation and difficulty in understanding social norms.
- *Health concerns*: Limited access to healthcare and nutritious food during their journey and in refugee camps can affect Martin's physical growth and development.

Support strategies

1 *Trauma-informed care*: Providing Martin with psychological support, including therapy, to address trauma and build resilience.
2 *Stable environment*: Ensuring a stable and secure living environment to foster a sense of safety and stability.
3 *Language support*: Offering language learning programmes to help Martin develop English language skills.
4 *Cultural integration*: Encouraging activities that promote cultural understanding and social integration with peers.
5 *Access to education*: Ensuring continuous access to early childhood education programmes to support cognitive and social development.
6 *Healthcare access*: Providing regular health check-ups and nutritional support to address any physical health concerns.

Being critical

- What specific elements of the case study did you question or challenge? Reflect on why you disagreed with certain aspects of the case study.
- Identify any insights, strategies or approaches from the case study that you can incorporate into your practice.
- What specific practices from the holistic approach and play-based learning can you adapt to support the development of children and young people?

Reflection points

- Reflect on how historical theories of child development, such as those proposed by Piaget and Erikson, may be influenced by the cultural contexts in which they were developed.
- Consider the limitations of applying these theories universally, especially in non-WEIRD societies. Think about the importance of incorporating diverse cultural perspectives to create more inclusive and accurate developmental models.

(Continued)

- Reflect on the historical evolution of child development theories and how they have been shaped by changing societal norms and scientific advancements. Consider how contemporary research is challenging and expanding traditional theories, particularly in light of global diversity.

Chapter summary

This chapter provided a comprehensive review of human development, focusing on several key areas:

- Historical perspective:
  - o Exploration of human development from a historical viewpoint.
  - o Examination of the origins of the science of development.
- Current perspectives:
  - o Analysis of contemporary views on human development in the 21st century.
  - o Consideration of the advantages brought by technological advancements.
- Key theories in development:
  - o Summary of influential theories in development, including cognitive, social and biological neuroscience psychology.
- Criticism of key theories:
  - o Discussion on the emphasis on Western, Educated, Industrialised, Rich and Democratic (WEIRD) research.
  - o Review of ethical considerations in developmental studies.

Further reading

Slater, A., & Bremner, G. (2017). *An Introduction to Developmental Psychology* (3rd ed.). John Wiley & Sons, Inc.

Useful websites

www.verywellmind.com/child-development-theories-2795068

While not a peer-reviewed journal, *Verywell Mind* is a reliable educational resource reviewed by mental health professionals.

References

Arduini-Van Hoose, N. (2021). *Child Psychology*. Pressbooks.

Baltes, P. B., Reese, H., & Lipsett, L. (1980). Lifespan developmental psychology. *Annual Review of Psychology*, *31*, 65–110.

Banks, G. C., Knapp, D. J., Lin, L., Sanders, C. S., & Grand, J. A. (2022). Ethical decision making in the 21st century: A useful framework for industrial-organizational psychologists. *Industrial and Organizational Psychology*, *15*(2), 220–235. doi:10.1017/iop.2021.143

Beck, L., & Grayot, J. D. (2021). New functionalism and the social and behavioral sciences. *European Journal for Philosophy of Science*, *11*, 103. https://doi.org/10.1007/s13194-021-00420-2

Bickhard, M. H. (2006). Developmental normativity and normative development. In L. Smith & J. Vonèche (Eds.), *Norms in human development* (pp. 105–133). Cambridge University Press.

Cherry, K. (2023). Support and Criticism of Piaget's Stage Theory. *Verywell Mind*. www.verywellmind.com/support-and-criticism-of-piagets-stage-theory-2795460

Daum, M. M., & Manfredi, M. (2022). Developmental psychology. In J. Zumbach, D. A. Bernstein, S. Narciss, & G. Marsico (Eds.), *International handbook of psychology learning and teaching* (pp. 239–272). Springer. https://doi.org/10.1007/978-3-030-28744-3_10

Fassin, D. (2019). Humanism: A critical reappraisal. *Critical Times*, *2*(1), 29–38.

Fivush, R. (2022). Sociocultural perspectives on autobiographical memory. In M. L. Courage & N. Cowan (Eds.), *The Development of Memory in Infancy and Childhood* (3rd ed., pp. 262–285). Routledge.

Freud, S. (1900). *The Interpretation of Dreams*. New York, NY: Macmillan.

Gauvain, M. (2022). *Cognitive Development in Infancy and Childhood*. Cambridge University Press.

Jakelić, S. (2021). Humanism and its critics. In A. B. Pinn (Ed.), *The Oxford Handbook of Humanism*. Oxford University Press.

James, W. ([1890] 1983). *The Principles of Psychology, Volumes I and II*. Cambridge, MA: Harvard University Press.

Jiwen, C. (2024). Idiographic approach. In K. Zhang (Ed.), *The ECPH encyclopedia of psychology*. Springer. https://doi.org

Maslow, A. H. (1943). A theory of human motivation. *Psychological Review*, *50*(4), 370–396. https://doi.org/10.1037/h0054346

McLeod, S. (2025, November 6). *Humanistic psychology*. SimplyPsychology. https://www.simplypsychology.org/humanistic.html

Miller, P. H. (2022). Developmental theories: Past, present, and future. *Developmental Review*, *66*, 101049. https://doi.org/10.1016/j.dr.2022.101049

Munsey Mapel, B. (1977). Philosophical criticism of behaviorism: An analysis. *Behaviorism*, *5*(1), 17–32. Published by: Cambridge Center for Behavioral Studies (CCBS).

Ormerod, R. (2019). The history and ideas of sociological functionalism: Talcott Parsons, modern sociological theory, and the relevance for OR. *Journal of the Operational Research Society*, *71*(12), 1873–1899. https://doi.org/10.1080/01605682.2019.1640590

Pelaez, M., Gewirtz, J. L., & Wong, S. E. (2008). A critique of stage theories of human development. In B. A. Thyer, K. M. Sowers, & C. N. Dulmus (Eds.), *Comprehensive Handbook of Social Work and Social Welfare. Vol. 2: Human Behavior in the Social Environment* (pp. 503–518). John Wiley & Sons, Inc.

Rogers, C. R. (1951). *Client-centered therapy: Its current practice, implications, and theory*. Boston, MA: Houghton Mifflin.

Rogers, C. R. (1961). *On becoming a person: A therapist's view of psychotherapy*. Boston, MA: Houghton Mifflin.

Seligman, M. E. P., & Csikszentmihalyi, M. (2000). Positive psychology: An introduction. *American Psychologist, 55*(1), 5–14.

Singh, L. K. (2024). *Concept of Maturation [E-content]*. Department of Psychology, University of Lucknow. https://udrc.lkouniv.ac.in/Content/DepartmentContent/SM_f87e4bd3-8ac7-4d6c-a12c-cfaf2db2efa0_17.pdf

Spielman, R., Dumper, K., Jenkins, W., & Lovett, M. D. (2021). *Psychology* (2nd ed.). OpenStax.

van Ijzendoorn, M. H., & Sagi-Schwartz, A. (2008). Cross-cultural patterns of attachment: Universal and contextual dimensions. In J. Cassidy & P. R. Shaver (Eds.), *Handbook of attachment: Theory, research, and clinical applications* (2nd ed., pp. 880–905). The Guilford Press.

Vygotsky, L. S. (1978). *Mind in Society: The Development of Higher Psychological Processes*. Harvard University Press.

Watson, J. B., & Rayner, R. (1920). Conditioned emotional reactions. *Journal of Experimental Psychology, 3*(1), 1.

2

Key debates in child development

Cathryn Knight and Ioanna Palaiologou

Chapter objectives

By the end of this chapter, you should be able to:

- Critically evaluate key debates in child development.
- Understand development as a lifelong, multidimensional and multidirectional process.
- Explore child development through different disciplinary lenses, including psychology and sociology.
- Recognise the complexity of development and its individual variations.

Overview of the chapter

This chapter will use a critical lens to examine the key debates in child development and will explore development as a lifelong, multidimensional process, emphasising that it cannot be fully understood through a single criterion. Both quantitative measures (e.g., increase or decrease) and qualitative factors (e.g., attitudes, dispositions or behaviours) must be considered to capture the complexity of development. Additionally, the chapter will highlight that development is multidirectional, meaning that various abilities progress in different directions for each individual; in other words, development can vary for each of us. Taking multidisciplinary lenses, we will critically examine debates such as development as a psychological construct (e.g., nature vs nurture, active vs passive, continuous vs discontinuous, stage like development and stability vs change) and development as a sociological construct. It will conclude that not all development can be explained only by one discipline, such as psychology. Other disciplines, such as sociology or anthropology, can help us to understand the breadth and depth of child development.

Why should you read this chapter?

This chapter challenges traditional, single-discipline explanations of development, highlighting the interplay between biological, environmental and social influences, and provides a critical perspective on nature versus nurture, continuous versus discontinuous change, and stability versus change. By considering both psychological and sociological constructs, you will develop a well-rounded understanding of how children grow and learn.

Development as a psychological construct

As discussed in Chapter 1, child development has traditionally been examined through a psychological lens. Within the psychological perspective, there are a number of long-standing debates about the drivers of development. Using research evidence, this chapter will examine some of these historic debates and consider their relevance in understanding child development today.

Nature versus nurture

The question of 'what makes us who we are?' is a fiercely contested one within the study of child development. Psychologists question whether we are a product of our genes (nature) or a product of our environment (nurture). While it is now broadly understood that both nature and nurture interact during development, research continues to examine which has the strongest influence.

Consider this 2.1

- If someone has a natural talent for music or sports, would they still succeed without proper training and practice?
- Can a child with no family history of aggression become violent due to their environment?

The theory of evolution

Charles Darwin's theory of evolution by natural selection is a cornerstone of biological science and has significant implications for the nature versus nurture debate. Darwin (1859) argued that species evolve over time due to the survival and reproduction of individuals with advantageous traits. This concept, known as natural selection, suggests that biological characteristics, including physical and behavioural traits, are primarily shaped by genetics. These traits increase an organism's chances of survival in its environment. His ideas strongly support the nature side of the debate, suggesting that human characteristics – including intelligence, personality and behaviour – are influenced by genetics and evolutionary history.

Ultimately, Darwin's work contributed to the ongoing debate by demonstrating that both biological inheritance (nature) and environmental influences (nurture) play essential roles in human development.

John Locke (1632–1704)

John Locke's theory of nature versus nurture centres on his concept of tabula rasa, or the idea that the human mind is a blank slate at birth. He rejected the notion of innate behaviours, arguing instead that all knowledge and understanding come from experience. According to Locke (1847), individuals acquire knowledge through sensation (gathering information from the senses) and reflection (processing and analysing sensory input). This empiricist view places him firmly on the side of nurture, as he believed that human development is shaped primarily by external influences rather than inborn traits.

Stability versus change- the 21st century debate

As mentioned, psychologists in the 21st century agree that neither nature nor nurture alone are likely to be fully accountable for the development of a child. Instead, research is more interested in whether characteristics are *stable* or *change* over time. Some theorists suggest, for example, that children who show certain characteristics (e.g., anxiety) will continue to show these characteristics at later ages (Weems, 2008). The *stability* of a trait leads people to argue for the importance of heredity and of early experiences establishing behaviour.

Some researchers argue that personality and behaviour can *change* significantly due to life experiences, social influences and personal development (more in Chapter 3). Longitudinal studies have shown, for instance, that while early temperament may predict certain traits in adulthood, environmental factors such as parenting styles, education and peer interactions can lead to substantial shifts over time (Basilio & Rodríguez, 2017; Colliver et al., 2022; Zhang & Whitebread, 2021).

The debate over stability and change is particularly relevant in developmental psychology, as it influences our understanding of intervention strategies, education and mental health support. If traits are stable, early interventions become crucial, whereas if traits are malleable, ongoing support and environmental changes can have lasting effects.

Continuous versus discontinuous development

Another debate in developmental psychology is whether development occurs in a smooth, gradual process or through distinct stages. This debate is often framed as continuous versus discontinuous development.

Two key theorists who had differing perspectives on whether development is continuous or discontinuous were Jean Piaget and Lev Vygotsky.

Jean Piaget: Development as a discontinuous process

Jean Piaget was a pioneer in developmental psychology, best known for his stage theory of cognitive development (Piaget, 1932, 1936, 1945, 1957). He proposed that children move through four distinct stages of cognitive growth: the *sensorimotor stage* (birth to 2 years), the *preoperational stage* (2 to 7 years), the *concrete operational stage* (7 to 11 years) and the *formal operational stage* (11 years and older). Each stage represents a qualitative shift in how children think and understand the world, making Piaget's theory an example of discontinuous development.

Piaget believed that children do not simply accumulate knowledge over time; instead, they undergo fundamental transformations in their thinking at specific points in their development. During the transition from the preoperational stage to the concrete operational stage, for example, children move from egocentric thinking to being able to consider multiple perspectives. This shift does not happen gradually but rather in a distinct way when the child reaches the necessary level of cognitive maturity. Piaget also argued that children actively construct their knowledge through *assimilation* (integrating new information into existing mental frameworks) and *accommodation* (adjusting those frameworks when new information does not fit). These processes drive movement through the stages, supporting the idea that development occurs in distinct phases rather than as a continuous process.

Lev Vygotsky: Development as a continuous process

Unlike Piaget, Lev Vygotsky viewed development as a continuous and dynamic process, driven by social interaction and cultural influences (Vygotsky, 1978). He rejected the idea that cognitive development occurs in universal stages and instead emphasised the role of learning through guidance from others. His concept of the Zone of Proximal Development (ZPD) highlights how children learn best when they receive support from more knowledgeable individuals, such as parents, teachers or peers. According to Vygotsky, as children gain new skills and knowledge, their ZPD shifts, allowing them to take on increasingly complex tasks. This perspective suggests that learning happens gradually over time rather than in distinct jumps from one stage to another.

Over time, as children become more proficient, the support is gradually removed, allowing for independent problem-solving. This idea aligns with the concept of continuous development, as it suggests that cognitive growth happens incrementally through repeated social interactions rather than sudden, stage-like transitions.

The universal application of Piaget and Vygotsky

While Piaget and Vygotsky had differing views on whether development is continuous or discontinuous, both made lasting contributions to our understanding of how children learn and play (see Chapter 13). Piaget's stage theory suggests that cognitive abilities emerge in distinct phases, whereas Vygotsky's sociocultural theory views development as a gradual process shaped by interaction with others. Both Piaget and Vygotsky have been criticised, however, for basing their theories on research that reflects WEIRD psychology (see Chapter 1). It has led to concerns that their theories may not be universally applicable to all cultures and social contexts (Matusov & Hayes, 2000; Pramling, 2022).

Piaget's theory of cognitive development was largely developed based on observations of Swiss children from middle-class, Western backgrounds. His experiments focused on how children interacted with objects and solved problems independently, leading to the assumption that cognitive development follows a universal, stage-like pattern. However, cross-cultural research has shown that cognitive development can be heavily influenced by environmental and cultural factors (Rakesh et al., 2024; Stevenson et al., 1978).

Studies in non-WEIRD societies, for example, suggest that children's cognitive development is often shaped by their everyday experiences, which may not align with Piaget's rigid stages (Hwang, 2023). In many indigenous cultures, children learn through observation and participation in real-world tasks, rather than through the structured, self-guided discovery that Piaget emphasised. Additionally, some studies suggest that not all children reach Piaget's formal operational stage, particularly in societies where abstract scientific thinking is less emphasised (Ahmad et al., 2016; Mangan, 1978; Maynard, 2008). This finding challenges the universality of Piaget's claims and suggests that his model may reflect a WEIRD bias rather than a true global perspective on development.

Vygotsky's theory places a strong emphasis on social interaction and guided learning, which makes it more adaptable to cultural variation compared to Piaget's theory. Vygotsky's ideas, however, were shaped by the socio-political context of early 20th-century Soviet Russia, and much of his work assumes that learning occurs through formal schooling and structured mentorship. This focus on teacher–student or parent–child interactions aligns closely with Western educational models but may not fully capture learning processes in societies where children acquire skills through more informal or observational learning.

In many non-WEIRD cultures, children learn through participatory learning, where they engage in tasks alongside adults rather than being explicitly 'taught' in a structured manner. In indigenous communities in Mexico, for instance, children learn by observing and participating in daily activities such as cooking, farming and weaving. They acquire skills and knowledge through active involvement and collaboration with adults, rather than through formal instruction (Cohen et al., 2023). It raises questions about whether Vygotsky's concept of ZPD is as universally relevant as he suggested.

Re-examining continuous and discontinuous development

The paper 'Re-examining developmental continuity and discontinuity in the 21st century: Better aligning behaviors, functions, and mechanisms' (Petersen, 2024) explores the complex nature of developmental change over time. It challenges the assumption that similar behaviours across different ages always reflect the same underlying psychological processes. The paper highlights that continuity is not always straightforward. A child's early shyness, for example, may develop into social anxiety in adulthood, an example of *heterotypic continuity*, where different behaviours over time stem from the same underlying process. Conversely, the same behaviour, such as aggression, may arise from different causes at different ages, an example of *phenotypic continuity*, where the same behaviour occurs over time but originates from different underlying causes. Petersen argues that developmental researchers often overlook the possibility of discontinuity or misinterpret continuity due to the use of the same measurement tools over time, which can mask genuine changes in the underlying processes driving behaviour. Petersen therefore encourages researchers to look beyond surface-level behaviours and instead to investigate the functions and mechanisms behind them.

Development as a sociological construct

Over the last few decades, the study of child development has arguably become more contextually aware. As discussed in reference to Piaget and Vygotsky, many of the debates within psychology are based on research studies conducted in WEIRD contexts. The sociological perspective on child development emphasises the role of social structures, cultural norms and institutions in shaping how children grow, learn and develop their identities (James & Prout, 2003). Unlike psychological perspectives, which often focus on internal cognitive processes or biological maturation, sociology views development as a product of social interactions, family dynamics, education, economic systems and broader societal influences. Understanding childhood through a sociological lens allows us to critically examine how policies, institutions and cultural norms shape children's lives, as well as how children themselves may challenge and redefine the meaning of childhood in contemporary society.

The social construction of childhood

Many sociologists would argue that childhood is a social construct, meaning that society shapes our understanding of what it means to be a child, rather than it being solely defined by biological age. A sociological perceptive of childhood suggest that the concept of 'childhood' is not a fixed, universal stage of life but rather a socially constructed phenomenon that varies across time, cultures and social contexts. Sociologists argue that childhood is not solely determined by biological age or psychological development but is shaped by social norms, historical contexts and power structures. What it means to be a child, what is expected of children, and how they are treated differs significantly across societies, reflecting broader cultural, economic and political influences.

Childhood as a social category

Childhood is often perceived as a natural stage of life, distinct from adulthood, in which children are dependent, innocent and in need of protection. Sociologists challenge this assumption, however, arguing that the meaning of childhood is defined by social expectations rather than biological necessity. The perspectives of Philippe Ariès and Hugh Cunningham (discussed below) suggest that childhood is not a universal, biologically determined stage but a concept that changes based on social and historical conditions.

Philippe Ariès ([1962] 1965), *Centuries of Childhood*

In *Centuries of Childhood* (Aries, 1965), historian Philippe Ariès argued that childhood, as we understand it today, is a relatively recent social construct rather than a universal, natural stage of life. Using historical evidence, particularly from medieval Europe, he suggested that childhood was not always seen as distinct from adulthood. Instead, societal changes over time, such as shifts in education, family structures and economic systems, helped shape modern perceptions of childhood. Ariès found that in medieval society, children were often treated as 'miniature adults': they were expected to work and participate in daily life as soon as they were physically capable. There was little distinction between child and adult clothing, responsibilities or behaviour. High infant mortality rates may have also influenced parenting, with weaker emotional bonds between parents and children. The idea of childhood as a protected, dependent phase had not yet emerged.

He argued that it was not until the 16th to 18th centuries that childhood began to be seen as a separate stage, particularly among the middle and upper classes. The rise of formal education created a structured period of dependency, reinforcing the idea that children needed instruction before entering adulthood. Ariès suggests that during this time family dynamics, influenced by growing middle-class values, led to a greater emotional investment in children, emphasising their moral and intellectual development. By the 19th century, the Industrial Revolution and social reform movements further solidified modern ideas of childhood. Campaigns for compulsory education and child labour laws helped to establish childhood as a protected phase, distinct from the adult workforce. Children's literature, toys and clothing also became more specialised, reinforcing the belief that childhood should be a time of innocence and learning.

Hugh Cunningham (2006), *The Invention of Childhood*

In *The Invention of Childhood* (Cunningham, 2006), historian Hugh Cunningham examined how childhood has evolved over the past 1,000 years, particularly in Western societies. He argued that childhood is not a natural, unchanging phase of life but a social construct that is shaped by historical, economic and cultural factors. Cunningham built on the work of Philippe Ariès but provided a more nuanced perspective, recognising that while childhood has changed over time, certain fundamental aspects, such as children's dependence on adults, have remained consistent.

Cunningham explored how childhood has historically been defined by adult needs and expectations. In pre-industrial societies, children were often viewed as economic contributors, working alongside adults in agriculture or trades. During the Industrial Revolution, however, attitudes towards children shifted, particularly in response to growing concerns about child labour. Legal reforms, such as restrictions on child labour and the expansion of compulsory education, helped to construct the modern idea of childhood as a time of learning, play and emotional development rather than work.

Unlike Ariès, who focused primarily on cultural representations of childhood, Cunningham emphasised the role of institutions and the state in shaping children's lives. He argued that governments, through policies on education, welfare and child protection, have played a major role in defining what childhood should be. The introduction of compulsory schooling in the 19th and 20th centuries, for example, extended the period of dependency, reinforcing the idea that children should be protected and gradually prepared for adulthood. Child welfare laws further reinforced the perception of children as being vulnerable individuals in need of care and supervision.

Childhood and power relations

Sociologists also explore the power dynamics inherent in the social construction of childhood. The concept of childhood often positions children as passive, dependent and lacking agency, which can justify adult control over children's lives.

Chris Jenks (2005) and the adult-centric perspective of childhood

In his influential work, Jenks (2005) argued that the way we conceptualise and understand childhood is often shaped by an adult-centric perspective. Jenks suggested that society's ideas and expectations about childhood are heavily influenced by the views, concerns and needs of adults, rather than reflecting the actual experiences and voices of children themselves. This viewpoint reflects the dominant tendency in many societies to treat children as dependent, incomplete or less-than-adult beings, who are largely shaped by external forces such as parental guidance, education systems and social institutions.

Jenks emphasised that childhood is not simply a natural, universal stage of development but is instead socially constructed and subject to adult definitions. According to his analysis, adults often impose their own ideals and concerns onto childhood, which results in a view of children as objects of adult care, protection and moral guidance. In other words, the adult world has a significant impact on how children are perceived, how they are treated, and what roles they are expected to play in society. This adult-centric perspective can lead to a narrow and limiting understanding of childhood, one that disregards the agency and individuality of children.

The adult-centric view of childhood has implications for policies, laws and social practices related to children. In this framework, childhood is often defined by its separation from adulthood, leading to policies that emphasise education, protection and special rights for children, often excluding them from adult roles and responsibilities. It can be manifested in laws that restrict child labour, mandate schooling and control children's behaviour through rules and regulations. While these policies are often well intentioned, Jenks highlighted that they are shaped by adult concerns about childhood innocence, vulnerability and the perceived need for parental authority.

In Jenks' view, for example, child protection laws are designed with the adult idea that children are inherently vulnerable and must be shielded from harm. They can often result in the infantilisation of children, denying them opportunities to take on responsibilities or participate fully in social life. Additionally, policies that extend compulsory education into the teenage years may reflect adult desires to control how children are raised and how they transition into adulthood rather than fully accommodating children's own interests or developmental needs.

Jenks also critiqued the adult-centric narrative that excludes the child's voice and perspective from discussions about childhood. This approach, according to Jenks, assumes that children are incapable of understanding or participating in decision-making about their lives. He argued that childhood should not merely be seen as a stage of preparation for adulthood, but instead that children should be recognised as active agents in their own development. This argument includes acknowledging that children can, and do, form their own identities and can actively shape their own social environments in ways that may not always align with adult expectations.

Feminist and postmodernist critiques of childhood and social hierarchies

Feminist and postmodernist scholars have critically examined how childhood is socially constructed, arguing that these constructions often reinforce existing social hierarchies, particularly along lines of gender, class and race. By deconstructing traditional narratives of childhood, these scholars highlight the ways in which societal norms and expectations shape children's experiences and identities, perpetuating systemic inequalities.

Gender and childhood: Feminist perspectives

Feminist scholars argue that childhood is inherently gendered, with societal expectations dictating distinct roles and behaviours for boys and girls. These gendered constructions limit children's potential and perpetuate gender inequalities. Feminist theorists argue that the gendered construction of childhood has long-term implications for individuals and society and can limit children's potential by discouraging them from pursuing interests and careers that do not align with traditional gender roles. This theory perpetuates gender inequalities in various fields, including the workforce, politics and academia. Additionally, it reinforces harmful stereotypes that can affect individuals' self-esteem, relationships and overall wellbeing. Feminist scholars advocate for a more inclusive and equitable approach to childhood that allows all children to explore their full potential, free from restrictive societal expectations (Brown & Bigler, 2016; De Lair & Erwin, 2000; Smith et al., 2017).

Class and childhood: Social reproduction of inequality

From a Marxist or socio-economic perspective, childhood is often constructed in ways that reproduce class inequalities. Marxist scholars argue that childhood is a stage of life that is deeply influenced by the economic conditions and class position of children. Children born into wealthy families often experience childhood in ways that provide them with privilege and access to resources and educational opportunities, while children from working-class or poor backgrounds may face a childhood marked by scarcity, fewer educational opportunities and a greater likelihood of early entry into the workforce.

Race, ethnicity and childhood: Postcolonial critiques

Critical race theorists highlight that the social construction of childhood is deeply influenced by racial and ethnic factors, often reflecting colonial histories and contemporary power dynamics. Even in modern societies, race continues to shape childhood experiences, often in ways that mirror historical patterns of exclusion and discrimination. Black and indigenous, children are more likely to face criminalisation, surveillance and harsher discipline in schools compared to their white peers. Studies show that Black children in the USA and the UK, for example, are often seen as older, less innocent and more threatening than white children, a phenomenon known as adultification (Epstein et al., 2017). It has been argued that this perception leads to Black children being disproportionately punished in schools, as they are more likely to be suspended or expelled and are more frequently targeted by law enforcement.

Critical race theorists advocate for challenging dominant Eurocentric views of childhood by recognising the diverse ways childhood is experienced across cultures and communities. They call for inclusive policies that address racial disparities in education, criminal justice and child welfare.

Intersectionality in childhood studies

The concept of intersectionality is crucial in understanding how overlapping identities, such as gender, class and race, collectively shape children's experiences. Postmodernist scholars argue that childhood should not be viewed through a singular lens but rather as a complex interplay of various social categories. This perspective acknowledges that children's experiences are multifaceted and cannot be fully understood by examining one aspect of their identity in isolation.

Case study 2.1: Dyslexia

The International Dyslexia Association (IDA) defines dyslexia as a neurobiological learning disability that affects word recognition, spelling and decoding. The definition states that it stems from a phonological processing deficit that is unexpected given other cognitive abilities and adequate instruction and that secondary effects may include reading comprehension difficulties and limited vocabulary growth due to reduced reading exposure (Lyon et al., 2003, p. 2). This understanding of dyslexia suggests that it is a biological and inherited neurodevelopmental condition. Research has found, however, that dyslexia identification is clustered in particular demographic groups. Knight and Crick (2021) found that being male, being from a more advantaged social background and having higher parental income, and being younger in the year group were significant predictors of being identified with dyslexia. Odegard et al. (2020) found that African American learners were half as likely as white learners to be identified as dyslexic.

Therefore, while there may be a biological component to dyslexia, environmental aspects also impact whether it is being identified in practice. It raises important questions about whether those with the highest level of need are getting support. It also allows us to explore the key debates in development that have been highlighted within this chapter:

Nature versus nurture

The definition provided by the IDA frames dyslexia as a neurobiological condition, implying that it is largely inherited and innate, a perspective that aligns with the nature side of the debate. However, research findings that dyslexia identification is more common in boys, in children from advantaged backgrounds and in white learners suggest that environmental factors (nurture) play a significant role in whether dyslexia is recognised and supported. Disparities in dyslexia diagnosis based on socio-economic status and race, for instance, indicate that access to assessments and interventions is not purely a reflection of biological need but is also shaped by educational policies, cultural perceptions and systemic biases. It reinforces the idea that both biological predisposition (nature) and environmental context (nurture) interact to shape developmental outcomes.

Continuous versus discontinuous development

Dyslexia also contributes to the debate on whether development occurs gradually (continuous) or in distinct stages (discontinuous). If dyslexia were purely a biological condition, one might expect that its effects on learning would emerge in a predictable, linear way. However, research suggests that the timing of dyslexia identification

(Continued)

varies, often depending on external factors such as age, socio-economic status and educational setting. Instead, dyslexia may manifest at different points in development, depending on the interaction between a child's cognitive abilities and their learning environment. It suggests that development is not entirely continuous but can be shaped by critical periods and external interventions.

Dyslexia and the social construction of childhood

The fact that white and wealthier children are more likely to be identified as dyslexic suggests that not all children's struggles with reading and learning are equally recognised or responded to. It raises the question of whether dyslexia is viewed as a legitimate learning difficulty in all groups or whether societal assumptions about intelligence, race and ability influence who is perceived as having a learning disability. If dyslexia were purely a biological condition, we would expect to see more even identification rates across demographic groups. Instead, its diagnosis is embedded in social and institutional contexts, reinforcing the idea that childhood experiences – including access to educational support – are not universal but are shaped by societal structures.

Conclusion

While dyslexia is often framed as a biological condition, research on its identification highlights the importance of environmental, social and systemic factors. This finding reinforces key debates in development, showing that nature and nurture interact, that development is influenced by social structures, and that childhood is not a fixed biological stage but is shaped by cultural and institutional contexts.

Being critical

- Identify any statements or conclusions in the case study that you found questionable or problematic. Think about the reasons for your disagreement and whether they stem from different interpretations of the data, personal experiences or alternative perspectives.
- Consider how the information and insights from the case study can be applied in your professional practice. Reflect on specific strategies, approaches or considerations that could enhance your work with children, young people and families, particularly in supporting those with dyslexia.

Reflection points

- Consider how your own beliefs about child development have been shaped by dominant psychological or sociological perspectives. How has this chapter challenged or reinforced those views?

- Think about the real-world implications of the theories explored and consider how recognising both psychological and sociological perspectives may influence the way professionals support children in education, healthcare or social work?
- Additionally, consider the role of societal structures in shaping developmental opportunities. Are certain children more likely to receive support than others, and if so, why? How can we ensure that all children, regardless of background, have access to the resources they need to thrive?

Chapter summary

This chapter critically examined the key debates in child development, emphasising that development is a lifelong, multidimensional and multidirectional process. The chapter highlights that development varies for each individual and cannot be fully understood through a single criterion.

Key debates explored

- Nature versus nurture:
  - The chapter discusses the ongoing debate about whether genetics (nature) or environment (nurture) has a stronger influence on child development. It acknowledges that both factors interact during development, offering examples from the theories of Charles Darwin and John Locke.
- Stability versus change:
  - This debate focuses on whether characteristics remain stable or change over time.
- Continuous versus discontinuous development:
  - The chapter contrasts the views of Jean Piaget, who proposed distinct stages of cognitive development, and Lev Vygotsky, who emphasised continuous development through social interaction and cultural influences.
- Multidisciplinary perspectives:
  - The chapter argues that child development cannot be explained solely by psychology. Other disciplines, such as sociology, provide valuable insights into the breadth and depth of development.
- Sociological constructs:
  - The chapter explores how childhood is socially constructed and influenced by social norms, historical contexts and power structures. It discusses the perspectives of Philippe Ariès and Hugh Cunningham on the social construction of childhood and the role of institutions and the state in shaping children's lives.

Further reading

Elliott, J. G., & Grigorenko, E. L. (2024). *The Dyslexia Debate Revisited*. Cambridge University Press.

Suggate, S., & Reese, E. (2012). *Contemporary Debates in Childhood Education and Development*. Routledge.

Wild, M., & Street, A. (2013). *Themes and Debates in Early Childhood*. Sage/Learning Matters.

Useful websites

Timeless Debates in Psychology, *Psychology Today*, www.psychologytoday.com/us/blog/darwins-subterranean-world/202101/5-timeless-debates-in-psychology

This website explores five enduring debates in psychology, including nature versus nurture, free will versus determinism and the impact of early experiences on development. It provides insights into how these debates continue to shape our understanding of human behaviour.

References

Ahmad, S., Ch, A. H., Batool, A., Sittar, K., & Malik, M. (2016). Play and cognitive development: Formal operational perspective of Piaget's theory. *Journal of Education and Practice*, 7(28), 72–79.

Ariès, P. ([1962] 1965). *Centuries of Childhood: A Social History of Family Life*. Vintage Books.

Basilio, M., & Rodríguez, C. (2017). How toddlers think with their hands: Social and private gestures as evidence of cognitive self-regulation in guided play with objects. *Early Child Development and Care*, 187(12), 1971–1986. https://doi.org/10.1080/03004 430.2016.1202944

Brown, C. S., & Bigler, R. S. (2016). Feminist perspectives on gender development: Contributions to theory and practice. In T.-A. Roberts, N. Curtin, L. E. Duncan, & L. M. Cortina (Eds.), *Feminist Perspectives on Building a Better Psychological Science of Gender* (pp. 61–78). Springer International. https://doi.org/10.1007/978-3-319-32141-7_5

Cohen, N. B., Cooper, A., & Mackaway, H. D. (2023). (Re) Imagining children's participatory rights with decolonial learning. *O Social em Questão*, 26(56), 61–88.

Colliver, Y., Harrison, L. J., Brown, J. E., & Humburg, P. (2022). Free play predicts self-regulation years later: Longitudinal evidence from a large Australian sample of toddlers and preschoolers. *Early Childhood Research Quarterly*, 59, 148–161. https://doi.org/https://doi.org/10.1016/j.ecresq.2021.11.011

Cunningham, H. (2006). *The Invention of Childhood*. BBC Books.

Darwin, C. (1859). *On the Origin of Species by Means of Natural Selection, or, the Preservation of Favoured Races in the Struggle for Life*. Harvard Botany Libraries – Biodiversity Heritage Library digitization project.

De Lair, H. A., & Erwin, E. (2000). Working perspectives within feminism and early childhood education. *Contemporary Issues in Early Childhood, 1*(2), 153–170. https://doi.org/10.2304/ciec.2000.1.2.4

Epstein, R., Blake, J., & González, T. (2017). Girlhood interrupted: The erasure of Black girls' childhood. *SSRN Electronic Journal.* http://dx.doi.org/10.2139/ssrn.3000695

Hwang, K.-K. (2023). An epistemological strategy for initiating scientific revolution against WEIRD psychology. *Integrative Psychological and Behavioral Science, 57*(2), 361–380. https://doi.org/10.1007/s12124-022-09681-9

James, A., & Prout, A. (2003). *Constructing and Reconstructing Childhood: Contemporary Issues in the Sociological Study of Childhood.* Routledge.

Jenks, C. (2005). *Childhood* (2nd ed.). Routledge. https://doi.org/10.4324/9781003060345

Knight, C., & Crick, T. (2021). The assignment and distribution of the dyslexia label: Using the UK Millennium Cohort Study to investigate the socio-demographic predictors of the dyslexia label in England and Wales. *PLoS ONE, 16*(8), e0256114. https://doi.org/10.1371/journal.pone.0256114

Locke, J. (1847). *An Essay Concerning Human Understanding.* Kay & Troutman.

Lyon, G. R., Shaywitz, S. E., & Shaywitz, B. A. (2003). A definition of dyslexia. *Annals of Dyslexia, 53*(1), 1–14.

Mangan, J. (1978). Piaget's theory and cultural differences: The case for value-based modes of cognition. *Human Development, 21*(3), 170–189. http://www.jstor.org/stable/26764475

Matusov, E., & Hayes, R. (2000). Sociocultural critique of Piaget and Vygotsky. *New Ideas in Psychology, 18*(2–3), 215–239. https://doi.org/10.1016/S0732-118X(00)00009-X

Maynard, A. E. (2008). What we thought we knew and how we came to know it: Four decades of cross-cultural research from a Piagetian point of view. *Human Development, 51*(1), 56–65. https://www.jstor.org/stable/26763968

Odegard, T. N., Farris, E. A., Middleton, A. E., Oslund, E., & Rimrodt-Frierson, S. (2020). Characteristics of students identified with dyslexia within the context of state legislation. *Journal of Learning Disabilities, 53*(5), 366–379. https://doi.org/10.1177/002221942091455

Petersen, I. T. (2024). Reexamining developmental continuity and discontinuity in the 21st century: Better aligning behaviors, functions, and mechanisms. *Developmental Psychology, 60*(11), 1992–2007. https://doi.org/10.1037/dev0001657

Piaget, J. (1932). *Le jugement moral chez l'enfant.* Presses Universitaires de France.

Piaget, J. (1936). *Origins of Intelligence in the Child.* Routledge & Kegan Paul.

Piaget, J. (1945). *Play, Dreams and Imitation in Childhood.* Heinemann.

Piaget, J. (1957). *Construction of Reality in the Child.* Routledge & Kegan Paul.

Pramling, N. (2022). Vygotsky and Piaget as twenty-first-century critics of early childhood education philosophizing. In N. Veraksa & I. Pramling Samuelsson (Eds.), *Early Childhood Research and Education: An Inter-theoretical Focus. Vol 4: Piaget and Vygotsky in XXI Century.* Springer International. https://doi.org/10.1007/978-3-031-05747-2_11

Rakesh, D., McLaughlin, K. A., Sheridan, M., Humphreys, K. L., & Rosen, M. L. (2024). Environmental contributions to cognitive development: The role of cognitive stimulation. *Developmental Review, 73*, 101135. https://doi.org/https://doi.org/10.1016/j.dr.2024.101135

Smith, K., Alexander, K., & Campbell, S. (2017). *Feminism(s) in Early Childhood: Using Feminist Theories in Research and Practice* (Vol. 4). Springer.

Stevenson, H. W., Parker, T., Wilkinson, A., Bonnevaux, B., Gonzalez, M., & Greenfield, P. M. (1978). Schooling, environment, and cognitive development: A cross-cultural study. *Monographs of the Society for Research in Child Development, 43*(3), 1–92. https://doi.org/10.2307/1166040

Vygotsky, L. S. (1978). *Mind in Society: The Development of Higher Psychological Processes.* Harvard University Press.

Weems, C. F. (2008). Developmental trajectories of childhood anxiety: Identifying continuity and change in anxious emotion. *Developmental Review, 28*(4), 488–502. https://doi.org/https://doi.org/10.1016/j.dr.2008.01.001

Zhang, H., & Whitebread, D. (2021). Identifying characteristics of parental autonomy support and control in parent–child interactions. *Early Child Development and Care, 191*(2), 307–320. https://doi.org/10.1080/03004430.2019.1621303

3

Researching child development

Maria Tsapali

Chapter objectives

By the end of the chapter, you will gain:

- An understanding of the main research designs used in developmental psychology and their respective strengths and limitations.
- Familiarity with a variety of data collection and analysis methods used in child development research.
- Insight into the ethical and practical challenges of conducting research with children.
- A foundation for designing, evaluating or engaging critically with developmental research studies.

Overview of the chapter

This chapter will focus on the methodological, ethical and practical considerations guiding developmental research with young populations. The first part of this chapter will cover the different methodological approaches and data collection, and the analysis methods commonly used in child developmental psychology research. Different data collection (e.g., standardised tasks and tests, experiments, observations, case studies) and data analysis methods (quantitative and qualitative) will be problematised. The second part of the chapter will focus on the ethical and practical considerations in researching child development. It will cover topics such as informed consent and assent, respect for the child's agency, power dynamics, ensuring the use of age-appropriate methodologies and conducting research in diverse cultural contexts. The chapter will conclude with a discussion on the future directions and evolution in the ethical, methodological and scientific aspects of studying child development.

Why should you read this chapter?

This chapter offers a comprehensive and up-to-date overview of how developmental research is conducted responsibly and effectively and will equip you with both the theoretical insight and practical tools needed to navigate the complex landscape of researching child development.

Methodological approaches in studying child development

The following section will consider the different methodological approaches used in studying child development, the contexts in which they may be used, as well as some of the benefits and drawbacks of each approach.

Longitudinal versus cross-sectional research designs

Researching child development processes requires methodological approaches that can capture changes over time and the variability among children. Two commonly used research designs in child development research are longitudinal and cross-sectional designs. Each design offers strengths and caveats and can address different types of research questions.

Longitudinal research involves following the same group of individuals over extended time periods (which can vary from months to years). This design allows child development researchers to track individual change over time and offers rich data on the developmental trajectories involved as well as the context that surrounds them (e.g., family environment, school, etc.).

Case study 3.1: The Avon Longitudinal Study of Parents and Children (ALSPAC)

A foundational longitudinal study in child development is the Avon Longitudinal Study of Parents and Children (ALSPAC). The project has followed the development of more than 12,000 children born in 1991 and 1992 in the Bristol and Bath area in the UK. One of the areas that ALSPAC tracks is changes in father involvement in raising children over time, highlighting their importance in child development. Scourfield et al. (2016), for example, found that potential paternal abuse when children were toddlers was associated with increased odds of depressive symptoms at age 16 (see also Chapters 4 and 9 on issues around factors that influence development). The longitudinal nature of the study allowed researchers to examine the influence of parental factors (e.g., father abuse) in a specific time period (toddlerhood) on children's mental health outcomes in another time period (adolescence).

Being critical

- To what extent can findings from the ALSPAC cohort be generalised to other populations or cultural contexts?
- How does the timing of paternal involvement or abuse during early childhood influence long-term mental health outcomes in adolescence?

Despite the popularity of longitudinal designs in child development research, they come with a set of challenges. They require many resources in terms of the researchers' time and research funding, and they often face issues with participant attrition, especially when they span many years.

In contrast, cross-sectional research involves studying individuals from different age groups at a single point in time, allowing researchers to capture age-related differences among participants. For example, a cross-sectional study by Alloway and Alloway (2013) explored age-related differences in the development of working memory functions (see also Chapter 11). The sample consisted of 1,070 participants aged between 5 and 80 years old. The findings revealed that there is a considerable growth in working memory abilities in childhood, with performance peaking in 30-year-olds, and little change is found in older adults. Although the cross-sectional approach followed in this study yielded important findings about the development of working memory across the lifespan, it could not provide information about individual developmental trajectories.

Although cross-sectional designs are time efficient in capturing snapshots of developmental differences, they offer little information about individual children's developmental trajectories and the factors that influence them. Moreover, they are prone to cohort effects, where differences captured between children of different ages may be due to generational influences (e.g., technological advancements, economic changes) rather than true developmental change (Atingdui, 2011).

Overall, longitudinal and cross-sectional research designs each distinctively contribute in advancing scientific knowledge about child development. To mitigate each approach's caveats, researchers increasingly use integrative approaches to produce rich and robust data.

Observational research

Two common types of observational methodology used in child development research are naturalistic and structured observations. Naturalistic observations include observing children in their natural environment with minimal interference from the researcher. Observing how young children interact during free play can, for instance, provide insights into their social development and conflict resolution skills. This method allows researchers to gather rich information about children's natural behaviour in real-world contexts and produces findings that are applicable in everyday settings and situations. The researcher does not have a strict control of the variables involved, however, and there is potential for researcher bias (the presence of the researcher or a camera in the setting can influence children's behaviour and bias the data).

Structured observations take place in a controlled environment (e.g., a psychology lab) where the researcher has strict control of the variables involved and can manipulate them to observe their influence on the participants' behaviour. For example, in attachment research (see also Chapter 9), the Strange Situation test devised by Mary Ainsworth has been used to study attachment styles in infants. The Strange Situation is typically conducted in a laboratory setting and involves the infant, the mother and a stranger. The mother and the stranger leave or return in a series of structured episodes and the child's reactions are observed when they are left alone or with the stranger. Although structured observations allow for the control of extraneous variables and can be replicated easily, they often lack ecological validity, as the artificial setting can influence the child's natural behaviour.

Experimental research

Experimental designs are used to determine cause-and-effect relationships by manipulating one variable and measuring its effect on another variable. The two main types of experiments used in child development research include laboratory experiments and field experiments.

Similar to structured observations, laboratory experiments take place in a controlled environment and allow precision in the measurement of cause-and-effect relationships between the variables of interest. The results may not always generalise well to real-word settings, however, due to the artificiality of the procedure and the laboratory's environment.

Field experiments occur in natural settings but, unlike unstructured observations, they include the manipulation of variables by the researchers, blending in this way the high ecological validity of real-world settings and the control of laboratory settings. An example of a field experiment would be to study the effect of positive teacher reinforcement in children's prosocial development, with a group of students getting oral positive teacher feedback when a child engaged in prosocial behaviour (e.g., 'I really liked how you helped your friend clean up') and another group of students interacting with teachers as usual.

Ethnographic and case studies approaches

Ethnographic studies are qualitative research approaches that seek to understand social practices, meanings, and experiences within their real-life contexts. They typically involve sustained engagement in the research setting and draw on methods such as participant observation, interviews, and field notes to capture participants' perspectives and everyday interactions.

Case studies allow in-depth exploration of an individual child or small group of children and yield rich qualitative data about their development. Although case studies produce findings that are not generalisable, they are important for generating hypotheses and for studying how the context can influence a child's behaviour and development (Yin, 2014). Ethnography and case studies methods are often used to provide a deep understanding of a child's cultural and contextual understanding as the researchers often immerse themselves in the child's environment over extended periods of time. Moreover, they can provide useful data on children's neurodevelopmental differences, such as autism, dyslexia, for example. Dawson et al. (2000), for instance, used a case study method to explore and closely observe the development of an infant from birth to two years of age. The study produced a comprehensive report of how autistic traits demonstrated themselves at different points of the child's development, highlighting the nature of autism at its earliest stages.

Data collection and analysis methods

To produce robust and reliable data and results child development researchers employ a variety of data collection and data analysis methods that allow them to observe, quantify and interpret the complex developmental processes children undergo as they grow. This section discusses a range of data collection methods, including standardised tests, questionnaires, interviews and neuroimaging tools. It also examines how the data obtained by these methods are analysed using quantitative and qualitative approaches.

Standardised tests and assessments

Standardised tests and assessments are often used to measure children's cognitive, socioemotional and behavioural development. These tools are designed and administered in a uniform way, ensuring consistent scoring and comparison across individuals and groups. They can provide normative data that facilitate the comparison to a larger representative sample. They are considered objective as they rely less on subjective judgement and are rigorously evaluated to establish their validity (i.e., they measure what they are designed to measure) and reliability (i.e., they produce consistent results over time).

Tests like the Wechsler Intelligence Scale for Children (WISC) (Weschler, 1974), for instance, assess general cognitive abilities, including memory, reasoning and language. Tools like the Ages and Stages Questionnaire (ASQ) (Bricker et al., 1995) are often used by paediatricians and researchers to evaluate developmental milestones and identify delays. Although standardised tests are valuable in measuring children's development, they are often developed and standardised on specific populations, which can lead to biases when applied to other groups with different backgrounds or experiences and inaccurate or unfair assessments of individuals from underrepresented groups.

Surveys and questionnaires

Surveys and questionnaires are widely used in child development research due to their efficiency in gathering large amounts of data in a short time. They are typically completed by parents, teachers or older children themselves:

- Parent-report questionnaires: They are useful for gathering data on children's behaviours happening at home and parents' perspectives on children's development.
- Teacher-report questionnaires: They provide data on children's behaviour and social interactions at school.
- Child self-report: Older children can provide direct information about their experiences and ideas on various aspects of their lives.

Although surveys and questionnaires are fast to administer, they come with limitations. These include low response rates, the potential for bias in responses due to participants responding in the way they believe will be viewed favourably by others (social desirability), unclear wording, difficulty in interpreting questions, and limitations in capturing nuanced or complex information.

The Child Behaviour Checklist (CBCL) (Achenbach, 1991), for example, is a questionnaire that is used to evaluate a wide range of emotional and behavioural issues in children. It includes different versions for preschool and school-age children and it has forms that can be completed by the child, parent and/or teacher about the child.

Interviews

Interviews are often used in child development research to gather information from parents, teachers or children themselves about children's lives and development. Interviews provide rich and in-depth data but are time consuming to administer and can be subject to researcher bias (e.g., the interviewer may unconsciously give more attention or positive feedback to a participant who shares their views or ideas about the topic of interest). There are two main types of interviews typically employed by researchers:

- Structured interviews: These follow a fixed set of questions and are used to ensure consistency across participants. This method is ideal for comparative studies that aim to compare responses between different age groups (cross-sectional studies) or between different time-points (longitudinal studies).
- Semi-structured or unstructured interviews: These interviews follow a flexible structure with the researcher being able to ask follow-up questions and explore different topics based on the participants' experiences, responses and interests. They are commonly used in qualitative research that aims to explore different aspects of child development in depth.

For younger children, techniques such as puppet interviews or drawing tasks are often employed for better understanding their unique perspectives and experiences (Clark, 2005). For instance, the Berkeley Puppet Interview (BPI) has been developed to obtain structured children's self-reports on multiple domains of mental health and social wellbeing (Measelle et al., 1998). The BPI, which is a structured interviewing method, uses two identical puppets that make opposing statements about themselves and then ask children to describe themselves. For instance, the first puppet says 'I have a lot of friends', then the second puppet says 'I don't have a lot of friends' and finally the first puppet asks the child 'How about you?'. This method makes children feel comfortable and elicits natural responses from them.

Neuroimaging, biophysical and digital tools

With the advancement in technology, researchers have increasingly been using technological tools to study child development. These tools range from neuroimaging and biophysical measures to eye tracking and wearable devices. Tools like magnetic resonance imaging (MRI) help researchers to study how a child's brain changes (see also Chapter 6). For example, how areas of the brain become more connected as the child grows – as a result of thinking and learning (Sowell et al., 2004). Functional MRI (fMRI) shows which parts of the brain are active during tasks like solving problems, helping researchers to understand how brain function becomes more organised with age (Casey et al., 2005). Researchers also use tools like electroencephalography (EEG) to measure brain waves, which can show how quickly children's brains respond to different stimuli (e.g., sights or sounds). In addition to brain scans, researchers often measure things like heart rate, sweat and stress hormones (like cortisol) to understand how children's bodies react to their environment, especially in response to things like parenting or stress (Obradović et al., 2010). Eye-tracking is also used to monitor where and how long a child looks at stimuli, and is a useful technique in language and attention research. Finally, mobile and wearable sensors are often used to collect data on children's physical activity and sleep in real time (e.g., Pini et al., 2024). By combining all these methods, researchers get a fuller picture of how both the brain and body develop – and how different experiences can shape that development.

Data analysis methods

Child development researchers use both quantitative and qualitative methods to study how children grow, learn and interact with their environment. Quantitative methods involve collecting numerical data (e.g., standardised test scores) and using statistical models to analyse them. Longitudinal data analysis, for instance, is widely used in studies to track developmental changes over time, often utilising techniques such as growth curve modelling and latent growth modelling. On the other hand, data collected through interviews are often analysed through qualitative methods such as thematic analysis and phenomenology to explore children's experiences and views in more depth. These approaches are useful for understanding the reasons and context behind children's behaviours and experiences (Creswell & Poth, 2018). Increasingly, child development researchers are using mixed methods approaches which combine both quantitative and qualitative data in a single study. Mixed methods approaches can create a more complete picture of child development by providing both breadth (statistical methods) and depth (qualitative analysis methods) in the topic of interest. Mixed-method approaches combine the strengths of both qualitative and quantitative approaches and overcome their limitations (Creswell & Plano Clark, 2017).

Ethical and practical considerations

Research involving children presents ethical and practical challenges due to their developmental stage, dependence on adults and legal status as minors. It is essential that researchers adopt child-centred approaches that prioritise the rights, safety and wellbeing of young participants, while also ensuring the collection of valid and meaningful data.

Ethical considerations

Research organisations such as the Society for Research in Child Development (SRCD), the British Psychological Society (BPS) and the British Educational Research Association (BERA) produce ethical guidelines and standards that guide research practices involving children. Primary ethical considerations include informed consent, anonymity and confidentiality, and minimisations of risk and power dynamics.

A key consideration in child development research is the issue of informed consent and assent. While informed consent must be obtained from a parent or guardian after they have been informed in detail about the goals, the activities and the potential risks of the research study, researchers must also seek the child's assent (agreement to participate in the study) in ways that are developmentally appropriate. This involves clearly explaining the study's purpose, procedures and potential risks or benefits in language that the child can understand (Johnson et al., 2014). Children should also be informed of their right to withdraw or pause/stop the research activity at any point, even if parental consent has been obtained. Rather than conducting research *on* children, many child development researchers now seek to engage *with* children in research, reflecting a participatory rights approach that considers children's agency and their right to have a say in the research process (Dockett & Perry, 2011).

Confidentiality, participant anonymity and data protection are also important. Children may disclose personal or sensitive information, and researchers have a duty to maintain confidentiality. They must also be transparent about the limits of confidentiality, however, particularly in situations involving abuse, neglect or imminent harm where mandatory reporting laws apply (Alderson & Morrow, 2020). Ensuring secure data storage (e.g., a password-protected laptop) and the anonymisation of data (e.g., through assigning a participant number instead of using names) are crucial practices in protecting participant anonymity.

Another critical ethical concern is the minimisation of risk. Children are considered to be a vulnerable population under research ethics guidelines due to their limited capacity to understand and evaluate risks. Researchers must therefore carefully weigh the potential risks and benefits of the research, prioritising the child's wellbeing, and design studies that involve only minimal risk, unless the research holds the prospect of direct benefit for the child or for other children in similar circumstances (American Psychological Association, 2017). Even with a prospect of direct benefit, the research should still be designed to minimise unnecessary risks.

Institutional Review Boards play a critical role in reviewing research proposals and ensuring ethical standards are met. Risk can take various forms, including emotional distress from discussing sensitive topics or physical discomfort from experimental procedures. Researchers should have clear guidelines for handling distress during the research activity (e.g., instantly terminating the interview).

Additionally, power dynamics between adult researchers and child participants must be carefully managed. Researchers should create environments where children feel safe, valued and empowered to express their views freely. Managing aspects of the physical environment by using child-friendly furniture and decoration, for example, can make children feel at ease during an interview session. Moreover, researchers can ensure that children have more power in the research process, for instance, by setting their own agenda or taking an active role in decision-making related to the study (Montreuil et al., 2021). To conclude, it is essential to strike a balance between ethical integrity and participatory approaches in research, ensuring that children are both empowered and actively involved in the process (Palaiologou, 2013; Salamon & Palaiologou, 2022).

Consider this 3.1

- How can researchers ensure that children's assent is truly informed and voluntary, especially when power dynamics with adults may influence their responses?
- What ethical dilemmas might arise when a child discloses sensitive information during a study, and how should researchers balance confidentiality with mandatory reporting obligations?

Practical considerations

Beyond ethical considerations, child development researchers need to consider various practical issues when designing and conducting child development research studies. A key consideration is the selection of age-appropriate and development-appropriate methods and instruments. As will be seen in Chapters 7–12, children's cognitive, lin-guistic and emotional skills vary widely across age groups and research tools need to be adapted accordingly. Young children may benefit from interactive and visual methods, such as drawing, role-playing or storytelling, for instance, while older children and adolescents may engage better with interviews or questionnaires (Greene & Hogan, 2005). This is especially challenging in longitudinal and cross-sectional studies that, on the one hand, involve children of different age groups and, on the other hand, need to use the same research instrument to ensure reliable comparisons between age groups (Paes et al., 2019; Tsapali, 2024). Selecting a tool that has been reliably used and tested with different age groups as well as engaging in pilot testing, during which the researcher tests the appropriateness of the tool with a few participants from each group before the main study, can effectively ensure the feasibility of the study.

Another practical challenge lies in the recruitment and retention of child participants. Researchers often gain access to child participants though gatekeepers such as parents and teachers, which can make the process more time consuming and complicated. Schools and teachers operate on a busy schedule which can sometimes make the communication between researchers and schools slow. Thus, it is critical that researchers operate on a flex-ible research time frame that can allow them to recruit an adequate sample size while also working around the school schedule and teacher commitments (Tsapali et al., 2020). Retaining the participants over multiple rounds of data collection is a common challenge that longitudinal studies face. Child development researchers ensure retention in children through strategies like regular contact, flexible data collection methods (e.g., flexibility around the timing and location of the research activity) and by establishing rapport with families (Graziotti et al., 2012). These strategies aim to maintain engagement, address chal-lenges like mobility and make it easy for participants to continue contributing to the study.

Future directions

The main challenge ahead for developmental psychology is how to update its current methods and develop new ones towards inclusive, open and sustainable practices.

A growing priority for child development research is to become more inclusive. Historically, as mentioned in the previous chapters, child development studies have often focused on WEIRD samples, resulting in a skewed account of children's develop-ment that is unrepresentative of the full population (Henrich et al., 2010). Recently, studies have broadened their scope to include children from diverse cultural, linguistic and socio-economic backgrounds. This shift requires not only diverse samples, but also the development of culturally appropriate research tools and methods (Awad et al., 2016). Möller et al. (2022), for instance, investigated Japanese and German preschool-ers' emotion understanding. Using an emotion recognition task employing European-American and East Asian child's faces, the researchers showed that Singaporean preschoolers outperformed their German counterparts in recognising emotions from facial stimuli, a finding that highlights the role of culture in shaping emotion understanding and the need for researchers to consider the adaptability of their research tools for different cultural backgrounds.

One area that the developmental psychology field will move towards is how to incorporate sustainability in research practices. Sustainability refers to the practice of conducting research in ways that minimise negative environmental, social and economic impacts, while contributing positively to society, the environment and future knowledge production. Sustainability in research has become a prominent topic of discussion and multiple research organisations and funding bodies have developed guidelines and policies for researchers (e.g., UK Research and Innovation, 2023). Calculating the carbon footprint of a research project/study, turning to online data collection to minimise travelling and utilising energy-efficient appliances, to name a few, can become the norm in future years. One of the main challenges that developmental psychologists will face on that front is data collection with infants and young children, which is challenging to do online. Thus, alternative solutions need to be sought. For instance, setting up a portable testing lab in a van that can visit early years settings to collect data from young participants in one session, rather than requiring each family to travel back and forth to the psychology lab.

Moreover, although multiple efforts have been made to devise more transparent developmental research, there is still room for researchers to incorporate open and reproducible practices in their research processes. This includes openly sharing data, materials, research protocols and results. Openness in research contributes to transparency and trust in developmental research. For students and researchers, it means becoming familiar with digital platforms that enable open sharing and access to research, and learning to document their research in a way that is accessible to others.

Reflection points

- What are the strengths of longitudinal versus cross-sectional designs in understanding child development issues?
- To what extent should developmental research studies produce generalisable results rather than a rich, context-specific understanding of a topic? Do you think it is possible to achieve both?
- How can child development researchers ensure that their choice of methods is ethical and appropriate for the cultural context they are investigating?

Chapter summary

This chapter explored key research methods in child development, alongside practical and ethical considerations when undertaking research.

- Longitudinal studies offer insights into developmental change but are time-intensive and risk participant dropout. Cross-sectional designs are more efficient but may be affected by cohort differences. Researchers also use observational, experimental and case study approaches.

- Data collection methods include standardised tests, interviews, surveys and neuroimaging, and both quantitative and qualitative analyses were discussed.
- Ethical guidelines from bodies like the BPS and BERA emphasise informed consent, child assent, confidentiality and minimising risk. Researchers should also address power dynamics and create child-friendly environments.
- Practically, studies must be tailored to children's developmental levels, with careful tool selection and flexible planning to support recruitment and retention. Building rapport with participants and gatekeepers is essential.
- Looking ahead, child development research should embrace inclusive, sustainable and transparent practices. Diverse samples, low-impact methods and open science principles will enhance generalisability, collaboration and reproducibility.

Further reading

Jones, N. A., Platt, M., Mize, K. D., & Hardin, J. (2020). *Conducting Research in Developmental Psychology: A Topical Guide for Research Methods Utilized across the Lifespan.* Routledge.

Palaiologou, I. (Ed.). (2012). *Ethical Practice in Early Childhood.* Sage. https://doi.org/10.4135/9781446250938

Useful websites

www.bps.org.uk/guideline/code-ethics-and-conduct
www.bera.ac.uk/publication/ethical-guidelines-for-educational-research-fifth-edition-2024

For guidance on ethical considerations, researchers can refer to the standards provided by the BPS and BERA, which offer comprehensive frameworks for conducting responsible and respectful research with children.

References

Achenbach, T. M. (1991). *Manual for the Child Behavior Checklist/4–18.* University of Vermont.

Alderson, P., & Morrow, V. (2020). *The Ethics of Research with Children and Young People: A Practical Handbook* (2nd ed.). Sage.

Alloway, T. P., & Alloway, R. G. (2013). Working memory across the lifespan: A cross-sectional approach. *Journal of Cognitive Psychology*, *25*(1), 84–93. https://doi.org/10.1080/20445911.2012.748027

American Psychological Association. (2017). *Ethical Principles of Psychologists and Code of Conduct.* APA. www.apa.org/ethics/code/

Atingdui, N. (2011). Cohort effect. In S. Goldstein & J. A. Naglieri (Eds.), *Encyclopedia of Child Behavior and Development.* Springer. https://doi.org/10.1007/978-0-387-79061-9_617

Awad, G. H., Patall, E. A., Rackley, K. R., & Reilly, E. D. (2016). Recommendations for culturally sensitive research methods. *Journal of Educational and Psychological Consultation, 26*(3), 283–303. https://doi.org/10.1080/10474412.2015.1046600

Bricker, D., Squires, J., Mounts, L. et al. (1995). *Ages & Stages Questionnaires (ASQ): A Parent-Completed, Child-Monitoring System.* Paul H. Brookes Publishing Co.

Casey, B. J., Tottenham, N., Liston, C., & Durston, S. (2005). Imaging the developing brain: What have we learned about cognitive development? *Trends in Cognitive Sciences, 9*(3), 104–110. doi: 10.1016/j.tics.2005.01.011

Clark, A. (2005). Listening to and involving young children: A review of research and practice. *Early Child Development and Care, 175*(6), 489–505. https://doi.org/10.1080/03004430500131288

Creswell, J. W., & Plano Clark, V. L. (2017). *Designing and Conducting Mixed Methods Research* (3rd ed.). Sage.

Creswell, J. W., & Poth, C. N. (2018). *Qualitative Inquiry and Research Design: Choosing among Five Approaches* (4th ed.). Sage.

Dawson, G., Osterling, J., Meltzoff, A. N., & Kuhl, P. (2000). Case study of the development of an infant with autism from birth to two years of age. *Journal of Applied Developmental Psychology, 21*(3), 299–313. https://doi.org/10.1016/S0193-3973(99)00042-8

Dockett, S., & Perry, B. (2011). Researching with young children: Seeking assent. *Child Indicators Research, 4*, 231–247. https://doi.org/10.1007/s12187-010-9084-0

Graziotti, A. L., Hammond, J., Messinger, D. S., Bann, C. M., Miller-Loncar, C., Twomey, J. E., … & Alexander, B. (2012). Maintaining participation and momentum in longitudinal research involving high-risk families. *Journal of Nursing Scholarship, 44*(2), 120–126. doi: 10.1111/j.1547-5069.2012.01439.x

Greene, S., & Hogan, D. (Eds.). (2005). *Researching Children's Experience: Approaches and Methods.* Sage.

Henrich, J., Heine, S. J., & Norenzayan, A. (2010). The weirdest people in the world? *Behavioral and Brain Sciences, 33*(2–3), 61–83. https://doi.org/10.1017/S0140525X0999152X

Johnson, V., Hart, R., & Colwell, J. (2014). *Steps for Engaging Young Children in Research: The Toolkit.* Education Research Centre, University of Brighton. www.bernardvanleer.org/steps-to-engaging-young-children-in-research

Measelle, J. R., Ablow, J. C., Cowan, P. A., & Cowan, C. P. (1998). Assessing young children's views of their academic, social, and emotional lives: An evaluation of the self-perception scales of the Berkeley Puppet Interview. *Child Development, 69*(6), 1556–1576. https://doi.org/10.1111/j.1467-8624.1998.tb06177.x

Möller, C., Bull, R., & Aschersleben, G. (2022). Culture shapes preschoolers' emotion recognition but not emotion comprehension: A cross-cultural study in Germany and Singapore. *Journal of Cultural Cognitive Science, 6*(1), 9–25. https://doi.org/10.1007/s41809-021-00093-6

Montreuil, M., Bogossian, A., Laberge-Perrault, E., & Racine, E. (2021). A review of approaches, strategies and ethical considerations in participatory research with children. *International Journal of Qualitative Methods, 20*, 1609406920987962.

Obradović, J., Bush, N. R., Stamperdahl, J., Adler, N. E., & Boyce, W. T. (2010). Biological sensitivity to context: The interactive effects of stress reactivity and family adversity on socioemotional behavior and school readiness. *Child Development, 81*(1), 270–289. https://doi.org/10.1111/j.1467-8624.2009.01394.x

Paes, T. M., Tsapali, M., & Ellefson, M. R. (2019). Studying cognitive development in school-aged children. In G. Westerman (Ed.), *The Encyclopaedia of Child and Adolescent Development* (pp. 1–12). John Wiley & Sons. https://doi.org/10.1002/9781119171492. wecad107

Palaiologou, I. (2013). 'Do we hear what children want to say?' Ethical praxis when choosing research tools with children under five. *Early Child Development and Care, 184*(5), 689–705. https://doi.org/10.1080/03004430.2013.809341

Pini, N., Fifer, W. P., Oh, J., Nebeker, C., Croff, J. M., Smith, B. A., & Novel Technology/Wearable Sensors Working Group. (2024). Remote data collection of infant activity and sleep patterns via wearable sensors in the HEALthy Brain and Child Development Study (HBCD). *Developmental Cognitive Neuroscience, 69*, 101446. https://doi.org/10.1016/j.dcn.2024.101446

Salamon, A., & Palaiologou, I. (2022). Infants' and toddlers' rights in early childhood settings: Research perspectives informing pedagogical practice. In F. Press & S. Cheeseman (Eds.), *(Re)conceptualising Children's Rights in Infant–Toddler Early Childhood Care and Education: Transnational Conversations* (pp. 45–58). Springer.

Scourfield, J., Culpin, I., Gunnell, D., Dale, C., Joinson, C., Heron, J., & Collin, S. M. (2016). The association between characteristics of fathering in infancy and depressive symptoms in adolescence: A UK birth cohort study. *Child Abuse & Neglect, 58*, 119–128. https://doi.org/10.1016/j.chiabu.2016.06.013

Sowell, E. R., Thompson, P. M., Leonard, C. M., Welcome, S. E., Kan, E., & Toga, A. W. (2004). Longitudinal mapping of cortical thickness and brain growth in normal children. *Journal of Neuroscience, 24*(38), 8223–8231. https://doi.org/10.1523/JNEUROSCI.1798-04.2004

Tsapali, M. (2024). Child development: The psychological perspective. In I. Palaiologou (Ed.), *The Early Years Foundation Stage: Theory and Practice* (5th ed., pp. 197–207). Sage.

Tsapali, M., Paes, T. M., & Ellefson, M. R. (2020). Researching cognitive development in primary schools: Methods and practical considerations. *Journal of the Chartered College of Teaching, 8*, 52–55. https://impact.chartered.college/article/researching-cognitive-development-primary-schools-methods/?fbclid=IwAR1BhdfNREKC-yyoc97TrgK6hF4SyILWLmZkKSEiIkt-vwIAVNr4fjj7DFY

UK Research and Innovation. (2023). *UKRI Environmental Sustainability Strategy*. www.ukri.org/publications/ukri-environmental-sustainability-strategy/

Weschler, D. (1974). *Weschler Intelligence Scale for Children-Revised*. Psychological Corporation.

Yin, R. K. (2014). *Case Study Research: Design and Methods* (5th ed.). Sage.

4

Influential factors for child development

Olga Fotakopoulou

Chapter objectives

By the end of this chapter, you will gain an understanding of:

- The role of ecological systems in shaping child development, with a focus on Bronfenbrenner's model and the interplay between microsystems, mesosystems and macrosystems.
- The impact of family structures, parenting styles and caregiving networks (including allocaregiving and fathering) on children's emotional, cognitive and social development across diverse cultural contexts.
- How environmental and societal factors – such as poverty, digital media exposure and cultural expectations – affect developmental outcomes.
- The concept of resilience in early childhood, identifying protective factors and support systems that help children cope with adversity and thrive in challenging environments.

Overview of the chapter

This chapter will examine the diverse and interconnected factors that influence child development, using Bronfenbrenner's Ecological Systems Theory as a guiding framework. It will explore how children's growth is shaped by interactions within immediate environments – such as families, schools and peer groups – as well as broader societal and cultural contexts. The chapter will highlight the importance of relationships, especially within families, and will discuss how different parenting styles and caregiving structures, including extended kin networks, contribute to developmental outcomes. It will also consider the evolving roles of fathers and the impact of changing family structures, such as single-parent households and stepfamilies. Cultural expectations and socio-economic conditions will be shown to shape parenting goals and child-rearing practices globally. The chapter will also address the influence of digital media, emphasising both its educational potential and its risks to social and emotional development. A key focus will be on resilience – how children adapt and thrive despite adversity. The chapter will explore the protective factors that support resilience, particularly for children with special educational needs (SEND) or those experiencing trauma, such as family separation.

Why should you read this chapter?

This chapter provides essential insights into the complex factors that shape child development. It also highlights the concept of resilience, showing how children adapt to adversity and what supports help them to thrive – especially those with special educational needs (SEN). Through a real-life case study, it encourages critical reflection on how life events, such as parental separation, impact development and wellbeing. It aims to equip you with the knowledge to understand and support children in diverse contexts.

Introduction

As mentioned in Chapters 1 and 2, children's development unfolds within a complex and dynamic system of interconnected environments – including families, neighbourhoods, schools, communities, governments and the media – all of which shape their experiences, opportunities and developmental outcomes. As shown in Table 1.1, Bronfenbrenner's Ecological Systems Theory provides a valuable framework for understanding how these multiple layers of context influence a child's growth (see also Chapter 5). His model identifies a series of nested systems, ranging from the immediate settings of daily life (microsystem) to the broader cultural and societal structures (macrosystem) (Bronfenbrenner, 1979).

At the core is the microsystem, which encompasses the environments children interact with directly from birth, such as the home, early years settings, schools, places of worship and extended family networks. The mesosystem refers to the interconnections between these settings, such as the relationship between parents and educators or the influence of family dynamics on school engagement. The macrosystem represents the overarching cultural, economic, legal and political contexts that shape all the other systems. It reflects the values, ideologies and societal norms of the culture in which a child lives. Importantly, this system also includes the influence of technological advancements and media, which have become increasingly central to children's lives.

In today's digital age, children are growing up immersed in a media-rich environment. From a very young age, they are surrounded by screens – smartphones, tablets, computers and televisions – which have become integral to their daily routines. While digital technologies offer vast educational and entertainment opportunities, they also raise important questions about their impact on children's social development, communication skills and overall wellbeing (Massaroni et al., 2024; Ren, 2023; Rocha & Nunes, 2020).

Recent research shows that children under the age of 8 now spend an average of 2.5 hours per day engaged in screen-based activities, with touchscreen devices accounting for an increasing share of this time (Common Sense Media, 2025). These trends highlight the need to consider how digital media, as part of the broader macrosystem, interacts with other developmental contexts and contributes to shaping children's early experiences.

Early environmental influences

Early childhood development is profoundly shaped by the interplay between biological maturation and environmental context (see also Chapter 2). The developing brain, particularly during the pre-natal period and the first years of life, is highly sensitive to environmental influences (see Chapter 6). Experiences during this critical window can lead to lasting changes in brain structure and function through epigenetic mechanisms, thereby influencing long-term developmental and mental health outcomes (Miguel et al., 2019). Early experiences not only shape neural architecture but also contribute to individual differences in behaviour and susceptibility to chronic conditions across the lifespan (see Chapter 9).

From an evolutionary perspective, the human brain's rapid post-natal growth is a direct consequence of adaptations to bipedalism, a form of movement in which an organism walks on two legs. In humans, it is the primary mode of locomotion and is a defining characteristic of our species. To accommodate both upright locomotion and increasing brain size, human infants are born at an earlier stage of neurological development compared to other primates (see also Chapter 6). At birth, the brain is approximately 25% of its adult weight, reaching about 75% by age 2. This growth is driven not by an increase in neuron number but by the expansion of axons, dendrites and the myelination of neural pathways – processes that are essential for cognitive and motor development (Feldman, 2015). Initially, the lower brain regions (e.g., brainstem, cerebellum, limbic system) are more developed, supporting vital functions such as breathing, feeding and sleep (Sussman et al., 2016). In contrast, the cerebral cortex, which is responsible for higher-order thinking, undergoes significant post-natal development, requiring adequate nutrition, sleep and environmental stimulation. Research has shown that enriched environments promote dendritic growth and synaptic connectivity, while deprivation or malnutrition can hinder brain development and cognitive outcomes. Animal studies, for instance, demonstrate that rats raised in stimulating environments develop heavier and more complex brains than those in deprived settings (Han et al., 2022).

These findings emphasise the vital influence of both biological and environmental factors in shaping early physical, cognitive, social and emotional development. They highlight the importance of nurturing, enriched environments during the earliest stages of life. The family serves as the primary context in which development is initiated, supported and actualised, playing a central role in fostering a child's potential.

The power of the family

Family structures around the world vary widely, but they are often categorised into two primary forms: nuclear families, consisting of parents (including single parents) and their children, and extended families, which include additional relatives such as grandparents, aunts, uncles and cousins. In many Western societies, where nuclear families are more common, the quality of close, intimate relationships between parents and children becomes especially significant due to the relative isolation of the household unit. In contrast, extended families, which are more prevalent in many African, Asian, Latin American and Middle Eastern cultures, offer a broader and often more resilient support network (Norman, 2024).

For young children, particularly those from economically disadvantaged or minority backgrounds, extended families can provide critical resources for problem-solving and emotional support, helping to buffer the effects of stress and adversity (Kazeem & Jensen, 2017; Pieloch et al., 2016). In sub-Saharan Africa, for example, children orphaned by the HIV/AIDS epidemic or famine often thrive better when cared for within extended family systems (Lightfoot et al., 2018). Similarly, in Middle Eastern contexts, where political violence and forced migration have disrupted traditional family units, extended kin networks continue to play a vital role in maintaining stability and continuity for displaced children.

A systematic review of peer-reviewed studies conducted between 2000 and 2018, which examined resilience among children and adolescents across 18 sub-Saharan African countries, revealed that resilience is a multifaceted, socio-ecological process underpinned by relational, personal, structural, cultural and spiritual enablers (Theron, 2020). Across cultures, extended kin networks often play a vital role by offering tangible support, such as food, childcare and household assistance, as well as intangible contributions like emotional guidance and informal counselling. These findings resonate with anthropological and evolutionary theories of allocaregiving, which refer to caregiving provided by individuals other than a child's biological parents. Allocaregivers may include siblings, grandparents, uncles, and even foster children (Norman, 2024). In many indigenous and collectivist societies, such caregiving is not only common but expected, reflecting deeply embedded cultural values around communal responsibility and social interdependence. Empirical evidence suggests that allocaregiving boosts maternal reproductive success and has also been observed across various non-human species (Konner, 2018).

From an evolutionary standpoint, the human capacity for extended childhood is thought to have developed as a response to the need for acquiring complex cognitive, linguistic, symbolic and cultural skills, which are essential for long-term survival and societal participation (Shen et al., 2025). Large human brains are possible, in part, because of prolonged periods of childhood dependency – periods during which extended kin networks provide the support necessary for the maturation of advanced neurocognitive functions. These networks, in effect, create the conditions for brain evolution by enabling sustained learning and skill acquisition (Tooley et al., 2021).

Anthropological perspectives suggest that while childrearing practices differ markedly across ecological, cultural and historical contexts, caregivers around the world generally strive towards common goals. Robert LeVine (2010; LeVine et al., 1988) has emphasised the cultural dimensions of parenting and child development, particularly in Africa, Asia, Latin America and other global regions (Gaines, 2015). He identified three core goals shared by caregivers: the *survival goal*, which centres on ensuring children's health and safety; the *economic goal*, which relates to equipping them with skills for future productivity; and the *cultural goal*, which focuses on transmitting core values and norms.

LeVine (Lightfoot et al., 2018) observed that in environments where children's physical survival is under constant threat – as in parts of Africa, South America and Indonesia – parents often maintain close physical contact with their infants and toddlers, prioritising protection. Under such conditions, there tends to be less emphasis on fostering cognitive, social, emotional or linguistic development. Conversely, in more stable environments where survival is largely assured, parents are more likely to focus on cognitive stimulation, academic preparation and emotional autonomy. In industrialised societies, this has translated into a strong emphasis on formal education, early learning and academic achievement. It has also spurred the growth of commercial markets for educational toys, digital apps and developmental resources (Lightfoot, 2018).

LeVine's work (Page et al., 2021) has significantly contributed to our understanding of both the universality of parental aims and the vast diversity of caregiving strategies shaped by cultural context. Globally, parenting styles vary along key dimensions – emotional warmth, control and autonomy support – reflecting a complex interplay of tradition, values and circumstance. The theme of sociocultural context is also key, in that parenting practices are strongly influenced by cultural beliefs, biases and goals and are related to different outcomes for children in different cultures (Sorkhabi & Mandara, 2013). Different parenting styles, child-rearing practices and family structures are associated, therefore, with differences in children's social and emotional development (Hastings et al., 2015).

Finally, Table 4.1 provides an overview of Baumrind's (2013) influential framework for categorising parenting styles based on three key dimensions: emotional warmth, autonomy support and behavioural control. Each parenting style – authoritative, authoritarian, permissive and neglectful – is characterised by distinct approaches to nurturing, discipline and the encouragement of independence. This classification helps to illuminate how different parental behaviours can shape children's development and social outcomes.

Table 4.1   Baumrind's (2013) parenting styles

Parenting style	Emotional warmth	Autonomy support	Behavioural control
Authoritative parenting pattern	Demanding and reciprocal relationships	Encourage independence	Favour reasoning
Authoritarian parenting pattern	Favour punitive methods over reasoning,	Stress obedience over independence	Demanding and controlling
Permissive parenting pattern	Express their warmth	Do not demand the same levels of achievement or standards of behaviour from their children	Do not exercise control or exercise a less explicit control
Neglectful parenting pattern	Emotionally distant	Allow children to learn through neglect	Do not exercise control

Fathering and child outcomes

Anthropological research emphasises the significant, though variable, role of fathers in child development across cultures. For example, in hunter – gatherer societies such as the BaYaka, an Indigenous group of hunter – gatherers living primarily in the Congo Basin region of Central Africa (Gettler et al., 2021) found that children whose fathers were less effective providers and less generous sharers exhibited elevated cortisol levels, a physiological marker of stress. This finding highlights the psychological and material importance of paternal support.

While in some populations, such as the Aka of Central Africa, paternal involvement in direct childcare is notably high (Hewlett, 1991), cross-cultural studies suggest that fathers most commonly specialise in provisioning roles (Crittenden & Marlowe, 2008). Consistent with this, research across pre-industrial societies has linked father absence to increased child mortality (Hill & Hurtado, 1996).

This pattern is not universal, however, and only 47% of the statistically controlled studies reviewed by Sear and Mace (2008) found a significant association between paternal presence and child survival, which was likely due to the compensatory roles played by other caregivers, or 'allomothers', within the kinship network (Meehan et al., 2014). These findings reinforce that, while fathers matter, they are part of a broader social matrix supporting child development.

Contemporary fathering also reflects this diversity. While paternal involvement in childrearing has increased globally, substantial differences persist between mothers' and fathers' caregiving behaviours. In many Western societies, although childcare responsibilities are nominally shared, fathers tend to spend less time with their children than mothers. In countries such as Estonia, Finland, Russia, South Korea and the United States, for example, mothers engage in more play with their children, whereas in countries like

Brazil and Malaysia, no significant difference in parental playtime has been observed (Khaleque & Rohner, 2012; Roopnarine & Davidson, 2015). These variations highlight how caregiving practices continue to be shaped by cultural norms, gender expectations and broader socio-economic contexts.

Relationships with peers

From the earliest stages of life, infants begin acquiring new behaviours, skills and capacities simply through exposure to other children. Peers – and especially siblings – act as powerful socialising agents. Among all human relationships, sibling bonds are often the most enduring, stretching across the lifespan and evolving over time. Developmental research is now shedding light on the nuanced dynamics within these relationships, highlighting how factors such as age spacing, birth order and gender composition shape social learning and emotional development (Yu & Yan, 2023).

One foundational mechanism that facilitates this learning is imitation. The capacity for infants to mimic others appears to be innate, a finding that is supported by the discovery of mirror neurons – specialised brain cells that activate not only when an individual performs an action but also when observing another perform the same behaviour. This neurobiological basis enables infants and young children to learn not just through direct instruction, but by watching and engaging with the world around them, including the everyday actions, emotions and language modelled by siblings and peers. These early peer interactions contribute significantly to the development of empathy, cooperation, conflict resolution and identity formation. In essence, siblings and other children provide a natural laboratory for navigating the complexities of human relationships.

Day care: Changes in the family structures

Family structures have undergone significant transformations over recent decades. Compared to the 1960s and 1970s, children today are far less likely to live with two married parents and far more likely to be raised by single mothers. This shift has considerable implications for household income and child wellbeing: in the United States, approximately 34% of children in single-parent families live below the federal poverty line. Economic constraints and time scarcity often mean that single parents – especially those balancing multiple jobs – have less opportunity to engage directly with their children.

Parenting demographics have also changed. First-time parents are now older than in previous generations. This trend brings certain advantages, as older parents tend to have attained higher levels of education, occupy higher-status jobs and possess greater financial stability than younger parents. Another notable change is the increasing number of children being raised by grandparents, either with or without the presence of their biological parents. While grandparent caregiving provides essential support, it also presents challenges, particularly when navigating generational differences in values, energy and parenting approaches (Atış Akyolet al., 2023; Zhao et al., 2025).

Family size has generally declined, a pattern influenced by women opting to delay childbearing due to career aspirations and broader access to contraception. Additionally, family configurations have become more fluid. High rates of divorce, remarriage and marital conflict can expose children to a range of developmental risks – sometimes making separation less harmful than maintaining a discordant household. There has also been a rise in same-sex couples raising children, often with offspring biologically related to one parent. Although many legal obstacles have been reduced, same-sex couples still face practical challenges when building families. Nonetheless, growing societal acceptance has supported broader recognition of diverse parenting arrangements (Bos et al., 2021; Farr et al., 2022).

Stepfamilies are now increasingly common, and are typically formed following divorce, remarriage or the loss of a biological parent. These complex family landscapes reflect evolving definitions of kinship, caregiving and the roles families play in children's development.

Societal influences on development: Poverty, culture and asylum

Human development is shaped by a dynamic interplay between individual capacities and the broader societal context. While traditional developmental theories, such as those of Piaget, Vygotsky and Erikson, offer foundational insights into cognitive, social and emotional growth, they often assume stable environments and may underrepresent the impact of societal disruptions. Contemporary research increasingly highlights how poverty, cultural expectations and forced displacement significantly shape developmental trajectories (see also Chapter 9 for adverse childhood experiences).

Poverty and development

Poverty exerts a profound influence on child development, affecting cognitive, emotional and physical outcomes. Children in low-income families are more likely to experience developmental delays, reduced academic achievement and behavioural challenges due to limited access to resources and chronic stress exposure. Neurobiological research shows that socio-economic adversity can alter brain structures related to executive functioning and language (see Chapter 6).

Cultural expectations

Culture shapes developmental pathways by influencing parenting practices, educational norms and social expectations. Collectivist cultures, for instance, may prioritise interdependence and social harmony, while individualist cultures emphasise autonomy and self-expression. Cultural psychology offers a lens through which developmental milestones can be understood as culturally situated experiences. Heiphetz and Oishi (2022) argue that developmental stages themselves can function like cultural groups, each with distinct norms and expectations, thereby influencing cognition and behaviour.

Asylum-seeking and forced displacement

Children exposed to forced displacement face heightened risks for adverse developmental outcomes. A systematic review by Bernhardt et al. (2024) found that young asylum-seeking children often experience disrupted peer relationships, delayed language acquisition and emotional dysregulation due to trauma, instability and limited access to supportive environments. Protective factors, such as stable housing, access to education and caregiver support, are critical in mitigating these risks. The review emphasises the importance of early integration policies and trauma-informed care to support developmental recovery.

Integrating traditional and societal perspectives

Traditional developmental theories remain valuable but must be contextualised within the realities of diverse and often marginalised populations. Vygotsky's sociocultural theory, for example, provides a bridge between individual development and societal context, emphasising the role of social interaction and cultural tools in learning (Vygotsky, 1978). Integrating these perspectives allows for a more holistic understanding of development, one that accounts for structural inequalities, cultural diversity and the lived experiences of displaced and impoverished children.

Consider this 4.1

- In what ways can educators and practitioners adapt their approaches to support the developmental needs of children from marginalised or displaced backgrounds, while remaining sensitive to cultural and individual differences?

Case study 4.1: Charlie, age 4

Charlie is a 4-year-old White British child who attends nursery at a preschool in the Midlands. Charlie was referred for a psychological evaluation because his parents and teachers are worried about how he is feeling and behaving, especially after his parents separated.

At home, Charlie has been showing signs of being very upset. He sometimes hits things like furniture or throws toys when he feels angry. His parents say this happens

(Continued)

more often now and they are worried about him. At nursery, Charlie sometimes gets angry with other children and teachers. He might shout or push when he doesn't get his way or when he feels frustrated.

Charlie's teachers have noticed that he finds it hard to join in learning activities. He struggles with early reading and writing skills, like recognising letters and matching them to sounds. He also finds counting and understanding numbers difficult. Charlie often needs more time than other children to finish tasks and sometimes gives up when things feel too hard.

Charlie also has trouble sleeping. His parents say he sometimes wakes up crying or screaming, and he talks about hearing scary voices at night. These things are making it hard for Charlie to feel safe and calm.

Because of these concerns, Charlie's parents and teachers agreed that he should see a psychologist to better understand what Charlie is going through and to find ways to help him feel better and learn more easily.

Being critical

- How might an important and life-changing event – like a divorce – affect a very young child like Charlie?
- How could changes at home (like separation, conflict or instability) affect Charlie's experience at nursery?
- What does resilience look like in a 4-year-old? What kinds of support (from family, school or community) might help Charlie feel stronger and more secure?
- Are there things that might make it harder for Charlie to bounce back from difficult experiences?

Reflection points

- Reflect on Bronfenbrenner's model and consider how the microsystem, mesosystem and macrosystem interact to influence a child's experiences. How might changes in one system (e.g., family separation in the microsystem) ripple through others (e.g., school engagement in the mesosystem)?
- Think about the roles of nuclear versus extended families, allocaregiving and fathering across cultures. How do these structures help children to cope with adversity, and what might be the implications for children from marginalised or displaced backgrounds?
- Consider the dual impact of digital technologies on young children. What are the educational advantages and what are the potential risks to social, emotional and cognitive development? How can educators and caregivers strike a balance?
- Using Baumrind's framework, reflect on how authoritative, authoritarian, permissive and neglectful parenting styles differ in emotional warmth, autonomy support and behavioural control. How do cultural values shape these styles, and what are the implications for children's development?

Chapter summary

This chapter examined factors that influence development, focusing on:

- Ecological Systems Theory:
  - Bronfenbrenner's model is used to understand how nested environments (microsystem, mesosystem, macrosystem) shape child development.
  - It emphasises the dynamic interaction between children and their immediate and broader contexts.
- Digital media and technology:
  - Children are increasingly immersed in screen-based environments.
  - Digital media offers educational benefits but also poses risks to social and emotional development.
- Early environmental influences:
  - Early brain development is highly sensitive to environmental conditions.
  - Enriched environments promote cognitive and emotional growth; deprivation can hinder development.
- Family structures and caregiving:
  - Nuclear and extended families offer different forms of support.
  - Extended kin networks and allocaregiving play vital roles in resilience and development, especially in collectivist cultures.
- Parenting styles:
  - Baumrind's framework categorises parenting into authoritative, authoritarian, permissive and neglectful styles.
  - Each style varies in emotional warmth, autonomy support and behavioural control, influencing developmental outcomes.
- Fathering and child outcomes:
  - Fathers contribute variably across cultures, often through provisioning.
  - Paternal involvement affects stress levels and child wellbeing, but other caregivers can compensate for absence.
- Peer relationships:
  - Siblings and peers are key socialising agents.
  - Imitation and interaction foster empathy, cooperation and identity formation.
- Changing family dynamics:
  - There is a rise in single-parent households, older first-time parents and grandparent caregiving.
- Resilience in childhood:
  - Resilience is defined as the ability to adapt and thrive despite adversity.
  - It is supported by protective factors such as stable relationships, community support and enriched environments.

- Societal influences on development: poverty, culture and asylum
  - o Development is not solely shaped by internal psychological processes but is deeply influenced by external societal factors such as poverty, cultural norms and displacement. A comprehensive understanding of development requires integrating traditional theories with contemporary insights into social and environmental contexts.

Further reading

Lansford, J. E., French, D. C., & Gauvain, M. (2021). *Child and Adolescent Development in Cultural Context.* American Psychological Association.

Mastergeorge, A. M., & Barnett, M. A. (Eds.). (2026). *The Impact of Poverty on Early Development: Implications for Practice and Policy.* American Psychological Association.

Useful websites

Resources for Families: Supporting Your Child's Growth: www.zerotothree.org/resources/for-families/

This website provides extensive resources for families and caregivers. It emphasises responsive caregiving, developmental milestones and strategies for managing challenging behaviours. Its materials are evidence-based and tailored for children from birth to age 3.

Tools to maximise your child's development: https://pathways.org/

This website provides expert-reviewed tools and videos to support early development through inclusive caregiving. It includes milestone tracking, sensory development guides and tips for caregivers beyond parents, such as grandparents and childcare providers.

References

Atış Akyol, N., Atalan Ergin, D., & Kallitsoglou, A. (2023). The pathway from grandparental support with childcare in the early years to child socioemotional outcomes in middle childhood: evidence from the Millennium Cohort Study. *Early Child Development and Care, 193*(9–10), 1067–1082. https://doi.org/10.1080/03004430.2023.2218596

Baumrind, D. (2013). Authoritative parenting revisited: History and current status. In R. Larzelere, A. Morris, & A. Harrist (Eds.), *Authoritative Parenting: Synthesizing Nurturance and Discipline for Optimal Child Development* (pp. 11–34). American Psychological Association. https://doi.org/10.1037/13948-002

Bernhardt, A. et al. (2024). Young children's development after forced displacement: A systematic review. *Child and Adolescent Psychiatry and Mental Health, 18,* Article 711. https://doi.org/10.1186/s13034-024-00711-5

Bos, H., Carone, N., Rothblum, E., Koh, A., & Gartrell, N. (2021). Long-term effects of homophobic stigmatization during adolescence on problem behavior in emerging adult offspring of lesbian parents. *Journal of Youth and Adolescence, 50*, 1114–1125.

Bronfenbrenner, U. (1979). *The Ecology of Human Development: Experiments by Nature and Design.* Harvard University Press.

Common Sense Media. (2025). *The Common Sense Census: Media use by kids zero to eight* (5th ed.). Common Sense Media. https://www.commonsensemedia.org/sites/default/files/research/report/2025-common-sense-census-web-2.pdf

Crittenden, A., & Marlowe, F. (2008). Allomaternal care among the Hadza of Tanzania. *Human Nature, 19*, 249–262. doi:10.1007/s12110-008-9043-3

Farr, R., Tornello, S., & Rostosky, S. (2022). How do LGBTQ+ parents raise well-adjusted, resilient, and thriving children? *Current Directions in Psychological Science, 31*(6), 526–535.

Feldman, R. (2015). The adaptive human parental brain: Implications for children's social development. *Trends in Neurosciences, 38*(6), 387–399.

Gaines, A. (2015). Culture, development and self: The work of Robert A. LeVine. *Culture, Medicine, and Psychiatry, 39*, 584–596.

Gettler, L., Lew-Levy, S., Sarma, M., Miegakanda, V., Doxsey, M., Meyer, J., & Boyette, A. (2021). Children's fingernail cortisol among BaYaka foragers of the Congo Basin: Associations with fathers' roles. *Philosophical Transactions of the Royal Society, 376*, 20200031. doi:10.1098/rstb.2020.0031

Han, Y., Yuan, M., Guo, Y., Shen, X.., Gao, Z., & Bi, X. (2022). The role of enriched environment in neural development and repair. *Frontiers in Cellular Neuroscience, 16*, 890666.

Hastings, P., Miller, J., & Troxel, N. (2015). Making good: The socialization of children's prosocial development. In J. E. Grusec & P. D. Hastings (Eds.), *Handbook of Socialization: Theory and Research* (2nd ed., pp. 637–660). Guilford Press.

Heiphetz, L., & Oishi, S. (2022). Viewing development through the lens of culture: Integrating developmental and cultural psychology to better understand cognition and behavior. *Perspectives on Psychological Science, 17*(1), 62–77. https://doi.org/10.1177/1745691620980725

Hewlett, B. (1991). *Intimate Fathers: The Nature and Context of Aka Pygmy Paternal Infant Care.* University of Michigan Press.

Hill, K., & Hurtado, A. (1996). *Aché Life History: The Ecology and Demography of a Foraging People.* Aldine de Gruyter.

Kazeem, A., & Jensen, L. (2017). Orphan status, school attendance, and their relationship to household head in Nigeria. *Demographic Research, 36*, 659–690.

Khaleque, A., & Rohner, R. (2012). Pancultural associations between perceived parental acceptance and psychological adjustment of children and adults: A meta-analytic review of worldwide research. *Journal of Cross-Cultural Psychology, 43*(5), 784–800.

Konner, M. (2018). Nonmaternal care: A half-century of research. *Physiology & Behavior, 193*, 179–186.

LeVine, R. (2010). Plasticity and variation: Cultural influences on parenting and early child development within and across populations. In C. Worthman, P. Plotsky, D. Schechter, & C. Cummings (Eds.), *Formative Experiences: The Interaction of Caregiving, Culture and Developmental Psychobiology.* Cambridge University Press.

LeVine, R., Miller, P., & West, M. (Eds.). (1988). *Parental Behavior in Diverse Societies: New Directions for Child Development Sourcebook, No. 40.* Jossey-Bass.

Lightfoot, C., Cole, M., & Cole, S. (2018). *The Development of Children.* Worth Publishers/ Macmillan Education.

Massaroni, V., Delle Donne, V., Marra, C., Arcangeli, V., & Chieffo, D. P. R. (2024). The relationship between language and technology: How screen time affects language development in early life – a systematic review. *Brain Sciences, 14*(1), 27. https://doi.org/10.3390/brainsci14010027

Meehan, C., Helfrecht, C., & Quinlan R. (2014). Cooperative breeding and Aka children's nutritional status: Is flexibility key? *American Journal of Physical Anthropology, 153,* 513–525. doi:10.1002/ajpa.22415

Miguel, P., O Pereira, L., Silveira, P., & Meaney, M. (2019). Early environmental influences on the development of children's brain structure and function. *Developmental Medicine & Child Neurology, 61.* doi: 10.1111/dmcn.14182

Norman, A. (2024). Alloparenting – a historical perspective on infant 'loving' care relationships. *Norland Educare Research Journal, 2*(1), 1–11.

Page, A., Emmott, E., Dyble, M., Smith, D., Chaudhary, N., Viguier, S., & Migliano, A. B. (2021). Children are important too. *Philosophical Transactions: Biological Sciences, 376*(1827), 1–11.

Pieloch, K., McCullough, M., & Marks, A. (2016). Resilience of children with refugee statuses: A research review. *Canadian Psychology/psychologie canadienne, 57*(4), 330.

Ren, W. (2023). The influence of screen media usage on child social development: A systematic review. *Journal of Education Humanities and Social Sciences, 8,* 2110–2117. https://drpress.org/ojs/index.php/EHSS/article/view/4655/4509

Rocha, B., & Nunes, C. (2020). Benefits and damages of the use of touchscreen devices for the development and behavior of children under 5 years old – a systematic review. *Psicol Reflex Crit.* 2020 Oct 31;33(1):24. doi: 10.1186/s41155-020-00163-8. PMID: 33128692; PMCID: PMC7603436.

Roopnarine, J., & Davidson, K. (2015). Parent–child play across cultures: Advancing play research. *American Journal of Play, 7,* 228–252.

Sear, R., & Mace, R. (2008). Who keeps children alive? A review of the effects of kin on child survival. *Evolution and Human Behavior, 29*(1), 1–18. https://doi.org/10.1016/j.evolhumbehav.2007.10.001

Shen, J., Zhu, Y., & Zhang, G. (2025). The relationship between parental adverse childhood experiences and offspring preschool readiness: The mediating role of psychological resilience. *BMC Psychology, 13*(1), 136.

Sorkhabi, N., & Mandara, J. (2013). Are the effects of Baumrind's parenting styles culturally specific or culturally equivalent? In R. E. Larzelere, A. S. Morris, & A. W. Harrist (Eds.), *Authoritative Parenting: Synthesizing Nurturance and Discipline for Optimal Child Development* (pp. 113–135). American Psychological Association. https://doi.org/10.1037/13948-006

Sussman, D., Leung, R., Chakravarty, M., Lerch, J., & Taylor, M. (2016). The developing human brain: Age-related changes in cortical, subcortical, and cerebellar anatomy. *Brain and Behavior, 6*(4), e00457.

Theron, L. (2020). Resilience of sub-Saharan children and adolescents: A scoping review. *Transcultural Psychiatry*, *60*(6), 1017–1039. doi:10.1177/1363461520938916

Tooley, U., Bassett, D., & Mackey, A. (2021). Environmental influences on the pace of brain development. *Nature Reviews Neuroscience*, *22*(6), 372–384.

Vygotsky, L. (1978). *Mind in Society: The Development of Higher Psychological Processes*. Harvard University Press.

Yu, W., & Yan, H. (2023). Effects of siblings on cognitive and socio-behavioral development: Ongoing debates and new theoretical insights. *American Sociological Review*, *88*(6), 1002–1030.

Zhao L, Tian M, Wang Z, Hu D. (2025). Associations of Grandparenting Dimensions/ Styles with Mental Health in Children and Adolescents: A Systematic Review and Meta-Analysis. Behav Sci (Basel). 2025 Feb 8;15(2):180. doi: 10.3390/bs15020180. PMID: 40001811; PMCID: PMC11851558.

5

Conceptualisations of neurodivergence

Emma Jenks, Philippa L. Howard and Felicity Sedgewick

Chapter objectives

By the end of this chapter, you will gain:

- An understanding of what neurodivergence is.
- An understanding of how to critically reflect on different framing models for neurodivergence.

Overview of the chapter

This chapter will focus on the different perspectives and paradigms through which developmental differences have been understood. Covering the medical model, social model, interactionist model and the neurodiversity paradigm, it will examine the assumptions each brings to understanding child development and the implications this has for educational and psychological practice. Taking autism as a case study, we will explore how each of these can be applied in practice.

Why should you read this chapter?

As diagnoses of neurodivergent differences continue to increase, practitioners are likely to encounter children with a range of different needs. You should read this chapter to gain insight into the ways in which policy and professional practice are shaped by the underlying assumptions around child development.

Neurodiversity and neurodevelopmental differences

Neurodiversity refers to the different ways in which people's minds function (Walker, 2021). When a person's brain functioning differs from the neurotypical norm within society, they are considered to be neurodivergent – in other words, their neurology diverges from what we expect from typically developing individuals (Pellicano & Houting, 2022). This term was developed from the neurodiversity movement in the 1990s (described later in this chapter), so earlier approaches do not use this terminology.

It should be noted that neurodivergence itself is not a recognised condition or diagnosis; rather, it is an umbrella term that covers a range of potential differences. Some definitions extend as far as any disability or difference in the brain (Walker, 2021) but, within this text, our focus will be on neurodevelopmental conditions. These are lifelong differences in brain development (see Chapter 6) that may include, but are not limited to, those listed in Table 5.1. They are varied in nature and may overlap with one another.

Table 5.1   Examples of neurodevelopmental differences

Neurodevelopmental difference	Summary of diagnostic criteria (American Psychiatric Association, 2013)	Examples of strengths
Autism	Differences in social communication and interaction (e.g., body language or eye contact) and restricted or repetitive behaviours (e.g., sensory sensitivities or focused interests)	Pattern recognition, expertise in areas of interest, attention to detail, honesty (Chow & Cooper, 2024; Woods & Estes, 2023)
Attention Deficit Hyperactivity Disorder (ADHD)	Appearing inattentive (e.g., difficulty with concentration or seeming not to listen) or hyperactive (e.g., needing to move around)	Creativity, ability to 'hyperfocus', energy, cognitive flexibility (Schippers, Greven et al., 2024; Schippers, Horstman et al., 2022)
Specific learning difficulty (e.g., dyslexia, dyscalculia)	Difficulty with learning and processing information or academic skills, such as word reading, spelling, number sense or mathematical reasoning	Visuospatial and abstract reasoning, problem-solving, team work (Kannangara et al., 2018)

Consider this 5.1

- How have you heard neurodiversity described in the past? Consider whether the definition above is in line with what you have been taught previously or how you have seen neurodiversity being described (e.g., in the media or online).

How do we frame neurodevelopmental differences?

There are various ways in which neurodevelopmental differences are conceptualised. The approach someone adopts may be influenced by the interaction of a wide range of factors, including cultural norms and traditions, educational environment, and knowledge and experience of neurodiversity (Babik & Gardner, 2021). What is important to understand is that the way that neurodevelopmental differences are conceptualised by an individual, society and institutions has implications for education policy and practice, stigmatisation and the wellbeing of the individual (e.g., Haegele & Hodge, 2016). Below we explore some of the primary conceptualisations of neurodevelopmental differences and the implications of each.

Medical model

The medical model of disability assumes that physical and psychological conditions are a direct consequence of an impairment within a person's mind or body. This view originates from the advancement of the physical health care systems in the Western world, where the primary goal was to identify and diagnose the direct cause of the symptoms a person is experiencing and provide treatment that will revert or eradicate the issue to return the person to 'normal functioning'. It is very clearly appropriate in physical healthcare contexts. If a person has a broken leg or a virus, for instance, it is optimal to act in a way to heal their leg or cure the infectious disease, which will remove unpleasant symptoms (e.g., pain, fever) and enable them to return to their usual activities and level of functioning (e.g., walking upstairs or leaving their bed).

The assumptions of the medical model have also been traditionally applied to psychological conditions more broadly and is the dominant lens through which neurodivergence is viewed in the global North (note that understanding of the conceptualisations of neurodivergence is Western-centric and there is much less understanding of the conceptualisations of disability in the global South; Grech, 2009). A simple piece of evidence for this is the development of the *Diagnostic and Statistical Manual of Mental Disorders* (American Psychiatric Association, 2013), which is used by medical professionals (e.g., psychiatrists, paediatricians and psychologists) to identify the mental disorder attached to an individual. Following diagnosis, an individual is likely to receive recommendations for treatment to reduce the impact of their condition on influencing their ability to function 'normally'. A child who is diagnosed with ADHD, for instance, may be prescribed stimulant medication to reduce their attentional difficulties with the aim to support their ability to engage in school (Castle et al., 2007; Swanson et al., 1991). An associated assumption of the medical model is that it is an individual's responsibility to seek out expert advice and follow treatment guidance. There is now a move away from the medical model when considering neurodiversity and psychological conditions more generally, because of the framing of neurodivergence as an abnormality and the consequential stigmatisation that has wide-reaching consequences on an individual's life (Haegele & Hodge, 2016; Kapp et al., 2013).

An example of the medical model in practice is Applied Behavioural Analysis (ABA), which was developed in the early 1980s. It uses the behaviourist approaches and operant conditioning to teach autistic children to communicate and behave more 'typically' in order to maximise their ability to learn; for example, increasing spontaneous verbal requests and eye contact, and reducing self-stimulating behaviour such as hand flapping. The aim of the original research on the ABA approach was for autistic children to complete preschool without their autism being recognised by school staff (Lovaas, 1987). In other words, the aim of ABA was to focus on changing the autistic children's behaviour so that they acted more like their neurotypical peers and is directly aligned with the medical model's approach in seeking to 'correct' psychological conditions. It should be noted that a Cochrane Review concluded that the evidence for the effectiveness of ABA is weak (Reichow et al., 2018). Moreover, ABA is a controversial intervention for a range of reasons. Autistic adults reflecting on the ABA approach reported it to be a traumatic experience that led to negative lifelong effects on their mental wellbeing (Leaf et al., 2022).

Social model

The social model was developed in the 1970s in response to a disability movement within the UK (Oliver, 1983, 2013). Like the medical model, the social model views disability or neurodiversity as related to an in-person impairment. However, the social model proposes that the difference does not cause disability; environmental, social and attitudinal barriers do (Oliver, 2013). A person who uses a wheelchair, for example, is only disabled if they are unable to travel independently because ramps are not available. This model therefore highlights the social construction of disability. It means that the approaches viewed as most optimal to alleviate any difficulties experienced is to adapt the environment to accommodate people with a range of abilities. In the context of neurodiversity, this may be removing a time limit for an exam to support dyslexic students or changing the sensory environment of a classroom to better meet the needs of an autistic student. It spreads the responsibility of care to go beyond medical professionals and the individual, and to include (but not be limited to) schools, policy makers and employers. This approach, therefore, fosters a sense of empowerment within the disabled and neurodiverse communities by emphasising the capabilities and rights of individuals (Shakespeare, 2006). There are criticisms, however, that this model can oversimplify the challenges the disabled community experience by proposing that disability is only caused by external barriers. It also idealises independence (Shakespeare, 2006).

Treatment and Education of Autistic and related Communication-handicapped Children (TEACCH) (Mesibov et al., 2004) is an example of an approach that supports autistic children within school. It reflects the social model, in that it does not attempt to change the individual, but instead adapts the school environment and systems to meet the needs of an individual; for example, using structured teaching, altering the physical space to better meet sensory needs, creating individual work schedules and using visual timetables that support a child to predict their day and reduce anxiety.

Meta-analyses report mixed findings as to whether TEACCH has a positive impact on outcomes (Sandbank et al., 2020; Virues-Ortega et al., 2013).

Interactionist model

The interactionist model, otherwise known as Ecological Systems Theory (Bronfenbrenner, 1979), was developed in the 1970s (see Chapter 4). The approach proposes that a person's experiences and outcomes will be influenced (either directly or indirectly) by several factors in their lives, from family and friends to the wider social context. The interactionist model is often visualised as a series of concentric circles (Figure 5.1). In Bronfenbrenner's model, each circle represents a level of environmental influence. These levels do not represent individual factors themselves; rather, they denote the contexts or environments within which multiple factors operate to shape individuals' development and lived experiences. The model focuses on the interactions between these levels and sees difficulties and disadvantage, including disability, as arising from ineffective, problematic or failed interactions between the levels rather than as having a single point of responsibility.

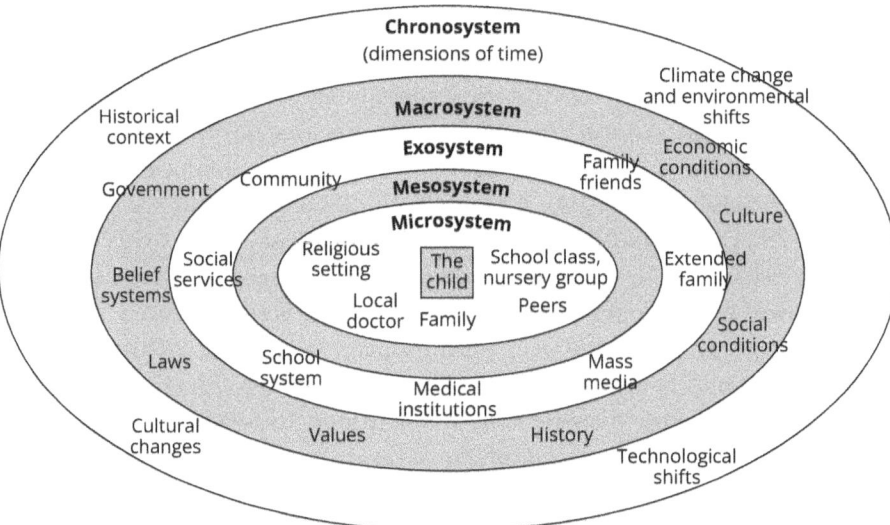

Figure 5.1   Illustration of the interactionist model (adapted from Carroll & McCulloch, 2018, p. 86)

The *individual* is the central point, containing the influences of their biology and psychology on their experiences – factors such as being neurodivergent, for example, would fit in this layer, as would genetics or personality traits.

Immediately surrounding the individual is the *microsystem*. It includes the family, friends, school settings and communities of which the individual is a part. Essentially, the microsystem comprises the local connections and places in which the individual spends a lot of time, and which can therefore influence them at close range and over an extended period of time.

After the microsystem comes the *mesosystem*. This layer is about the interactions between the individual and their microsystems or between the different microsystems themselves. For example, the interaction between a child (individual) and their teacher at school (microsystem) is part of the mesosystem. So is a parents' evening, where the family microsystem (parents/guardians) interacts with the school microsystem (teacher) in discussing the child (individual) – even if the child is not present for the conversation?

The next layer in the model is the *exosystem*. It focuses on the indirect influences on the individual – the factors and interactions which do not directly involve them but which impact others in their microsystem and, therefore, have a secondary effect on the individual. Parental stress at work, for example, can lead to anxiety for a child because of the changes it brings about in the family microsystem, but it is not the same as a child being stressed or anxious about their own school work (which would be a mesosystem pressure).

Surrounding all these layers in the model is the *macrosystem*. This outer layer represents the wider social, cultural, political, legal and religious systems in which the individual lives. These elements shape the opportunities and barriers applicable to each individual and microsystem, and thereby have an overarching influence on their lives. An example would be the amount of funding a government chooses to put into education – a decision from the political system – which is not made on the basis of the impact it will have on any individual child, but which will inevitably significantly change the school experience (microsystem) of every child in the country.

The final element of the model is the *chronosystem*. It represents the influence of time on everything else in the model – both the historical context for the society and systems in which an individual lives and the timespan of their own life and the ways in which things change during it. Examples of chronosystem influence can be the impact of the Victorian Industrial Revolution on many UK cities, meaning that large numbers of people live in terraced housing, which lends itself to a particular sense of your local community. Equally, the chronosystem influence is present on a smaller scale within an individual's life in terms of their own personal transitions, such as going through puberty or getting married, as these things change their sense of their self and their connections to people around them – the individual, micro- and mesosystem levels.

Taken together, the different system levels in this model seek to explain the whole range of possible influences on how a child develops and their experiences within the world. It has often been used to look at neurodiversity precisely because it actively and equally acknowledges the individual factor of developmental difference alongside the wider social context, rather than placing emphasis for cause and responsibility in just one part of the system.

A recent key development to Bronfenbrenner's original model has focused on the growing influence of the digital world. Known as the *neo-ecological theory*, it directly addresses the influence of the virtual environment on people's lives (Navarro & Tudge, 2022). In this addition to the model, the virtual microsystem includes things such as social media, gaming platforms and digital communication tools (anything from WhatsApp to Zoom). The virtual macrosystem is seen as the ways in which society at large uses, discusses and represents those same digital tools and experiences. The authors of the model argue that the virtual ecological system is distinct from the traditional, physical systems Bronfenbrenner described, while at the same time being unavoidably interwoven with them. The virtual ecological system enables individuals to participate in the creation of the virtual macrosystem in ways that were not previously possible, because they are now among those actively creating and curating online spaces and contributing to the discourses that operate within them. This is a new and emerging field of theoretical thinking and research, and further developments are likely to be added as new technologies emerge.

An example of the interactionist model in practice is Picture Exchange Communication Systems, known as PECS, which is a system that enables children to communicate with those around them even if they have minimal verbal language. Children have a set of picture cards that represent common requests and topics, such as foods, drinks, places they go, things they do and people they know. They learn to show these cards to adults (and other children) to communicate when they want a glass of water, for example, or to choose between a sandwich or a jacket potato for lunch, or to say that they want to go to the park after school.

The cards can be edited and personalised for each child (the individual in this intervention) and then family, teachers and other key adults learn to use them as well (the microsystem around the child). Parents and teachers discuss how to personalise the cards for each child and how to use the cards consistently between home and school (the mesosystem). The school may adopt the use of the cards more widely so that the child doesn't feel singled out compared to their speaking peers (a larger-scale element of the mesosystem). Although there is no government mandate that schools support PECS (a macrosystem consideration), it is often a highly successful intervention which significantly improves children's communication capabilities (Ganz et al., 2012; Pruneti et al., 2024). This beneficial effect has been shown cross-culturally, including in low-resource settings such as Brazil and Thailand (Wannapaschaiyong et al., 2025).

The neurodiversity paradigm

The previous three models are all used to talk about disability on a broader scale. The final model we will cover is more specific to neurodiversity.

The neurodiversity paradigm, and a wider social movement, developed as a response to the ongoing overarching medical understanding of neurodivergence, deficit-based narratives and attempts to find a cure (Dwyer, 2022; Walker, 2021). As many neurodivergent people were routinely denied agency or dismissed in both research and practice, there have been calls to place control back into their hands and recognise their expertise (Pellicano & Houting, 2022).

As the paradigm was not created by any single individual, the exact definition varies and continues to evolve (Dwyer, 2022; McLennan et al., 2025), but a common summary is as follows: neurodivergence is a natural and positive part of human variation, it is a core part of neurodivergent individuals' identities, and we should not aim to 'cure' or 'fix' these differences (Armstrong, 2015; Dwyer et al., 2024). This shift away from viewing neurodivergence merely as a problem or difficulty sets it apart from the other models but some overlapping ideas remain.

Similarly to the social model, proponents of this paradigm believe that many of the challenges faced by neurodivergent people are due to barriers within society, which can be addressed with appropriate accommodations (McLennan et al., 2025). However, few neurodiversity advocates argue that it is society alone which is disabling. Instead, they acknowledge that some challenges may remain even in a more supportive setting (den Houting, 2019; Dwyer et al., 2024). The neurodiverstity paradigm aligns with interactionist perspectives that see an overlap between society and the individual (Dwyer, 2022) and highlights the strengths associated with neurodivergence (Armstrong, 2015; Dwyer et al., 2024). According to the approach, interventions need to be based on the individual's preferences and to improve their quality of life, rather than to get them to fit neurotypical expectations (McLennan et al., 2025).

An example of an intervention that reflects the neurodiversity paradigm is the Learning About Neurodiversity at School (LEANS) project (Alcorn et al., 2022). It is a set of resources that educates primary school children about neurodiversity and what those differences may look like at school. The project materials are focused on strengths and highlighting areas of difference without suggesting that anyone's style of thinking is wrong or incorrect. Recent results demonstrate that the resources improve students' knowledge and attitudes around neurodiversity, as well as promoting positive intended actions towards their neurodivergent peers (Alcorn et al., 2024).

Consider this 5.2

- How might neurodevelopmental differences affect a child at school or in their day-to-day life? What advantages or challenges might they experience? Consider the examples in Table 5.1 or an example from your own practice if you have previously worked with neurodivergent people.
- How would you support a neurodivergent child? Think about your answers to the previous question and how you might support or encourage a child with these differences.

Case study 5.1: Greta

Greta is a 12-year-old girl who has been diagnosed as being autistic who attends a mainstream secondary school. She is performing well academically, particularly in English and science, which are her favourite subjects. Her teachers describe her as quiet and methodical, with an ability to remember specific facts and write creatively at a level beyond her years.

She had difficulty, however, with the transition from primary school and the related change in environment. She has had panic attacks in the busy corridors between classes and she gets upset when she has to change classrooms, especially when she cannot sit in her preferred seat.

(Continued)

She acts differently from her peers; she focuses on her own interests, does not make eye contact when having a conversation, and sometimes rocks back and forth on her feet or in her chair. When she is particularly stressed, she does not communicate verbally. She has experienced bullying and other students in her class tend to avoid spending time with her.

Greta has been sent home on multiple occasions for not wearing the correct uniform, complaining that it is uncomfortable, and has recently begun avoiding school altogether. Her parents say that she frequently describes having headaches and nausea on school days, despite no measurable signs of illness, but will happily get on with her schoolwork if allowed to stay at home.

Greta has friends outside school through a Girl Guides group, which she has been going to for several years. Her parents and the leaders of the group have spent time with Greta to work out how to make her time there a positive experience and she behaves very differently at Guides than at school. She takes part in almost all the activities, handles changes between activities with less anxiety and is popular with the other children.

Being critical

Think about the medical, social, interactionist and neurodiversity models/paradigms described in this chapter. For each of these:

- How does the model explain Greta's experiences?
- Are there any aspects of her case that are not addressed by the model?
- What recommendations could be made to support Greta, based on the model?

Reflection points

- Which model aligns best with your experiences? Reflect on what your views of neurodiversity were before you read this chapter and which models best represent them. Think about your own educational experiences or the places where you have worked. How do these models compare to the way in which neurodiversity was discussed, or how students were supported?
- What are your views on each of these models? Consider which assumptions from these models most resonate with you, or areas where you disagree. Think about how you would incorporate each of these approaches in your own practice and how well they would work.
- Have you ever seen these differences in your practice? Reflect on the approaches you, or others, have taken when working with neurodivergent students in the past. Consider which models these approaches were based on.

Chapter summary

This chapter explained the concept of neurodiversity and discussed examples of different perspectives we can take when considering neurodiversity in our practice. Each of these models has their own set of assumptions that affect the way we approach supporting neurodivergent learners.

Key models explored

- Medical model: The medical model is based on physical healthcare contexts and explains neurodivergence as a result of impairments within an individual person. The approach involves diagnosing and identifying symptoms, with the aim to treat them and reduce the impact of the condition on 'normal' functioning.
- Social model: The social model places more emphasis on barriers created by the environment or society. It proposes that supporting neurodivergent people should involve reducing the impact of those barriers with accommodations and adaptations to the environment.
- Interactionist model: The interactionist model takes into account a range of circumstances affecting the development of an individual. These circumstances are visualised as a series of concentric circles leading from the individual in the centre, through multiple layers, out to the wider social context. It incorporates not just the differences within an individual, but broader social and cultural influences and the effect of time.
- Neurodiversity paradigm: Developed as a response to the medical model, this approach recognises neurodivergence as a natural part of human variation to be respected and celebrated. It does not aim to 'cure' neurodivergence and instead recommends accommodations centred on the needs and preferences of the individual.

Further reading

Chapman, R., & Fletcher-Watson, S. (2026) *A Very Short Introduction to: Neurodiversity*. Oxford University Press.

Fielding, C., Streeter, A., Riby, D., & Hanley, M. (2025). Neurodivergent pupils' experiences of school distress and attendance difficulties. *Neurodiversity, 3*, 27546330251327056.

Haegele, J., & Hodge, S. (2016). Disability discourse: Overview and critiques of the medical and social models. *Quest, 68*(2), 193–206. https://doi.org/10.1080/00336297. 2016.1143849

Useful websites

ADHD UK: https://adhduk.co.uk/

ADHD UK: Provides information, resources, and support for individuals with ADHD and their families. Offers guidance on diagnosis, treatment, and living with ADHD.

British Dyslexia Association: www.bdadyslexia.org.uk/

British Dyslexia Association: A charity dedicated to supporting people with dyslexia. Offers advice, training, and resources for individuals, parents, and educators.

Dyspraxia Foundation: https://dyspraxiauk.com/dyspraxia-foundation

Dyspraxia Foundation: Supports individuals with dyspraxia and their families through advice, resources, and community engagement. Promotes awareness and understanding of the condition.

National Autistic Society: www.autism.org.uk/

National Autistic Society: Provides information, support, and advocacy for autistic individuals and their families. Offers resources for education, employment, and daily living.

References

Alcorn, A., Fletcher-Watson, S., McGeown, S., Murray, F., Aitken, D., Peacock, L., & Mandy, W. (2022). *Learning about Neurodiversity at School: A Resource Pack for Primary School Teachers and Pupils*. University of Edinburgh. https://salvesen-research.ed.ac.uk/leans

Alcorn, A., McGeown, S., Mandy, W., Aitken, D., & Fletcher-Watson, S. (2024). Learning About Neurodiversity at School: A feasibility study of a new classroom programme for mainstream primary schools. *Neurodiversity*, 2, 27546330241272186. https://doi.org/10.1177/27546330241272186

American Psychiatric Association. (2013). *Diagnostic and Statistical Manual of Mental Disorders (DSM)* (5th ed.). APA. https://doi.org/10.1176/appi.books.9780890425596

Armstrong, T. (2015). The myth of the normal brain: Embracing neurodiversity. *AMA Journal of Ethics*, 17(4), 348–352.

Babik, I., & Gardner, E. (2021). Factors affecting the perception of disability: A developmental perspective. *Frontiers in Psychology: Developmental Section*, 12. https://doi.org/10.3389/fpsyg.2021.702166

Bronfenbrenner, U. (1979). Contexts of child rearing: Problems and prospects. *American psychologist*, 34(10), 844.

Carroll, M., & McCulloch, M. (Eds.). (2018). *Understanding Teaching & Learning in Primary Education* (2nd ed.). Sage.

Castle, L., Aubert, R., Verbrugge, R., Khalid, M., & Epstein, R. (2007). Trends in medication treatment for ADHD. *Journal of Attention Disorders*, 10(4), 335–342. https://doi.org/10.1177/1087054707299597

Chow, C., & Cooper, K. (2024). What are the lived experiences of strengths in autistic individuals? A systematic review and thematic synthesis. *Autism in Adulthood*, aut.2023.0172. https://doi.org/10.1089/aut.2023.0172

den Houting, J. (2019). Neurodiversity: An insider's perspective. *Autism*, 23(2), 271–273. https://doi.org/10.1177/1362361318820762

Dwyer, P. (2022). The neurodiversity approach(es): What are they and what do they mean for researchers? *Human Development*, 66(2), 73–92. https://doi.org/10.1159/000523723

Dwyer, P., Gurba, A., Kapp, S., Kilgallon, E., Hersh, L., Chang, D., Rivera, S., & Gillespie-Lynch, K. (2024). Community views of neurodiversity, models of disability and autism intervention: Mixed methods reveal shared goals and key tensions. *Autism*, 13623613241273029. https://doi.org/10.1177/13623613241273029

Ganz, J., Davis, J., Lund, E., Goodwyn, F., & Simpson, R. (2012). Meta-analysis of PECS with individuals with ASD: Investigation of targeted versus non-targeted outcomes, participant characteristics, and implementation phase. *Research in Developmental Disabilities*, 33(2), 406–418.

Grech, S. (2009). Disability, poverty and development: critical reflections on the majority world debate. *Disability & Society*, 24(6), 771–784. https://doi.org/10.1080/09687590903160266

Haegele, J., & Hodge, S. (2016). Disability discourse: Overview and critiques of the medical and social models. *Quest*, 68(2), 193–206. https://doi.org/10.1080/00336297.2016.1143849

Kannangara, C., Carson, J., Puttaraju, S., & Allen, R. (2018). Not all those who wander are lost: Examining the character strengths of dyslexia. *Global Journal of Intellectual and Developmental Disabilities*, 4(5), 555648.

Kapp, S. K., Gillespie-Lynch, K., Sherman, L. E., & Hutman, T. (2013). Deficit, difference, or both? Autism and neurodiversity. *Developmental psychology*, 49(1), 59–71. https://doi.org/10.1037/a0028353

Leaf, J., Cihon, J., Leaf, R. et al. (2022). Concerns about ABA-based intervention: An evaluation and recommendations. *Journal of Autism and Developmental Disorders*, 52, 2838–2853. https://doi.org/10.1007/s10803-021-05137-y

Lovaas, O. (1987). Behavioral treatment and normal educational and intellectual functioning in young autistic children. *Journal of Consulting and Clinical Psychology*, 55(1), 3.

McLennan, H., Aberdein, R., Saggers, B., & Gillett-Swan, J. (2025). Thirty years on from Sinclair: A scoping review of neurodiversity definitions and conceptualisations in empirical research. *Review Journal of Autism and Developmental Disorders*. https://doi.org/10.1007/s40489-025-00493-2

Mesibov, G., Shea, V., & Schopler, E. (2004). *The TEACCH Approach to Autism Spectrum Disorders*. Springer Science & Business Media. http://dx.doi.org/10.1007/978-0-306-48647-0

Navarro, J., & Tudge, J. (2022). Technologizing Bronfenbrenner: Neo-ecological theory. *Human Development*, 66(1), 1–18. https://doi.org/10.1159/000524139

Oliver, M. (1983). *Social Work with Disabled People*. Macmillan.

Oliver, M. (2013). The social model of disability: Thirty years on. *Disability & Society*, 28(7), 1024–1026. https://doi.org/10.1080/09687599.2013.818773

Pellicano, E., & Houting, J. (2022). Annual research review: Shifting from 'normal science' to neurodiversity in autism science. *Journal of Child Psychology and Psychiatry*, 63(4), 381–396. https://doi.org/10.1111/jcpp.13534

Pruneti, C., Coscioni, G., & Guidotti, S. (2024). Evaluation of the effectiveness of behavioral interventions for autism spectrum disorders: A systematic review of randomized controlled trials and quasi-experimental studies. *Clinical Child Psychology and Psychiatry*, 29(1), 213–231.

Reichow, B., Hume, K., Barton, E., & Boyd, B. (2018). Early Intensive Behavioral Intervention (EIBI) for young children with autism spectrum disorders (ASD). *Cochrane Database of Systematic Reviews*, Issue 5. Art. No. CD009260. doi: 10.1002/14651858.CD009260.pub3

Sandbank, M., Bottema-Beutel, K., Crowley, S., Cassidy, M., Dunham, K., Feldman, J., Crank, J., Albarran, S., Raj, S., Mahbub, P., & Woynaroski, T. (2020). Project AIM: Autism intervention meta-analysis for studies of young children. *Psychological Bulletin*, 146(1), 1–29. https://doi.org/10.1037/bul0000215

Schippers, L., Greven, C., & Hoogman, M. (2024). Associations between ADHD traits and self-reported strengths in the general population. *Comprehensive Psychiatry*, 130, 152461.

Schippers, L., Horstman, L., van de Velde, H., Pereira, R., Zinkstok, J., Mostert, J., Greven, C. U., & Hoogman, M. (2022). A qualitative and quantitative study of self-reported positive characteristics of individuals with ADHD. *Frontiers in Psychiatry, 13*. https://doi.org/10.3389/fpsyt.2022.922788

Shakespeare, T. (2006). The social model of disability. In L. J. Davis (Ed.), *The Disability Studies Reader* (pp. 16–24). Routledge.

Swanson, J., Cantwell, D., Lerner, M., McBurnett, K., & Hanna, G. (1991). Effects of stimulant medication on learning in children with ADHD. *Journal of Learning Disabilities*, 24(4), 219–230, 255. https://doi.org/10.1177/002221949102400406

Virues-Ortega, J., Julio, F., & Pastor-Barriuso, R. (2013). The TEACCH program for children and adults with autism: A meta-analysis of intervention studies. *Clinical Psychology Review*, 33(8), 940–953. https://doi.org/10.1016/j.cpr.2013.07.005

Walker, N. (2021). *Neuroqueer Heresies: Notes on the Neurodiversity Paradigm, Autistic Empowerment, and Postnormal Possibilities*. Autonomous Press.

Wannapaschaiyong, P., Vivattanasinchai, T., & Wongkwanmuang, A. (2025). Predictors of successful Picture Exchange Communication System training in children with communication impairments: Insights from a real-world intervention in a resource-limited setting. *BMJ Paediatrics Open*, 9(1), e003282.

Woods, S., & Estes, A. (2023). Toward a more comprehensive autism assessment: The survey of autistic strengths, skills, and interests. *Frontiers in Psychiatry*, 14, 1264516.

6

The role of neuroscience in child development

Carolina Gordillo-Bravo

Chapter objectives

By the end of the chapter, you will gain an understanding of:

- How the brain develops, from the pre-natal to the post-natal stages, in order to perform its main functions.
- The key biological processes in the brain that support the development of cognitive and socio-emotional abilities.
- The uses of neuroscientific insights for explaining developmental trajectories and behaviour from childhood to adolescence, including neurodevelopmental differences.
- How the environment affects brain development and its effects on cognition and socio-emotional processing.

Overview of the chapter

This chapter will offer an overview of the stages of neural and brain development from conception to adolescence, providing explanations of the main brain structures and their associated cognitive functions involved in child development into adolescence. Key concepts stemming from neuroscience, such as neuroplasticity, synaptic pruning and critical periods will be introduced. Finally, the chapter will explore the factors that may affect such development at a brain and mind level, together with potential neuroscience-based applications to promote optimal child development.

Why should you read this chapter?

This chapter introduces key brain regions and their cognitive functions, explaining how neuroplasticity and critical periods shape development. It highlights how both biological and environmental factors influence neurodivergence and developmental pathways, offering insights into the complexity of child development from infancy to adolescence.

An overview of the brain

In the brain, we find two types of cells: neurons and glial cells. Neurons are the nerve cells that send and receive electrical signals carrying information throughout the brain. There are around 86 billion neurons in the brain (Herculano-Houzel, 2009). The glial cells do not carry information but they have a supporting role in the central nervous system. Different types of glial cells are involved in different tasks, such as providing a scaffolding for the neurons, speeding neuronal communication and protecting the brain by removing foreign matter from dying cells. The process of myelination is key for neuronal transmission. It is a developmental process that covers the axon of the neuron with an insulating layer of a fatty substance called myelin, making transmission of the electrical signal in the neuron more efficient and faster. The myelination of the axons follows an increasing trajectory into adulthood and up to the fifth decade, when a natural decline occurs, the most noticeable effect of which is a lower speed in cognitive processes.

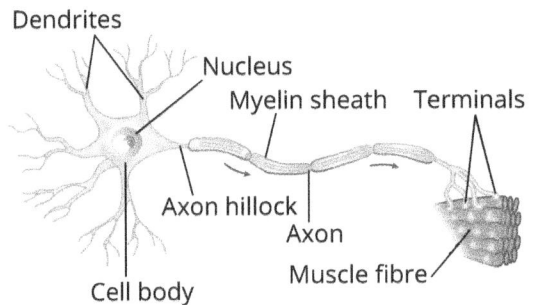

Figure 6.1 Parts of the neuron

Neurons communicate via two mechanisms of a different nature. Communication within the neuron is electrical whereas between neurons it is chemical. The dendrites of the neuron receive signals from other neurons and transmit its information to the cell body. The signal, in turn, is sent through the axon to the synaptic terminals on the other end of the neuron (see Figure 6.1) and across the synaptic cleft to reach the dendrites of the next neuron. The crossing to the next neuron is the result of a combination of chemical processes involving the release of neurotransmitters which are chemical messengers with specific functions.

The adult brain weighs approximately three pounds (1.4 kilos) and its size and weight changes dramatically in the first years of life. At birth, its weight is about 25% of that of an adult brain and it is only by the age of 2 that the brain reaches 75% of the weight of the adult brain.

One way to characterise the anatomical brain structure is to divide the cerebrum into lobes (see Figure 6.2), each with specific micro-structures and associated cognitive

functions. The occipital lobe is involved in visual processing; the frontal lobe is generally associated with higher order thinking and planning; the temporal lobe is involved
in language processing but also hearing and smell; and the parietal lobes are associated
with reading comprehension, logic and mathematical processing. The cerebrum has two
hemispheres which are connected by a bundle of fibres called the corpus callosum,
which helps communication between the two hemispheres.

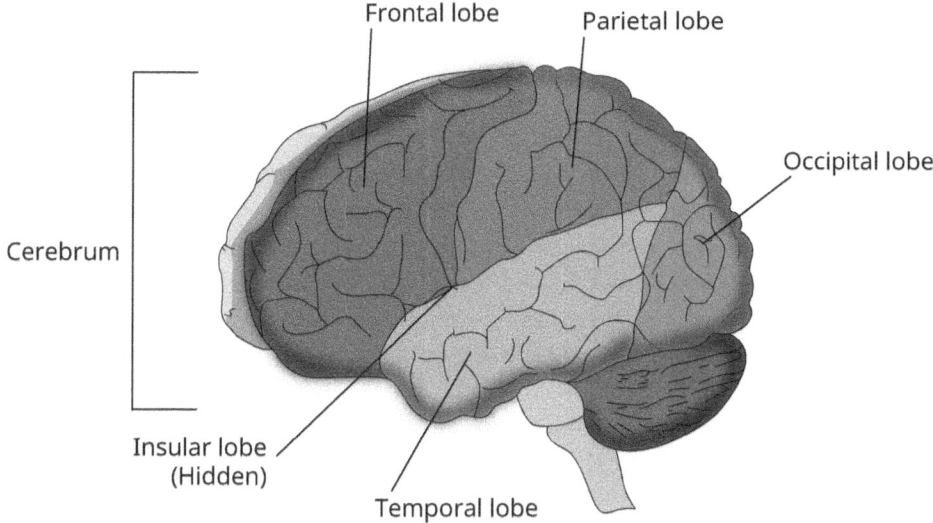

Figure 6.2   The cerebrum

The birth of a brain

The brain plays a central role in human development. As it grows and matures physically, and through its interactions with the environment, it drives a series of physical
and operational changes that sustain bodily processes and enable information processing. Through brain development, many of our abilities emerge, supporting learning,
adaptation, and transformation across the lifespan.

Pre-natal neural development

The brain starts its development from the moment of fertilisation, with the union of
cells and the multiple divisions that form the structures that will originate in the neural
plate around the third week of embryonic development. This plate folds into the neural
tube which becomes the foundation of the nervous system. The frontal part of the neural tube becomes the cerebrum and the other end corresponds to the spinal cord. The
frontal part develops into three distinctive swellings – the forebrain, the midbrain and
the hindbrain – and each will be associated with different functions. Each of these
regions will subdivide into functional brain regions – the prefrontal area, the basal
ganglia and the cerebellum, respectively.

The process of neurogenesis – of creating new neurons – begins around the fifth week of gestation and continues at a rate of up to 250,000 new neurons per minute at peak periods of pre-natal development (Meredith Weiss et al., 2024. The newly born neurons do not stay in the same place, however, and they embark on a neural migration to their final destination, which is determined by their specific cellular 'destiny'. This process is guided by specialised neurons – radial glial cells – and creates different layers of neurons within the cortex through a process of aggregation. The newest neurons will be located in the deep layers and the oldest neurons in the outer layers of the cortex. Once in their place, neurons begin a process of differentiation and, once they settle, they begin to network, leading to the development of synapses, a process that continues throughout a person's lifespan.

During the pre-natal period, the developing brain goes through several critical periods of vulnerability which may see a disruption in the development of brain structures (see also Chapter 4). External factors, such as toxins, nutrients, sensory stimulation and even maternal stress, affect the development of the brain structures and their potential function. As discussed in Chapter 4, it has been well noted in the literature that exposure to alcohol during the initial weeks of gestation can interfere with typical facial and brain development, and the potential to develop Fetal Alcohol Spectrum Disorders (FASD) (Riley et al., 2011). Similarly, maternal distress and poor nutrition have been documented to influence brain development *in utero* (Monk et al., 2013).

Post-natal brain development

Contrary to previous beliefs, the brain continues at a substantial rate of development after birth. At birth, the human brain contains nearly all the neurons it will ever have (86 billion approximately) but they have formed very few connections (Herculano-Houzel, 2009). It is during the post-natal period that these connections start to form as a result of a process denominated synaptogenesis – the formation of synapses between neurons.

Synaptogenesis dramatically increases after birth. By the age of two, the number of synapses per neuron is double that of an average adult brain (Huttenlocher & Dabholkar, 1997). This overproduction is followed by a process of synaptic pruning, where all the connections that are unused or redundant are eliminated, while those that are used and reinforced are strengthened. This process occurs in different stages of development and its aim is to prepare the brain, making it more efficient with specialised longer-reaching connections over time. Another process that continues during the post-natal brain development is the continuous insulation of the axon – myelination – which increases the speed of signal transmission among neurons. Myelination follows a predictable sequence that roughly corresponds to the emergence of various abilities (Deoni et al., 2011). For example, areas involved in sensory and motor processing myelinate earlier, while the prefrontal cortex, which is responsible for higher-order thinking, continues myelinating well into the second decade of life (Lebel et al., 2008).

Changes in the brain are influenced by both genetic and environmental factors, including social interactions, sensory experiences and learning (see Chapter 4). Plasticity, which enables the brain to adapt and reorganise in response to experience, allows the formation of new neural connections and even recovery from certain brain injuries. Most importantly, however, it enables the continuous acquisistion of new knowledge and skills (Kolb et al., 2017). Plasticity in the brain peaks during early childhood but continues throughout the lifespan (Pascual-Leone et al., 2005), making early childhood a critical period for cognitive, social and emotional development.

Structural and functional development of key brain regions

The following section outlines the structural and functional development of the key brain regions.

The cortex

The cerebral cortex is the outer layer of the brain that is responsible for higher-order functions and undergoes a protracted development compared to other brain regions. There are distinct timelines in the development of different cortical regions, but there is a common pattern that initiates in the posterior regions and moves to the anterior regions of the cortex (i.e., from the back to the front of the brain) (Gogtay et al., 2004).

First in maturation are the primary sensory and motor areas, which enable the processing of sensory information and movement control in infants. The association areas that contribute to the integration of information from multiple sources develop later (Casey et al., 2005). This sequential development explains why sensorimotor skills precede more complex cognitive abilities during childhood (Lenroot & Giedd, 2006).

The limbic system

The limbic system is a name given to a set of subcortical structures (Figure 6.3) that include the amygdala, the hippocampus and parts of the cingulate cortex, which together play a key role in the processing of emotion, motivation and memory (Tottenham & Sheridan, 2009). The amygdala is considered the centre of emotional processing, particularly fear and threat responses. This structure shows a significant development during the first few years of life and contributes to emerging emotional regulation abilities (Gee et al., 2013).

The hippocampus is widely regarded as the central structure for declarative memory – those memories that are consciously accessible (Ghetti & Bunge, 2012). This brain region continues to develop throughout childhood. During infancy, the hippocampus is still immature, which explains why we typically lack recollection of experiences from our earliest years. Nevertheless, even at this stage, the hippocampus plays a crucial role in enabling learning to occur at a remarkable pace (Alberini & Travaglia, 2017).

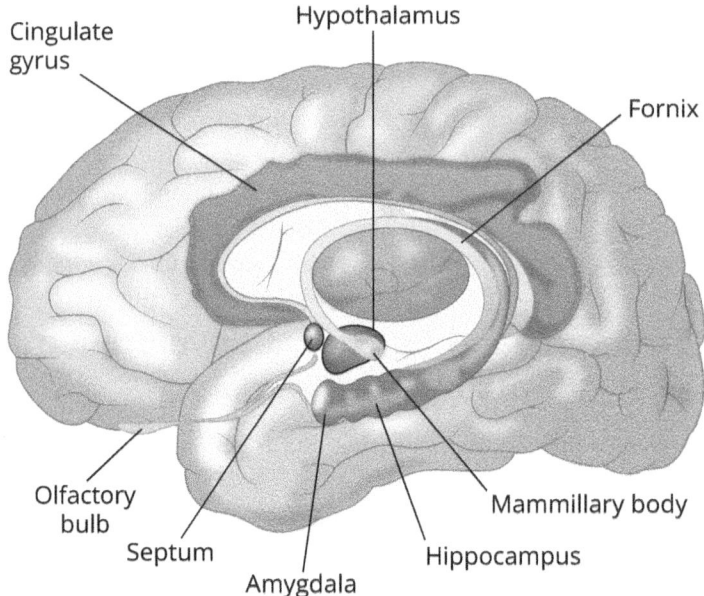

Figure 6.3 The limbic system

Source: Carolina Hrejsa/Body Scientific International.

Frontal lobe and the emergence of executive functions

The frontal lobes, specifically the prefrontal cortex, experience the most prolonged development of any brain region, which continues into early adulthood. This is the region that supports the executive functions. Executive functions are a set of higher-order cognitive processes that enable individuals to engage in goal-directed behaviour and adapt to changing environments. These processes are critical for children's learning and development, as they underpin skills such as self-regulation, problem-solving, and social interaction. Attentional control allows children to focus on relevant information while ignoring distractions, for example, concentrating on an instruction during a noisy classroom activity. Working memory enables them to hold and manipulate information, such as remembering the steps in a problem solving activity. Inhibitory control helps children resist impulsive actions, like waiting their turn in a game rather than interrupting. Planning involves setting goals and organising actions to achieve them, such as preparing materials for a project. Finally, cognitive flexibility allows children to shift perspectives or strategies when circumstances change, for instance, adapting to a new rule in a classroom game. Together, these functions form the foundation for academic success and social-emotional development in early childhood and beyond.

Children develop executive functions gradually over time. For instance, very young children often find difficult to wait for their turn, but as their cognitive abilities mature, they become increasingly capable of doing so. This gradual developmental trajectory reflects the maturation of the prefrontal cortex, which plays a central role in executive functioning. Neuroscience evidence provides valuable insights into this process, helping us understand how cognitive and emotional development unfolds from childhood into adolescence. Such knowledge is essential for designing appropriate environmental adaptations that support learning and promote self-regulation throughout these developmental stages.

Children need more support with their working memory, for example, as this cognitive ability has been shown to recruit activity in the prefrontal lobes, particularly the dorsolateral prefrontal cortex (DLPFC) (Figure 6.4), which has not fully developed at this stage. It would be natural, therefore, to break information into manageable chunks, reducing cognitive load and preventing overload of brain systems that are essential for learning.

Executive functions, such as impulse control, develop gradually and are supported by areas of the prefrontal cortex. These skills are also shaped by education and parental socialisation into social norms. For example, young children often find it hard to resist grabbing a toy they want, but with guidance and brain development, they learn

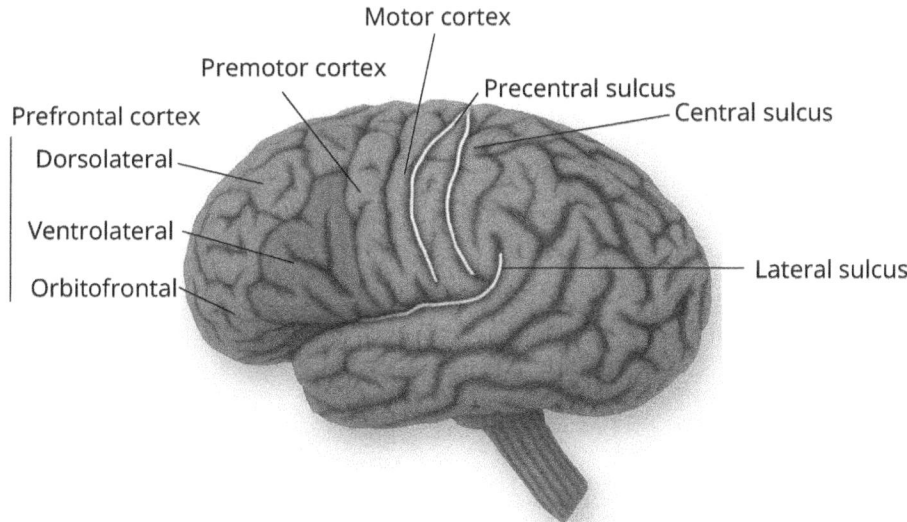

Figure 6.4   The prefrontal cortex and the dorsolateral prefrontal cortex (DLPFC)

to wait for their turn. During adolescence, however, there is a developmental mismatch: the prefrontal cortex, which supports planning, decision-making, and self-control, is still maturing, while the limbic system – responsible for emotions and reward – becomes highly sensitive. This imbalance makes teenagers more prone to sensation-seeking and high-risk behaviours, such as speeding or experimenting with substances, especially in emotionally charged situations. Although adolescents may appear intellectually mature, their ability to regulate impulses and make careful decisions is still developing. Neuroscience research (Casey et al., 2008) helps explain why these behaviours occur and highlights the importance of supportive environments that guide decision-making during this stage.

Temporal lobe and language development

The temporal lobes, which contain the primary auditory cortex and control the language areas (particularly in the left hemisphere), show significant development during early childhood (Lawton et al., 2023). This development corresponds with the speed of language acquisition (see Chapter 12) typically observed between the ages 1 to 5 (Lawton et al., 2023).

The strength of connections between Broca's area (which is involved in speech production) and Wernicke's area (which is involved in language comprehension) increases dramatically during this period, facilitating the integration of the different language functions (Friederici, 2009). Broca and Wernicke's areas (Figure 6.5) are an example of hemispheric specialisation as they only exist on the left hemisphere, unlike most other brain structures, which are bilateral. This does not mean that language functions are absent from the right hemisphere. In fact, the right hemisphere plays an important role during the early stages of learning a new language and when developing reading skills.

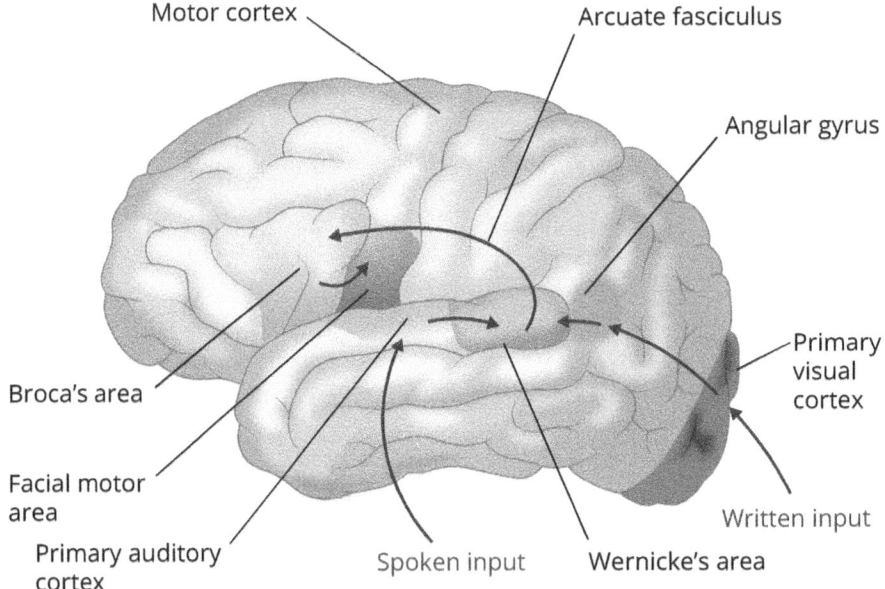

Figure 6.5   Broca and Wernicke's areas

Source: Carolina Hrejsa/Body Scientific International (adapted from 'Specializations of the human brain,' by N. Geschwind (1979), *Scientific American*, *241*(9), 180–199)

Visual and auditory processing systems

There is a rapid development of basic visual and auditory processing pathways during infancy. By approximately 6 months of age, infants can perceive visual acuity, depth and colour, similar to adults, although the ability to integrate visual information continues to develop throughout childhood (Johnson, 2011).

It is the auditory system that shows a remarkable early development, with evidence that fetuses can hear and respond to sounds in the womb (Hepper & Shahidullah, 1994). This early development supports the rapid discrimination of speech sounds in infancy, which is a crucial foundation for language acquisition (Kuhl et al., 2006).

Neurodevelopmental timeline summary

- *Infancy (0–2 years): Rapid growth and sensorimotor development*: Infancy marks the fastest period of brain growth, reaching 80% of adult volume by the age of two. Sensory and motor systems develop rapidly, shaped by environmental input. Critical periods mean that missing key experiences, such as visual stimulation, can result in lasting deficits. Motor milestones, such as sitting and walking, reflect maturing brain regions, including the cerebellum and the motor cortex.
- *Early Childhood (3–5 years): Language and emotion*: Language areas develop significantly, with vocabulary expanding from around 200 to over 2,000 words. Emotional regulation begins to emerge as connections between the prefrontal cortex and limbic system strengthen. Executive functions, such as attention and working memory, begin to develop, although preschoolers still require support with focus and rule-following.
- *Middle Childhood (6–11 years): Cognitive and social growth*: Myelination and synaptic refinement improve processing speed and cognitive efficiency at this stage, with children showing enhanced reasoning and problem-solving. Brain regions supporting social cognition mature, helping children to understand others' perspectives and manage complex relationships. Academic skills consolidate as neural networks become more specialised.
- *Adolescence (12–23 years): Executive function and risk*: Adolescence involves major changes in the prefrontal cortex and its links to emotional and reward systems. Limbic regions mature earlier, contributing to heightened emotional responses and risk-taking. Continued myelination supports abstract thinking and metacognition. Adolescents become more sensitive to peer influence due to changes in reward pathways.

The neurobiological foundations of key developmental processes

This section explores the neurobiological foundations of key developmental processes.

Attachment and social bonding

The formation of secure attachments between infants and caregivers has profound effects on neural development (Strathearn et al., 2009) (see Chapter 9). Positive caregiving experiences promote optimal development of the oxytocin system, which facilitates bonding and social connection and helps to regulate stress-response systems (Feldman, 2012). Research demonstrates that the oxytocin/vasopressin systems are involved in the formation of social, working, spatial and episodic memory, which are mediated by brain structures such as the hippocampus (particularly the CA2 and CA3 regions), the amygdala and the prefrontal cortex (Chini et al., 2018).

When infants experience consistent, sensitive caregiving, their hippocampus and prefrontal regions develop more favourably, promoting healthy stress responses and emotional regulation (Gunnar & Quevedo, 2007). Mothers who were securely attached to their caregivers show greater activation of brain reward regions, including the ventral striatum and the oxytocin-associated hypothalamus/pituitary region, when viewing their own infant's smiling and crying faces (Strathearn et al., 2009). Conversely, severe neglect or maltreatment can disrupt these systems, potentially leading to long-term alterations in stress reactivity and social functioning (Herrero-Roldán & Martín-Rodríguez, 2025).

Language acquisition and brain development

Language acquisition (see Chapter 12) represents a remarkable example of the interaction between genetic predispositions and environmental influences on brain development. Humans appear to have innate neural mechanisms that facilitate language learning, including specialised circuits for processing speech sounds (Friederici, 2009).

The left hemisphere typically develops specialisation for language, with key areas including Broca's area (inferior frontal gyrus), which is crucial for speech production, and Wernicke's area (posterior superior temporal gyrus), which is important for comprehension. The coordination between these regions improves dramatically during early childhood, supporting expanding language abilities through the development of white matter tracts, particularly the arcuate fasciculus (Huber et al., 2023).

Environmental exposure to language is essential for normal development; the quantity and quality of verbal input a child receives correlates with vocabulary development and later language outcomes (Fibla et al., 2023). Language development illustrates how experience shapes the brain within genetically guided boundaries, highlighting the gene–environment interactions that drive neural maturation.

Memory systems development

Different memory systems develop along distinct timelines (see Chapter 11), reflecting the maturation of underlying neural circuits (Stephens et al., 2020). Non-declarative or implicit memory systems, which operate largely outside conscious awareness and include procedural memory (skills and habits) and emotional conditioning, function from early infancy due to the early maturation of subcortical structures such as the basal ganglia and amygdala.

In contrast, declarative or explicit memory systems, which support conscious recollection of facts and experiences, develop more gradually due to the extended maturation of the hippocampus and its connections with cortical regions. It explains why children younger than 2–3 years typically cannot form lasting autobiographical memories despite considerable learning, a phenomenon known as infantile amnesia (Bauer, 2013.

Working memory is a type of memory that reflects the ability to temporarily hold and manipulate information. It follows an upward developmental trajectory and improves throughout childhood as prefrontal regions mature and form stronger connections with other brain areas (Blair & Diamond, 2008). This development supports numerous cognitive advances, from complex problem-solving to reading comprehension, and continues to develop into early adulthood.

Emotional regulation development

The neural systems supporting emotional regulation (see Chapter 8) experience a significant development throughout childhood and adolescence (Dumontheil, 2016). This development involves the maturation of the prefrontal cortex, which exerts top-down control over emotional reactivity, and its connections with limbic structures like the amygdala (Casey et al., 2008).

Young children rely heavily on external support from caregivers for emotional regulation, as their internal regulatory systems are still developing. As neural connections between prefrontal and limbic regions strengthen through myelination and synaptic refinement, children gradually develop a greater capacity for independent emotional regulation (Dumontheil, 2016).

The quality of early caregiving experiences shapes these developing systems; responsive caregiving that helps children to navigate emotions promotes optimal neural development for emotional regulation. The hormone oxytocin has a calming effect on the amygdala and can spur the prefrontal cortex to grow GABA-bearing fibres (GABA is a major inhibitory neurotransmitter) down to the amygdala and to suppress the fear response.

Development of executive functions

Executive functions emerge sequentially throughout childhood, corresponding to the gradual maturation of the prefrontal cortex and its connections with other brain regions. Simpler inhibitory control and attention shifting emerge earlier, while more complex planning and metacognition develop later, following a hierarchical pattern of development (Garon et al., 2008).

There is a particularly rapid development during two periods: first, during the ages 3–5 and then again during early adolescence. These spurts coincide with waves of synaptic pruning and myelination in prefrontal regions, particularly in areas responsible for cognitive control.

Environmental factors also significantly influence the executive function development. Activities that challenge emerging executive skills, such as imaginative play (see Chapter 13) in early childhood, or increasingly complex academic tasks in middle childhood, can promote the development of these neural systems (Diamond & Lee, 2011).

Environmental influences on brain development

This section explores environmental influences on brain development.

Role of experience-dependent plasticity

While our genes provide the basic blueprint for brain development, our experiences play a crucial role in fine-tuning neural connections. Imagine this as building a house where the genes provide the foundation and frame but experience determines how the rooms are furnished and connected. This process is called experience-dependent plasticity, where frequently used neural pathways become stronger, while unused connections are eliminated through a process called pruning (Fandakova & Hartley, 2020).

Time is also a key factor in the influence the environment plays on brain development. The ground-breaking work of David Hubel and Torsten Wiesel in the 1960s provided compelling evidence for the concept of critical periods (see Chapter 2). Their Nobel Prize-winning research investigated kittens whose vision in one eye was blocked during a critical developmental period. These kittens developed permanent visual problems in the deprived eye because the neural pathways serving that eye failed to develop normally (Hubel & Wiesel, 1970). These critical periods in development act as windows of time when the brain is especially sensitive to specific types of experiences. Although the evidence came from animal studies, the same principles apply to human development, which is why appropriate stimulation during these sensitive periods is so important for healthy brain development.

Consider this 6.1

- What are the ethical implications of studying brain development in young children? Consider issues such as consent, privacy, potential stress from procedures, and how findings are used in educational or clinical settings.
- How can neuroscience research in children be conducted responsibly while still advancing our understanding of development?

Effects of enriched versus deprived environments

An enriched environment – rich in sensory stimulation, physical activity, social interaction and learning – supports healthy brain development. In contrast, deprivation due to adverse life circumstances can lead to cognitive and socio-emotional delays. Animal studies show that enriched settings promote dendritic growth, synaptic density and even neurogenesis (van Praag et al., 2000).

Severe deprivation, such as in under-stimulating orphanages, can result in reduced prefrontal cortex volume and impaired attention, emotional regulation and social skills (Sheridan et al., 2022). Timing matters – early exposure to enrichment or deprivation has lasting effects, although brain plasticity allows for later improvement (Nelson et al., 2007).

Chronic stress is another negative influence. While short-term stress can be adaptive, prolonged exposure elevates cortisol, damaging brain areas like the hippocampus and over activating the amygdala, impairing emotional regulation (Lupien et al., 2009).

Epigenetic mechanisms in development

Epigenetics represents one of the most exciting recent discoveries in developmental science. Epigenetic mechanisms influence how genes are expressed without actually changing the DNA sequence itself. Think of them as dimmer switches that can turn genes up or down rather than completely on or off. The main epigenetic mechanisms include DNA methylation and histone modification. In the former, chemical tags, small chemical groups that attach to DNA or to proteins associated with DNA (such as histones) without altering the underlying genetic sequence play a role in epigenetic regulation, which controls how genes are turned on or off. These tags can silence genes. In the second case, they modify the proteins that package DNA, affecting how accessible the genes are.

Environmental factors ranging from nutrition to caregiving experiences can trigger epigenetic changes that influence neural development. For example, research shows that variations in maternal care in rats produce epigenetic modifications that affect the genes involved in stress regulation, which have lasting behavioural consequences that can even be passed to the next generation (Bagot et al., 2012; Weaver et al., 2004). This finding helps to explain how environmental factors experienced by one generation may affect the health and characteristics of a future generation.

This emerging field helps to explain how early experiences can have enduring effects on brain function and behaviour, reinforcing the profound connection between genetic and environmental factors in development.

Neurodevelopmental differences and the brain

Neurodevelopmental differences are lifelong conditions that affect how the brain develops and functions. They typically emerge in early childhood (see Chapter 5). These differences arise from variations in brain wiring and are influenced by complex genetic and environmental factors. The most common are:

Autism Spectrum Disorder (ASD), which involves atypical brain development and is often evident from infancy. Neuroimaging shows altered connectivity – excessive connectivity within local networks and reduced connectivity between distant regions – as well as accelerated early brain growth and structural differences in areas linked to social and language processing (Ha et al., 2015).

Attention Deficit Hyperactivity Disorder (ADHD), which affects attention, impulse control and activity regulation. It is linked to delayed maturation in the prefrontal regions, which are responsible for executive functions. Brain scans reveal atypical activation and connectivity patterns, particularly involving the striatum and motor areas.

Learning differences, such as dyslexia and dyscalculia, stem from specific neural variations. Dyslexia involves altered left-hemisphere activity in phonological processing, while dyscalculia is linked to reduced activation in the right intraparietal sulcus, affecting number sense (Kwok et al., 2023).

Case study 6.1: Pre-natal maternal stress and child development – Sarah and her daughter Alice

Sarah was 28 years old when she was pregnant and, while her pregnancy was medically uncomplicated, she experienced significant life stressors during this time. She lost her job at 20 weeks gestation; she experienced difficulties in her relationship with the baby's father and felt the stress of family pressures as her mother became ill. Due to her financial situation, she took over the care of her mother, adding another source of stress.

Observations

Alice was born to term in a natural delivery without major complications but, during infancy, she showed some delay in gross motor milestones, such as sitting and crawling, which is consistent with pre-natal stress exposure. At the cognitive level, Alice scored lower than the average child in standardised cognitive assessments for infants. Most importantly, she showed a high stress reactivity, especially in response to novel situations and separation from the mother.

At school, Alice experienced continuous challenges as she struggled to sustain attention. It was difficult for her to regulate herself and focus on the tasks the teacher demanded. Her working memory capacity was also impaired, which affected her ability to acquire new learning in the classroom. She, therefore, showed a lower academic performance compared to the group. She felt generally anxious in social situations, although her anxiety was progressively improved with emotional regulation support at school.

Analysis

This is a case that highlights how maternal stress during pregnancy is associated with atypical brain development and elevated risk for psychopathology in the child. Elevated pre-natal cortisol crossed the placental barrier and affected fetal brain development. Such exposure altered Alice's stress response system, leading to hypervigilance and elevated baseline cortisol.

Being critical

- Reflect on how some environmental factors can negatively affect fetal brain development and consider those factors that may have a positive influence in pre-natal brain development.
- Think about the cognitive functions that are affected as a result of pre-natal maternal stress and their impact in education.
- What are the real-world implications for designing pre-natal care and early intervention programmes?

Reflection points

- Reflect on how pre-natal and early post-natal experiences, such as maternal stress, nutrition and sensory input, can shape brain development. How can our understanding of these early influences change the way we support children and families during pregnancy and infancy?
- The brain's ability to adapt is greatest during early childhood but continues across the lifespan. What are the real-word implications of sensitive periods for designing learning and intervention programmes? Can you think of examples where the timing of learning or intervention made a difference in brain development or education?
- Neurodevelopmental differences, such as autism, ADHD and dyslexia, reflect natural variations in brain wiring. How can recognising neurodiversity influence your approach to supporting children's learning and behaviour?
- Neuroscience shows that executive functions like working memory and impulse control develop gradually. How can educators adapt classroom strategies to support children whose executive functions are still developing?

Chapter summary

This chapter explored:

- Stages of brain development from conception to adolescence
    - Pre-natal development: How the brain forms *in utero* and the impact of maternal health, nutrition and stress.

- o Infancy (0–2 years): Rapid brain growth, sensory development, the importance of early bonding and attachment.
- o Early childhood (2–6 years): Language acquisition, executive function development and the role of play.
- o Middle childhood (6–12 years): Refinement of cognitive skills, social learning and the impact of education.
- o Adolescence (12–18 years): Brain maturation, risk-taking behaviour and the role of the prefrontal cortex in decision-making.

- Key factors influencing brain development

  - o Genetics versus environment: The interplay between nature and nurture.
  - o Early experiences: How positive and negative experiences (e.g., maternal stress, neglect, enrichment) shape the brain structures, function and connectivity.
  - o Nutrition: The role of nutrients in brain development is key so it is important to avoid toxins that can disrupt brain development (e.g., alcohol consumption during pregnancy).
  - o Stress: The impact of chronic stress on brain structure and function.
  - o Social interaction: The importance of caregiver–child relationships, peer interactions and social learning.

Further reading

Howard-Jones, P. (2018). *Evolution of the Learning Brain: Or How You Got to Be So Smart...* Routledge. https://doi.org/10.4324/9781315150857

Useful websites

https://dana.org/

The Dana Foundation explores links between neuroscience and society's challenges.

https://neurosciencenews.com/

Neuroscience News is an open access science magazine.

www.brainfacts.org/

Brain Facts is a bank of resources on neuroscience presented by the Society for Neuroscience.

References

Alberini, C., & Travaglia, A. (2017). Infantile amnesia: A critical period of learning to learn and remember. *The Journal of Neuroscience, 37*(24), 5783–5795. https://doi.org/10.1523/JNEUROSCI.0324-17.2017

Bagot, R.C., Zhang, T.Y., Wen, X., Nguyen, T.T., Nguyen, H.B., Diorio, J., Wong, T.P. & Meaney, M.J. (2012). Variations in postnatal maternal care and the epigenetic regulation of metabotropic glutamate receptor 1 expression and hippocampal function in the rat. *Proc Natl Acad Sci U S A*. 2012 Oct 16;109 Suppl 2(Suppl 2):17200-7. doi: 10.1073/pnas.1204599109. Epub 2012 Oct 8. PMID: 23045678; PMCID: PMC3477397.

Bauer, P. (2013). Theory and processes in memory development: Infancy and early childhood. In R. E. Holliday & T. A. Marche (Eds.), *Child forensic psychology: Victim and eyewitness memory* (pp. 9–38). Palgrave Macmillan/Springer Nature. https://doi.org/10.1007/978-1-137-29251-3_2

Blair, C., & Diamond, A. (2008). Biological processes in prevention and intervention: The promotion of self-regulation as a means of preventing school failure. *Development and Psychopathology, 20*(3), 899–911. https://doi.org/10.1017/S0954579408000436

Casey, B., Getz, S., & Galvan, A. (2008). The adolescent brain. *Developmental Review, 28*(1), 62–77. https://doi.org/10.1016/j.dr.2007.08.003

Casey, B., Tottenham, N., Liston, C., & Durston, S. (2005). Imaging the developing brain: What have we learned about cognitive development? *Trends in Cognitive Sciences, 9*(3), 104–110. https://doi.org/10.1016/j.tics.2005.01.011

Chini, B., Verhage, M., & Grinevich, V. (2018). The action radius of oxytocin release in the mammalian CNS: From single vesicles to behavior. *Trends in Pharmacological Sciences, 39*(12), 1005–1018.

Deoni, S., Mercure, E., Blasi, A., Gasston, D., Thomson, A., Johnson, M., Williams, S., & Murphy, D. (2011). Mapping infant brain myelination with magnetic resonance imaging. *The Journal of Neuroscience, 31*(2), 784–791. https://doi.org/10.1523/JNEUROSCI.2106-10.2011

Diamond, A., & Lee, K. (2011). Interventions shown to aid executive function development in children 4 to 12 years old. *Science, 333*(6045), 959–964. https://doi.org/10.1126/science.1204529

Dumontheil, I. (2016). Adolescent brain development. *Current Opinion in Behavioral Sciences, 10*, 39–44. https://doi.org/10.1016/j.cobeha.2016.04.012

Fandakova, Y., & Hartley, C. (2020). Mechanisms of learning and plasticity in childhood and adolescence. *Developmental Cognitive Neuroscience, 42*, 100764. https://doi.org/10.1016/j.dcn.2020.100764

Feldman, R. (2012). Oxytocin and social affiliation in humans. *Hormones and Behavior, 61*(3), 380–391. https://doi.org/10.1016/j.yhbeh.2012.01.008

Fibla, L., Forbes, S.H., McCarthy, J., Mee, K., Magnotta, V., Deoni, S., Cameron, D., & Spencer, J.P. (2023) Language Exposure and Brain Myelination in Early Development. J Neurosci. 2023 Jun 7;43(23):4279–4290. doi: 10.1523/JNEUROSCI.1034-22.2023. Epub 2023 May 15. PMID: 37188518; PMCID: PMC10255048.

Friederici, A. (2009). Pathways to language: Fiber tracts in the human brain. *Trends in Cognitive Sciences, 13*(4), 175–181. https://doi.org/10.1016/j.tics.2009.01.001

Garon, N., Bryson, S., & Smith, I. (2008). Executive function in preschoolers: A review using an integrative framework. *Psychological Bulletin, 134*(1), 31–60. https://doi.org/10.1037/0033-2909.134.1.31

Gee, D., Humphreys, K., Flannery, J., Goff, B., Telzer, E., Shapiro, M., Hare, T., Bookheimer, S., & Tottenham, N. (2013). A developmental shift from positive to negative connectivity in human amygdala-prefrontal circuitry. *The Journal of Neuroscience, 33*(10), 4584–4593. https://doi.org/10.1523/JNEUROSCI.3446-12.2013

Geschwind, N. (1979, September). *Specializations of the human brain. Scientific American*, *241*(3), 180–199. https://doi.org/10.1038/scientificamerican0979-180

Ghetti, S., & Bunge, S. (2012). Neural changes underlying the development of episodic memory during middle childhood. *Developmental Cognitive Neuroscience, 2*(4), 381–395. https://doi.org/10.1016/j.dcn.2012.05.002

Gogtay, N., Giedd, J., Lusk, L., Hayashi, K., Greenstein, D., Vaituzis, A., Nugent, T., Herman, D., Clasen, L., Toga, A., Rapoport, J., & Thompson, P. (2004). Dynamic mapping of human cortical development during childhood through early adulthood. *PNAS, 101*(21), 8174–8179. https://doi.org/10.1073/pnas.0402680101

Gunnar, M., & Quevedo, K. (2007). The neurobiology of stress and development. *Annual Review of Psychology, 58*, 145–173. https://doi.org/10.1146/annurev. psych.58.110405.085605

Ha, S., Sohn, I., Kim, N., Sim, H., & Cheon, K. (2015). Characteristics of brains in autism spectrum disorder: Structure, function and connectivity across the lifespan. *Experimental Neurobiology, 24*(4), 273–284. https://doi.org/10.5607/en.2015.24.4.273

Hepper, P., & Shahidullah, B. (1994). Development of fetal hearing. *Archives of Disease in Childhood: Fetal and Neonatal Edition, 71*(2), F81–F87. https://doi.org/10.1136/fn.71.2.f81

Herculano-Houzel, S. (2009). The human brain in numbers: A linearly scaled-up primate brain. *Frontiers in Human Neuroscience, 3*, 31.

Herrero-Roldán, S. & Martín-Rodríguez, A. (2025) Neglect and Neurodevelopment: A Narrative Review Understanding the Link Between Child Neglect and Executive Function Deficits. Biomedicines. 2025 Jun 26; *13*(7):1565. doi: 10.3390/ biomedicines13071565. PMID: 40722641; PMCID: PMC12292309.

Hubel, D.H. & Wiesel, T.N. (1970) The period of susceptibility to the physiological effects of unilateral eye closure in kittens. J Physiol. 1970 Feb;*206*(2):419–36. doi: 10.1113/jphysiol.1970.sp009022. PMID: 5498493; PMCID: PMC1348655.

Huber, E., Corrigan, N.M., Yarnykh, V.L., Ferjan Ramírez, N. & Kuhl, P.K. (2023). Language Experience during Infancy Predicts White Matter Myelination at Age 2 Years. J Neurosci. 2023 Mar 1;*43*(9):1590–1599. doi: 10.1523/ JNEUROSCI.1043-22.2023. Epub 2023 Feb 6. PMID: 36746626; PMCID: PMC10008053.

Huttenlocher, P. R., & Dabholkar, A. S. (1997). Regional differences in synaptogenesis in human cerebral cortex. *Journal of Comparative Neurology, 387*(2), 167–178. https://doi. org/https://doi.org/10.1002/(SICI)1096-9861(19971020)387:2<167::AID-CNE1>3.0.CO;2-Z

Johnson, M. (2011). Interactive specialization: A domain-general framework for human functional brain development? *Developmental Cognitive Neuroscience, 1*(1), 7–21. https://doi.org/10.1016/j.dcn.2010.07.003

Kuhl PK, Stevens E, Hayashi A, Deguchi T, Kiritani S, Iverson P. (2006). Infants show a facilitation effect for native language phonetic perception between 6 and 12 months. Dev Sci. 2006 Mar; *9*(2): F13–F21. doi: 10.1111/j.1467-7687.2006.00468.x. PMID: 16472309.

Kolb, B., Harker, A., & Gibb, R. (2017). Principles of plasticity in the developing brain. *Developmental Medicine & Child Neurology, 59*(12), 1218–1223. https://doi.org/10.1111/ dmcn.13546

Kwok, F., Wilkey, E., Peters, L., Khiu, E., Bull, R., Lee, K., & Ansari, D. (2023). Developmental dyscalculia is not associated with atypical brain activation: A univariate fMRI study. *Human Brain Mapping*, *44*(18), 6308–6325. https://doi.org/10.1002/hbm.26495

Lawton, K., Araujo, M., & Kufaishi, A. (2023). Language environment and infants' brain structure: Evidence from left-hemispheric temporal regions. *The Journal of Neuroscience*, *43*(12), 2156–2168. https://doi.org/10.1523/JNEUROSCI.1234-22.2023

Lebel, C., Walker, L., Leemans, A., Phillips, L., & Beaulieu, C. (2008). Microstructural maturation of the human brain from childhood to adulthood. *NeuroImage*, *40*(3), 1044–1055. https://doi.org/10.1016/j.neuroimage.2007.12.053

Lenroot, R. K., & Giedd, J. N. (2006). Brain development in children and adolescents: Insights from anatomical magnetic resonance imaging. *Neuroscience & Biobehavioral Reviews*, *30*(6), 718–729. https://doi.org/https://doi.org/10.1016/j.neubiorev.2006.06.001

Lupien, S., McEwen, B., Gunnar, M., & Heim, C. (2009). Effects of stress throughout the lifespan on the brain, behaviour and cognition. *Nature Reviews Neuroscience*, *10*(6), 434–445.

Meredith Weiss, S., Aydin, E., Lloyd-Fox, S. & Johnson, M.H. (2024). Trajectories of brain and behaviour development in the womb, at birth and through infancy. *Nat Hum Behav*. 2024 Jul;8(7):1251–1262. doi: 10.1038/s41562-024-01896-7. Epub 2024 Jun 17. PMID: 38886534.

Monk, C., Georgieff, M., & Osterholm, E. (2013). Research review: Maternal prenatal distress and poor nutrition – mutually influencing risk factors affecting infant neurocognitive development. *Journal of Child Psychology and Psychiatry*, *54*(2), 115–130. https://doi.org/10.1111/jcpp.12000

Nelson, C., Zeanah, C., Fox, N., Marshall, P., Smyke, A., & Guthrie, D. (2007). Cognitive recovery in socially deprived young children: The Bucharest Early Intervention Project. *Science*, *318*(5858), 1937–1940. https://doi.org/10.1126/science.1143921

Pascual-Leone, A., Amedi, A., Fregni, F., & Merabet, L. B. (2005). The plastic human brain cortex. *Annual Review of Neuroscience*, *28*, 377–401. https://doi.org/10.1146/annurev.neuro.27.070203.144216

Riley, E., Infante, M., & Warren, K. (2011). Fetal alcohol spectrum disorders: An overview. *Neuropsychology Review*, *21*(2), 73–80. https://doi.org/10.1007/s11065-011-9166-x

Sheridan, M., Mukerji, C., Wade, M., Humphreys, K., Garrisi, K., Goel, S., Patel, K., Fox, N., Zeanah, C., Nelson, C., & McLaughlin, K. (2022). Early deprivation alters structural brain development from middle childhood to adolescence. *Science Advances*, *8*(40), eabn4316. https://www.science.org/doi/10.1126/sciadv.abn4316

Stephens, R.L., Langworthy, B.W., Short, S.J., Girault, J.B., Styner, M.A. & Gilmore, J.H. (2020) White Matter Development from Birth to 6 Years of Age: A Longitudinal Study. Cereb Cortex. 2020 Nov 3;30(12):6152–6168. doi: 10.1093/cercor/bhaa170. PMID: 32591808; PMCID: PMC7947172.

Strathearn, L., Fonagy, P., Amico, J., & Montague, P. (2009). Adult attachment predicts maternal brain and oxytocin response to infant cues. *Neuropsychopharmacology*, *34*(13), 2655–2666. https://doi.org/10.1038/npp.2009.103

Tottenham, N. & Sheridan, M. (2009). A review of adversity, the amygdala and the
    hippocampus: a consideration of developmental timing. *Frontiers in Human
    Neuroscience*. https://doi.org/10.3389/neuro.09.068.2009
van Praag, H., Kempermann, G., & Gage, F. (2000). Neural consequences of
    environmental enrichment. *Nature Reviews Neuroscience*, *1*(3), 191–198. https://doi.
    org/10.1038/35044558
Weaver, I.C., Cervoni, N., Champagne, F.A., D'Alessio, A.C., Sharma, S., Seckl, J.R.,
    Dymov, S., Szyf, M. & Meaney, M.J. (2004) Epigenetic programming by maternal
    behavior. Nat Neurosci. 2004 Aug;7(8):847–54. doi: 10.1038/nn1276. Epub 2004 Jun
    27. PMID: 15220929.

7

Physical development

Ioanna Palaiologou

Chapter objectives

By the end of this chapter, you will gain:

- An understanding of the stages of physical development from pre-natal growth through adolescence, including gross and fine motor skills and sensory maturation.
- Insight into the relationship between physical development and psychological wellbeing, including emotional regulation, social interaction, and cognitive growth.
- The ability to identify environmental, cultural, and health-related factors that influence physical development, including nutrition, caregiving practices, and neurodiversity.
- Recognition of the role of play and movement in supporting physical competence and holistic development in early childhood settings.

Overview of the chapter

The previous chapter explored the role of neuroscience in child development, highlighting how brain function underpins learning and behaviour. This chapter shifts the focus to physical development. While the two are deeply interconnected, here we will concentrate on the development of the body, the senses and the importance of physical activity for psychological wellbeing. The chapter will also explore the role of play, nutrition and the factors that impact physical development.

Why should you read this chapter?

Understanding physical development is essential for anyone working with or studying children and young people. This chapter provides key insights into how the body grows and changes, how the senses develop, and how physical activity supports not just physical health but also emotional and mental wellbeing.

Understanding physical growth and sensory development

Physical development is a continuous process that begins before birth and extends throughout the lifespan. It includes changes in the brain (see Chapter 6), in body size, shape, motor skills and the refinement of the senses. These developments are closely linked to cognitive and emotional growth and are especially significant during early childhood and adolescence.

Pre-natal development

Pre-natal development is a complex and dynamic process that unfolds across three distinct stages: the germinal, embryonic and fetal stages. The *germinal stage* begins at conception and lasts approximately two weeks. During this phase, the fertilised egg (zygote) undergoes rapid cell division, forming a blastocyst that implants into the uterine wall (Ma et al., 2024). This stage is critical for establishing the foundations of pregnancy, including the development of the placenta and amniotic sac. The *embryonic stage*, spanning from the third to the eighth week, is marked by significant cellular differentiation and organogenesis. The embryo forms three germ layers – ectoderm, mesoderm and endoderm – which give rise to major body systems, such as the nervous system, circulatory system and digestive tract. This period is particularly sensitive to teratogens, which can disrupt normal development and lead to congenital anomalies (Karacas, 2020). From the ninth week until birth, the *fetal stage* focuses on growth and maturation. The fetus develops functional organs, gains weight and exhibits reflexive behaviours such as sucking and swallowing. By the end of this stage, the fetus typically reaches full term, measuring around 50 cm in length and weighing approximately 3.4 kg.

Recent academic literature (e.g., Marceau et al., 2024) continues to emphasise the importance of these stages in understanding both typical and atypical developmental trajectories. Consider the following questions.

After studying Chapter 4 and 6:

1   How do environmental factors during the embryonic stage influence the risk of congenital anomalies and long-term health outcomes?
2   In what ways does prenatal development lay the foundation for neurological, physiological, and behavioural patterns observed after birth?

Early childhood (birth to 5 years)

In early childhood, similar to brain development (see Chapter 6), physical development is rapid and foundational. At birth, infants rely on primitive reflexes. Primitive reflexes are involuntary motor responses originating in the brainstem that are present at birth and play a crucial role in early child development. These reflexes are automatic and essential for survival, enabling newborns to respond to their environment before voluntary motor control is established. Examples include the rooting reflex, where an infant turns their head towards a touch on the cheek to help locate food, and the grasp reflex, where the baby instinctively clenches a finger placed in their palm. These responses are not learned but are hardwired into the nervous system, reflecting the early functioning of the central nervous system.

As the infant's brain matures (see Chapter 6), typically between 4 and 6 months of age, these reflexes are gradually inhibited and replaced by voluntary motor activities, such as reaching, grasping and crawling. This transition marks a critical phase in neurodevelopment, indicating healthy integration of higher brain functions. However, if primitive reflexes persist beyond the expected age or reappear later in life, it may signal neurological impairment or disease. The rapid physical and neurological development in early childhood, as discussed in Chapter 6, lays the foundation for more complex motor skills and cognitive functions. Monitoring these reflexes is therefore a key component in assessing infant health and developmental progress (Jaiswal & Morankar, 2017).

Physical development

Physical development involves gross motor skills and fine motor skills.

Gross motor skills involve the use of large muscle groups that control movements such as crawling, walking, running and jumping. These skills are essential for mobility, independence and active engagement with the environment. They develop in a predictable sequence, although the pace can vary between children.

In the first year of life, gross motor development begins with foundational movements such as lifting the head, neck and upper body muscles. By 6 months, many infants can roll over and begin to sit with support. Sitting independently often occurs by 8 months, followed by crawling, pulling to stand, and eventually walking normally around the completion of their first year.

Between 12 and 24 months, toddlers become increasingly mobile and begin to explore their surroundings with greater confidence. They learn to walk steadily, climb onto furniture and interact more actively with their environment, although frequent falls are common as they develop balance and coordination. This stage also sees significant progress in language development (see Chapter 12), with toddlers beginning to form simple words and phrases, enhancing their ability to communicate and engage socially (see Chapter 10). These developments reflect the ongoing maturation of the brain and the transition from reflexive to purposeful behaviour.

By age 3, most children can run with improved control, jump with both feet and climb stairs using alternating feet. They may also begin to pedal a tricycle and throw or kick a ball with direction. These skills allow for greater independence and participation in play, which is vital for social, emotional and cognitive development (see Chapters 8, 10, 11, 12 and 13).

As children grow, gross motor skills continue to refine. By age 5, many children can hop on one foot, skip and catch a ball with both hands. These abilities support physical confidence and a healthy lifestyle.

Fine motor skills involve the coordination of small muscles, particularly in the hands and fingers, to perform precise movements. These skills are essential for everyday tasks, such as feeding, dressing, writing and manipulating objects. Development begins in infancy and continues to refine throughout early childhood.

In the first few months, babies begin to show early signs of fine motor development. They may grasp a caregiver's finger reflexively and gradually learn to hold onto objects. By around 4–6 months infants can transfer items between hands and bring toys to their mouths, demonstrating improved hand–eye coordination.

By 9–12 months, babies start to use a pincer grasp, using the thumb and forefinger to pick up small items like cereal pieces. This is a key milestone that supports self-feeding and object exploration.

During toddlerhood (1–3 years), fine motor skills become more purposeful. Children begin to stack blocks, turn pages in board books and scribble with crayons. They may also start to use spoons and attempt to dress themselves with assistance, such as pulling off socks or placing arms through sleeves.

By age 4–5, children typically show greater control and precision. They can draw simple shapes, cut with child-safe scissors, button clothing and begin to form letters. These skills are crucial for entering school, as they support writing, art and independent self-care.

Fine motor development is closely linked to cognitive and sensory growth and it benefits greatly from activities like drawing, building, threading beads and playing with puzzles or construction toys.

Sensory development

Sensory development begins in the womb and continues rapidly through early childhood. The five senses – vision, hearing, touch, taste and smell – are essential for helping children to understand and interact with the world around them. Each sense develops at its own pace, contributing uniquely to a child's learning, emotional bonding and overall development.

At birth, a baby's *vision* is limited to short distances – around 20–30 centimetres – just enough to see a caregiver's face during feeding. Newborns are drawn to high-contrast patterns and bold shapes. By around 2 months, they begin to track moving objects with their eyes. By 6 months, most infants can recognise familiar faces and show interest in colourful toys. Depth perception and hand–eye coordination continue to improve throughout the first year, supporting activities like reaching and grasping. By age 3–5, children typically develop full visual acuity, enabling them to engage in more complex visual tasks, such as drawing or recognising letters.

Hearing is one of the most developed senses at birth. Babies respond to familiar voices, especially their mother's, and are soothed by rhythmic sounds and lullabies. By 3 months, they turn their heads towards sounds and by 6 months they begin to recognise their name and respond to tone of voice. Exposure to language through talking, reading and singing is crucial during this period, as it supports both auditory processing and early language development.

Touch is a primary sense in infancy and plays a vital role in emotional bonding and comfort. Newborns are highly sensitive to touch, particularly on the face, hands and feet. Skin-to-skin contact with caregivers helps to regulate body temperature, heart rate and stress levels. As babies grow, they use touch to explore their environment – grasping objects, feeling textures, learning about shape and temperature. By toddlerhood, touch becomes a key part of learning through hands-on play and sensory exploration.

Taste is functional from birth, with newborns showing a clear preference for sweet flavours, such as breast milk. They can also detect sour, bitter and salty tastes, although they may react negatively to strong or unfamiliar flavours. As children begin eating solid foods, usually around 6 months, they start to develop individual taste preferences. Repeated exposure to a variety of healthy foods helps to expand their palate and supports nutritional development.

Smell is closely linked to taste and is also well developed at birth. Newborns can recognise the scent of their mother and are comforted by familiar smells. This sense plays a role in early bonding and feeding. As children grow, their sense of smell becomes more refined, helping them to distinguish between pleasant and unpleasant odours. Smell also contributes to memory and emotional responses, often triggering strong associations with people, places or experiences.

Transition to adolescence

The transition from childhood to adolescence marks a significant shift in physical development. This period, typically beginning between ages 9 and 13, is characterised by puberty, a series of biological changes driven by hormonal activity.

In girls, puberty often begins with breast development, followed by the growth of pubic hair and the onset of menstruation. In boys, it usually starts with testicular enlargement, followed by voice deepening, facial hair growth and increased muscle mass. Both sexes experience growth spurts, with rapid increases in height and weight.

These changes are accompanied by shifts in body composition, such as increased fat distribution in girls and muscle development in boys. Adolescents may also experience changes in skin (e.g., acne), body odour and emotional sensitivity due to hormonal fluctuations.

Motor skills continue to refine during adolescence. Teenagers gain greater strength, speed and coordination, which supports more complex physical activities and sports. Fine motor skills also improve, allowing for more precise tasks, such as writing, drawing or playing musical instruments.

To conclude, understanding the stages of physical and sensory development, from reflexes and teething in infancy to the hormonal and structural changes of adolescence, provides valuable insight into how children grow and adapt. These developments are not only physical but also biological (see Chapter 6) and are deeply connected to emotional, social and cognitive wellbeing, forming the foundation for lifelong health and learning.

Factors impacting physical development

Physical development is influenced not only by genetics but also by a wide range of environmental and social factors (see Chapter 4). These influences can either support healthy growth or contribute to developmental delays and long-term health issues.

Neglect and its impact

Neglect, whether physical, emotional or medical, can have serious consequences for a child's physical development (see also Chapters 4 and 9). Children who experience neglect may suffer from malnutrition, poor hygiene and lack of medical care, all of which can stunt growth and delay motor skill development. Emotional neglect can also affect brain development, leading to difficulties in coordination, attention and sensory processing. In severe cases, neglect can result in failure to thrive, where a child does not gain weight or grow as expected.

Parental health and lifestyle

The health and lifestyle of parents, particularly during pregnancy and early childhood, play a critical role. Maternal nutrition, substance use, stress levels and access to pre-natal care all influence fetal development. For example, smoking or alcohol use during pregnancy can lead to low birth weight, premature birth or developmental disorders (see Chapter 6). Post-natally, parents who model healthy behaviours – such as under-taking regular physical activity and balanced eating – help to establish positive habits in their children.

Adverse environmental conditions

Living in environments with poor housing, limited access to nutritious food, unsafe outdoor spaces or exposure to pollution can hinder physical development. Children in low-income households may face food insecurity, leading to undernutrition or obesity due to a reliance on low-cost, high-calorie foods. Unsafe neighbourhoods may limit opportunities for outdoor play, reducing physical activity and motor skill development.

Illnesses and chronic conditions

Frequent or chronic illnesses can interrupt physical development. Conditions such as asthma, diabetes or congenital heart defects may limit a child's ability to engage in physical activity. Repeated hospitalisations or medical treatments can also disrupt routines and delay developmental milestones. Infections during early childhood, particularly those affecting the brain or nervous system, can have lasting effects on motor and sensory development.

Neurodiversity

Children with developmental disorders (see also Chapter 5) such as cerebral palsy, muscular dystrophy or genetic syndromes may experience delays or differences in physical development. These conditions often require specialised support and interventions to help children reach their full potential. Early diagnosis and access to therapies, such as physiotherapy or occupational therapy, are crucial in supporting physical progress.

Case study 7.1: Leo – the impact of environment on physical development

Leo is a 4-year-old boy living in an urban area with his single mother. He was born prematurely at 34 weeks and spent two weeks in neo-natal care. His mother has a history of depression and limited access to healthcare. The family lives in temporary accommodation with minimal outdoor space and limited access to nutritious food.

Observations

At nursery, staff noticed that Leo is smaller than his peers and appears tired and withdrawn. He struggles with gross motor tasks, such as running, jumping and climbing, and often avoids physical play. His fine motor skills are also delayed – he finds it difficult to hold a pencil or use scissors. Leo has frequent colds and has been hospitalised twice for respiratory infections.

Leo's diet consists mainly of processed foods and he is often hungry during the day. His mother, while loving, struggles to maintain routines due to her own mental health challenges. Leo has missed several health check-ups and has not received consistent dental care.

Analysis

Leo's case highlights the cumulative impact of multiple environmental risk factors on physical development. Premature birth, poor nutrition, limited physical activity and inconsistent healthcare have all contributed to his delayed growth and motor skills. Additionally, his mother's mental health and the family's living conditions have limited his access to stimulating and supportive environments.

(Continued)

> **Being critical**
>
> - Reflect on how these factors compound one another and consider which is the most urgent to address.
> - Think about how delays in his physical development can affect Leo's learning, social relationships and emotional wellbeing as he grows.
> - Consider the importance of a multi-agency approach and how collaboration can lead to more effective outcomes.

Why is physical development important?

The section discusses the key factors affecting physical development.

Cognitive, emotional and social development

As children develop their bodies serve as the primary medium through which they engage with and make sense of the world around them. From the earliest ability to lift their heads to the tentative steps of early walking, physical development lays the groundwork for subsequent cognitive, emotional and social growth (Berk & Meyers, 2023).

Each emerging motor skill, such as grasping objects, crawling or running, represents more than a physical milestone; it is also a cognitive endeavour. These actions require the integration of sensory input, motor planning and problem-solving. Reaching for an object, for instance, introduces concepts of cause and effect, while navigating under furniture fosters spatial awareness (Adolph & Hoch, 2019). Thus, the development of the body and brain is deeply interconnected, with each influencing and shaping the other.

Moreover, physical development plays a critical role in emotional regulation. As children gain mastery over their bodily movements, they also acquire tools for managing emotional experiences. A toddler who runs to a caregiver for reassurance, or a child who uses deep breathing to calm themselves, is demonstrating the use of physical strategies to navigate emotional states (Porges, 2011). Movement becomes a medium through which emotions such as joy, frustration and excitement are expressed. As physical competence increases, so too does self-confidence, fostering a sense of agency and resilience (Whitebread, 2020).

Social development is similarly intertwined with physical growth. The ability to move and interact physically enables children to participate in play, which is a fundamental context for social learning. Through physical play, children learn to negotiate, cooperate and interpret non-verbal cues such as gestures and facial expressions (Pellegrini & Smith, 2007). Even before verbal communication is fully developed, physical expression serves as a vital means of social interaction.

In sum, physical development is not merely concerned with the maturation of muscles and bones. It constitutes a foundational element of cognitive, emotional and social development. It acts as a silent yet powerful partner in every discovery, emotional experience and interpersonal relationship during early childhood.

Physical health and psychological wellbeing

Physical health and psychological wellbeing are intrinsically linked, with each exerting a significant influence on the other across the lifespan. Optimal physical health not only supports the physiological functioning of the body but also contributes to emotional stability, cognitive performance and overall life satisfaction (World Health Organization, 2022).

Physical activity is central to this relationship. Regular movement – whether through structured exercise, spontaneous play or routine tasks – enhances cardiovascular, respiratory, muscular and skeletal health. It also aids in maintaining a healthy weight and reduces the risk of chronic conditions such as obesity, diabetes and cardiovascular disease (Janssen & LeBlanc, 2010).

Beyond its physiological benefits, physical activity has a substantial impact on mental health. Exercise stimulates the release of endorphins and other neurochemicals that elevate mood and mitigate stress. It has been shown to alleviate symptoms of anxiety and depression, improve self-esteem and enhance the quality of sleep (Biddle et al., 2019). For children and adolescents, physical activity is also associated with improved concentration, memory and academic achievement (Singh et al., 2012).

Healthy lifestyle practices, including balanced nutrition, sufficient sleep and regular physical activity, form the basis for emotional resilience and self-regulation. Children who are physically healthy are more likely to engage positively with peers, cope effectively with challenges and develop a robust sense of identity and self-worth (Shanker, 2016).

In educational and care settings, the promotion of physical health extends beyond illness prevention. It encompasses the holistic development of the child. Facilitating active lifestyles, providing opportunities for movement and recognising the emotional and cognitive benefits of physical activity are essential for fostering lifelong wellbeing (Department for Education, 2021).

Consider the following questions:

1   How does regular physical activity during childhood and adolescence influence emotional resilience and self-regulation later in life?
2   In what ways can promoting physical health in educational settings contribute to improved psychological wellbeing and social engagement among children?

Nutrition and physical development

Nutrition is fundamental to healthy physical development from infancy to adolescence. It supplies the energy and essential nutrients required for growth, brain maturation, immune function and the development of bones and muscles. Nutritional deficiencies or excesses can have enduring consequences for both physical and psychological health (Black et al., 2013).

Breastfeeding

Breastfeeding is widely acknowledged as the optimal form of nutrition for infants. It delivers a balanced composition of nutrients, antibodies and enzymes that support early development and protect against infections. The World Health Organization (WHO) recommends exclusive breastfeeding for the first 6 months, followed by continued breastfeeding alongside complementary foods up to 2 years or beyond. Breastfed infants exhibit lower rates of gastrointestinal and respiratory infections and are less likely to develop obesity later in life (Victora et al., 2016).

Healthy eating

As children grow, a balanced diet becomes essential for sustained physical development. A nutritious diet comprising fruits, vegetables, whole grains, lean proteins and healthy fats supports energy levels, cognitive function and physical activity. Establishing healthy eating habits early in life can reduce the risk of chronic diseases and promote long-term wellbeing (Public Health England, 2020).

Obesity

Childhood obesity is an escalating concern, particularly in high-income countries. It is frequently associated with poor dietary habits, sedentary behaviour and environmental influences. Obesity increases the risk of conditions such as Type 2 diabetes, joint problems and cardiovascular disease, and can negatively impact self-esteem and mental health. Preventative strategies include promoting physical activity, reducing consumption of processed and sugary foods and encouraging family-based nutritional practices (Sahoo et al., 2015).

Malnourishment

Malnutrition, including undernutrition and micronutrient deficiencies, remains a global issue, especially in low-income regions. Malnourished children may experience stunted growth, delayed motor development and compromised immune function. Deficiencies in iron, iodine, vitamin A and zinc are particularly prevalent and can impair cognitive and physical development. Early intervention and access to nutrient-rich foods are critical to mitigating these effects (UNICEF, 2021).

Eating disorders

Eating disorders, such as anorexia nervosa, bulimia nervosa and avoidant/restrictive food intake disorder, can emerge during childhood or adolescence. These disorders are multifaceted and are often influenced by psychological, social and cultural factors. They can severely compromise physical health, leading to growth delays, nutrient deficiencies and long-term complications. Early identification and multidisciplinary interventions are essential for effective treatment and recovery (Treasure et al., 2020).

The importance of play for physical development

Play is a fundamental aspect of childhood and a key driver of physical development. Through play, children engage in activities that enhance strength, coordination, balance, and both gross and fine motor skills (see Chapter 13). Movement and exploration enable children to gain bodily control, test physical boundaries and build confidence in their abilities (Ginsburg, 2007).

Gross motor development is fostered through active play, such as running, jumping, climbing and cycling. These activities strengthen large muscle groups, improve balance and develop spatial awareness. Outdoor play, in particular, encourages vigorous movement, supporting cardiovascular health and overall fitness (Brussoni et al., 2015).

Fine motor skills are cultivated through activities involving small object manipulation, such as building with blocks, threading beads, drawing and using tools like scissors. These skills are essential for everyday tasks, including writing, dressing and feeding (Cameron et al., 2012).

Play also contributes to sensory development, as children interact with varied textures, sounds and movements. Sensory-rich activities, such as sand play, water play and messy play, stimulate sensory processing and integration.

Importantly, as will be shown in Chapter 13, play is not solely physical; it encompasses social, emotional and cognitive dimensions. It provides opportunities for risk-taking, problem-solving and self-expression, all while enhancing physical competence. For children of all abilities, play offers a joyful and meaningful context for growth, learning and holistic development (Whitebread, 2020).

Cultural perspectives on physical development: Beyond WEIRD norms

Much of the existing literature on physical development in children is derived from research conducted in WEIRD societies. These studies have significantly influenced global developmental norms, educational frameworks and health policies. However, such a culturally narrow perspective may obscure the diversity of developmental trajectories shaped by varying ecological contexts, caregiving practices and cultural values (Lansford et al., 2021).

In WEIRD contexts, physical development is often benchmarked against standardised milestones – such as crawling by 9 months or writing by age 5 – reflecting structured early education, healthcare access and a cultural emphasis on independence. Fine motor skills, for example, are frequently assessed through tasks like pencil grip or scissor use, which may not hold equivalent importance across cultures (Lansford et al., 2021).

Conversely, research in non-WEIRD settings reveals alternative developmental pathways. Studies in rural Kenya and South America, for example, suggest that children often acquire gross motor skills earlier due to increased autonomy and physical engagement in daily life (Adolph & Hoch, 2019). In some indigenous communities, observational learning and participation in communal tasks shape physical and sensory development differently from structured play environments.

Caregiving practices also vary widely. In cultures where infants are frequently carried, walking may be delayed, yet postural control and social bonding are enhanced (see Chapter 9). In contrast, early involvement in household responsibilities can foster strength, coordination and independence.

Recent research shows the role of positive childhood experiences (PCEs) in promoting physical and psychological resilience across cultures. A scoping review found that PCEs, measured through frameworks like the Benevolent Childhood Experience scale, have protective effects on health and development (Raghunathan et al., 2024).

These findings challenge the universality of WEIRD-based norms and highlight the importance of culturally responsive approaches in education, healthcare and policy.

Reflection points

- Reflect on how knowledge of typical development can inform your observations, planning and interactions with children in educational or care settings.
- Consider how early intervention and a supportive environment can mitigate risks and promote positive outcomes.
- Consider the impact of brain and physical development impact on other aspects of development.

Chapter summary

This chapter offered an overview of physical development, focusing on:

- Physical development includes growth in body size, motor skills and the refinement of the senses from birth to adolescence.
- Early childhood is marked by rapid development in both gross motor skills (e.g., crawling, walking, running) and fine motor skills (e.g., grasping, drawing, self-feeding).
- Sensory development begins in the womb and continues through early childhood, with each sense (vision, hearing, touch, taste, smell) playing a vital role in learning and interaction.
- Adolescence brings significant physical changes, including puberty, growth spurts and increased strength and coordination.

- Environmental and social factors, such as neglect, parental health, poverty, illness and housing, can significantly impact physical development, either supporting or hindering progress.
- Play is essential for physical development, offering opportunities to build strength, coordination and confidence through movement and exploration.
- Physical activity supports not only physical health but also psychological wellbeing, improving mood, reducing stress and enhancing cognitive function.
- Understanding physical development helps practitioners to identify typical and atypical patterns, enabling early intervention and tailored support.
- A holistic approach that includes nurturing environments, responsive caregiving and inclusive play opportunities is key to promoting healthy physical development in all children.

Further reading

Archer, C., & Siraj, I. (2015). *Encouraging Physical Development through Movement-Play*. Sage.

O'Connor, A., & Daly, A. (2016). *Understanding Physical Development in the Early Years: Linking Bodies and Minds*. Routledge.

Rico-González, M. (Ed.). (2025). *Physical Education in Early Childhood: Movement and Development from 3 to 6 Years*. Routledge.

Useful websites

EEF, Physical Development: https://educationendowmentfoundation.org.uk/early-years/evidence-store/physical-development

This website offers evidence-based strategies for supporting physical development in early years education. It includes practical guidance for educators on promoting motor skills, mark-making and movement through structured and play-based approaches.

References

Adolph, K., & Hoch, J. (2019). Motor development: Embodied, embedded, enculturated, and enabling. *Annual Review of Psychology, 70*, 141–164. https://doi.org/10.1146/annurev-psych-010418-102836

Berk, L., & Meyers, A. (2023). *Infants and Children: Prenatal through Middle Childhood* (9th ed.). Pearson.

Biddle, S., Ciaccioni, S., Thomas, G., & Vergeer, I. (2019). Physical activity and mental health in children and adolescents: An updated review of reviews and an analysis of causality. *Psychology of Sport and Exercise, 42*, 146–155. https://doi.org/10.1016/j.psychsport.2018.11.012

Black, R., Victora, C., Walker, S., Bhutta, Z., Christian, P., de Onis, M., & Uauy, R. (2013). Maternal and child undernutrition and overweight in low-income and middle-income countries. *The Lancet, 382*(9890), 427–451. https://doi.org/10.1016/S0140-6736(13)60937-X

Brussoni, M., Gibbons, R., Gray, C., Ishikawa, T., & Sandseter, E. B. H. (2015). What is the relationship between risky outdoor play and health in children? A systematic review. *International Journal of Environmental Research and Public Health*, *12*(6), 6423–6454. https://doi.org/10.3390/ijerph120606423

Cameron, C., Brock, L., Murrah, W., Bell, L., Worzalla, S., Grissmer, D., & Morrison, F. (2012). Fine motor skills and executive function both contribute to kindergarten achievement. *Child Development*, *83*(4), 1229–1244. https://doi.org/10.1111/j.1467-8624.2012.01768.x

Department for Education. (2021). *Statutory Framework for the Early Years Foundation Stage*. Department of Education. www.gov.uk/government/publications/early-years-foundation-stage-framework--2

Ginsburg, K. (2007). The importance of play in promoting healthy child development and maintaining strong parent–child bonds. *Pediatrics*, *119*(1), 182–191. https://doi.org/10.1542/peds.2006-2697

Jaiswal, M., & Morankar, S. (2017). Understanding primitive reflexes and their role in growth and development. *International Journal of Contemporary Pediatrics*, *4*(6), 2184–2189. https://doi.org/10.18203/2349-3291.ijcp20174745

Janssen, I., & LeBlanc, A. (2010). Systematic review of the health benefits of physical activity and fitness in school-aged children and youth. *International Journal of Behavioral Nutrition and Physical Activity*, *7*, 40. https://doi.org/10.1186/1479-5868-7-40

Lansford, J., French, D., & Gauvain, M. (2021). *Child Development in Cultural Contexts*. Routledge.

Ma, M., Zhang, L., Liu, Z., Teng, Y., Li, M., Peng, X., & An, L. (2024). Effect of blastocyst development on hatching and embryo implantation. *Theriogenology*, *214*, 66–72. https://doi.org/10.1016/j.theriogenology.2023.11.012

Marceau, K., Conradt, E., & Roubinov, D. (2024). Prenatal influences across the life course: Biobehavioral mechanisms of development. *Developmental Psychology*, *60*(9), 1533–1543. https://doi.org/10.1037/dev0001794

Pellegrini, A., & Smith, P. (2007). *The Nature of Play: Great Apes and Humans*. Guilford Press.

Porges, S. (2011). *The Polyvagal Theory: Neurophysiological Foundations of Emotions, Attachment, Communication, and Self-regulation*. W. W. Norton & Company.

Public Health England. (2020). *Health Matters: Child Obesity*. Public Health England. www.gov.uk/government/publications/health-matters-child-obesity/health-matters-child-obesity

Raghunathan, N., Lanier, P., & Maguire-Jack, K. (2024). Positive childhood experiences and child development: A scoping review. *Child Abuse & Neglect*, *150*, 106200. https://doi.org/10.1016/j.chiabu.2023.106200

Sahoo, K., Sahoo, B., Choudhury, A., Sofi, N., Kumar, R., & Bhadoria, A. (2015). Childhood obesity: Causes and consequences. *Journal of Family Medicine and Primary Care*, *4*(2), 187–192. https://doi.org/10.4103/2249-4863.154628

Shanker, S. (2016). *Self-reg: How to Help Your Child (and You) Break the Stress Cycle and Successfully Engage with Life*. Penguin.

Singh, A., Uijtdewilligen, L., Twisk, J., van Mechelen, W., & Chinapaw, M. (2012). Physical activity and performance at school: A systematic review of the literature including a methodological quality assessment. *Archives of Pediatrics & Adolescent Medicine, 166*(1), 49–55. https://doi.org/10.1001/archpediatrics.2011.716

Treasure, J., Stein, D., & Maguire, S. (2020). Eating disorders. *The Lancet Psychiatry, 7*(6), 487–498. https://doi.org/10.1016/S2215-0366(20)30036-9

UNICEF. (2021). *Nutrition.* UNICEF. www.unicef.org/nutrition

Victora, C., Bahl, R., Barros, A., França, G., Horton, S., Krasevec, J., & Rollins, N. (2016). Breastfeeding in the 21st century: Epidemiology, mechanisms, and lifelong effect. *The Lancet, 387*(10017), 475–490. https://doi.org/10.1016/S0140-6736(15)01024-7

Whitebread, D. (2020). *Developmental Psychology and Early Childhood Education* (2nd ed.). Sage.

World Health Organization. (2022). *Physical Activity.* WHO. www.who.int/news-room/fact-sheets/detail/physical-activity

8

Emotional development

Esmé Sung and Shazza Ali

Chapter objectives

By the end of the chapter, you will gain an understanding of:

- The experience and expression of basic and complex emotions.
- Temperament.
- Emotional regulation.
- Emotional intelligence.

Overview of the chapter

This chapter will start by exploring what emotions are and the developmental process of how basic and complex emotions are expressed, understood and differentiated. Next, it will cover the dimension of temperament – how it is measured and its influence on emotional and social development. This will be followed by an examination of emotion regulation and emotional intelligence – the strategies children use to understand and manage their emotions. The chapter will also highlight how societal and contextual influences, such as educational frameworks (e.g., the Collaborative for Academic, Social and Emotional Learning (CASEL) approach) and interventions (e.g., positive psychology) shape our emotional expression and experience.

Why should you read this chapter?

By reading this chapter, you will not only gain a broad understanding of emotional development, but also appreciate how emotional development intertwines with key developmental trajectories and milestones. It will underline some of the nuances of emotional development and encourage you to think critically about the influence of the wider society on emotional development.

Understanding, expression and differentiating emotions

This section explores the concept of emotions and the psychological processes that underpin their expression.

What are emotions?

One of the simplest ways to describe emotions is as a response to something in the environment. Emotions are considered to be automatic and unconscious. Occurring in episodes, they have a limited time span and they can change over the course of an event. It is helpful to think of emotions as adaptive motivational systems or processes that guide how we respond to our environments (Ekman, 1992; Izard, 2013).

Emotions are multifaceted, with different theories focusing on different aspects. Although there is no universally accepted definition, there is a general consensus that emotions are comprised of several components and it is changes in these components that form emotions (e.g., Frijda, 2017 [2007]; Shuman & Scherer, 2014). However, the set of components that an emotion *must* have and *how* the components relate to each other is debated.

- Unconscious physiological changes that are driven by the brain and the nervous system (e.g., body temperature).
- Cognitive appraisals of the environment that are influenced by our evolutionary and personal past (e.g., evaluations of what is happening).
- Motor expression, such as observable facial expression or body language (e.g., wider posture when experiencing pride).
- The conscious but subjective feeling of emotions.
- Distinct action tendencies or behavioural motivations.

Expressing and understanding emotions

The expression and perception of emotions form the basis of communication, which becomes increasingly complex as we develop. From birth, babies express two broad emotion responses – pleasure and displeasure. Displeasure is negatively valanced and is characterised by distress, crying and withdrawal, which communicates that the infant desires a change in their current environment. Pleasure is positively valanced and is characterised by attraction, attentiveness or a calm and relaxed posture. This response functions to maintain or increase contact with an object or person. Newborns seek comfort by snuggling with caregivers, for instance, and may begin to suck their thumb or fists to self-sooth. Infants may return a mother's gaze and show interest in faces or objects through focused attention and hyper-fixation (Kulke et al., 2017). As they grow, these broad emotional responses develop into distinct basic emotions. General displeasure, for example, morphs into more specific emotions, such as fear or sadness.

Expressing (basic) emotions

The emotions of fear, joy, disgust, sadness, anger and surprise are basic universal emotions, innate to humans and shared across cultures worldwide, as shown in Table 8.1 (Ekman, 1992). In other words, they are elicited by similar types of events and expressed in similar ways across cultures. Basic emotions are displayed early in life and are represented with facial expressions, gestures and vocalisations that map on to those of adults (e.g., Bennett et al., 2002; Sullivan & Lewis, 1989), which suggests that these emotions have adaptive functions that help humans to live and survive.

Table 8.1   Basic emotions

Emotion	Expression	Elicited by
Fear	Involuntary Startle or Moro reflex, extending arms and legs	Unsafe, unfamiliar circumstances; a sensation of falling
Disgust	Open mouth, protruding tongue, wrinkled nose	Unpleasant tastes
Joy	Smiles, laughter	Familiar faces, voices, touch and smells
Sadness	Whimpering, frowning, crying	Separation from caregiver
Anger	Fussing, crying, tantrums, aggression, violence	Unmet goals (e.g., hunger, tiredness, discomfort), perceived unfairness
Surprise	Wide eyes, raised eyebrows	Novel events

Crying is the most common reaction to negative stimuli and infants often express a range of negative emotions in the same crying episode (Messinger, 2002). Temperament, which is comprised of activity level, attention and adaptability (see more below), contributes to some of the variability in emotional development and expression.

Perceiving emotions

As motor, cognitive and visual systems continue to develop, infants not only express emotions but also start to respond to others' emotions. They begin to 'check in' with caregivers and use facial expressions and vocal cues to evaluate a situation, a process called social referencing. Studies like the Glass Cliff experiment show that infants look to their caregivers to evaluate the safety of an uncertain situation or novel object (Sorce et al., 1985; Walden & Ogan, 1988).

Empathy is shown early in infanthood and increases during early development. Empathy is described as an other-oriented emotional process that stems from the apprehension of another person's emotional state (Eisenberg & Miller, 1987). The affective (emotional) component refers to 'what the others are feeling' and the cognitive (perspective-taking) component refers to 'what the others are thinking'. Children whose parents model empathy and explain the reasons behind their actions are likely to display empathy and prosocial behaviour.

From basic to complex emotions

At around 2 years old, infants start using basic emotional language to describe how they feel (e.g., happy, sad, mad). As children's self-awareness and cognition develops, they start to express more complex emotions. In middle childhood, they experience mixed emotions and understand that the same experience can elicit two different emotions (e.g., excited and scared to jump in the pool). At around 3–5 years old, children understand that others have their own mental states, knowledge, intentions and beliefs. Theory of Mind (ToM) focuses on the ability to attribute mental states, such as thoughts, beliefs, desires and intentions, to oneself and others, and to understand that others may have perspectives that are different from one's own. This realisation is a key milestone in social and cognitive development and typically emerges between the ages of 3 and 5 (Baron-Cohen, 1991), when they begin to judge their own actions and understand that others will also judge their actions. A typical example of how ToM is tested is the Sally-Anne test:

- Sally places a marble in a basket and leaves the room.
- Anne moves the marble to a box.
- A child with ToM understands that Sally will look in the basket, not the box, because Sally doesn't know the marble was moved (Baron-Cohen, 1991).

Aquiring ToM facilitates secondary emotions, such as self-conscious and moral emotions (Lagattuta & Thompson, 2007).

Emotions such as shame, guilt, pride, honour and jealousy are rooted in social interactions and the understanding that individual experiences are intertwined with others' experiences. Shame and guilt, for example (see Table 8.2), require a more nuanced understanding of the validity of social and moral rules and the consequences of breaking them (Yoo & Smetana, 2022), which vary across contexts and cultures.

Table 8.2 Complex emotions

	Elicited by	Feeling	Motivation	Culture
Shame	Negative evaluation of the self (e.g., performing badly in front of others)	Exposed, bad, small, unworthy	To withdraw, avoid others, protect self from failure	More common in collectivist, interpersonal cultures, especially in Asia
Guilt	Negative evaluation of a behaviour (e.g., harming another, stealing a possession)	Concern for others, worthy	Resolve the wrong by repairing, confessing, apologising	More common in individualistic, intrapersonal cultures

The social constructivist perspective (see Chapter 1) views emotions as learned constructs which are determined by the larger social context (Barrett, 2017). That is, emotions are caused or constructed by our environments, such as our parents' rearing strategies, relationship experiences, gender roles, cultural norms and even the media. Parental styles (see Chapter 4) play a crucial role in the socialisation of self-conscious emotions. In relation to guilt, for example, children who feel safe and worthy may show concern about harming another person without directing negative feelings towards the self (Nikolić et al., 2023). As children grow older they spend less time with parents and teachers and more time with peers, which also influences how they express and manage emotions. Adolescents who spend time discussing the negative aspects and consequences (i.e., co-rumination) of their interactions are more likely to develop anxiety and depression, whereas friends who focus on understanding their interaction experiences (i.e., co-reflection) are at less risk of emotional problems (Bastin et al., 2014).

Social constructivists highlight the fact that languages include a varying number of emotion words. For instance, the English language contains up to 2,000 emotion words, whereas the Ifaluk language (in Western Pacific) contains up to 50 emotions words. Some emotions exist in some cultures/languages and not in others, and some emotion words are untranslatable. Thus, the emotions that we describe are tied to our socialisation experiences.

Consider this 8.1

- How do social and cultural contexts influence the way we experience, interpret and express complex emotions like shame, guilt and pride?
- To what extent are complex emotions learned through social interaction, and how may limited emotional vocabulary affect our ability to understand or communicate these emotions?

Temperament

Temperament refers to the biologically based individual differences in emotional reactivity, attention and self-regulation that appear early in life and remain relatively stable across time and situations. These temperamental traits significantly influence how emotions are experienced, expressed and managed, shaping an individual's emotional responses to their environment. Two widely recognised models – Chess and Thomas' classic framework (1996) and Rothbart's contemporary approach (2019) – offer valuable insights into how temperament is measured and expressed across various dimensions.

Chess and Thomas (1996) proposed that temperament is observable early in life and consists of nine dimensions:

- *Activity level*: Refers to the general level of physical energy and movement exhibited by the child.
- *Rhythmicity*: Describes the predictability of biological functions such as sleep, hunger and toileting.
- *Approach/withdrawal*: Indicates the initial response to new stimuli, including unfamiliar situations, people or environments.
- *Adaptability*: Reflects the ease with which a child adjusts to changes in routines, settings or expectations.
- *Threshold of responsiveness*: Measures sensitivity to sensory input; the amount of stimulation required to elicit a response.
- *Intensity of reaction*: Refers to the energy level or strength of emotional responses, whether positive or negative.
- *Quality of mood*: Represents the general tendency towards a predominantly positive or negative mood.
- *Distractibility*: Indicates the degree to which external stimuli interfere with ongoing behaviour or focus.
- *Attention span/persistence*: Relates to the duration of attention and the ability to persist with tasks despite challenges or distractions.

Following the New York Longitudinal Study (NYLS), Chess and Thomas (1996) identified three temperament types in infants:

- *Easy (40%)*: These children are generally happy, adaptable and have regular routines. They quickly establish sleep and feeding schedules, accept new foods, smile at strangers, adapt well to new environments and handle frustration with minimal fuss.
- *Difficult (10%)*: These children are intense, less adaptable and irregular in routines. They struggle with sleep and feeding schedules, resist new foods and take longer to adjust to changes. They often cry loudly, laugh intensely and may respond to frustration with tantrums.
- *Slow-to-warm-up (15%)*: These children are cautious, with low activity levels and mild reactions. They may initially respond negatively to new stimuli (e.g., food, people, places), but gradually show quiet interest and adapt positively over time.

There are two notable limitations in this model. First, not all children can be clearly categorised into the three temperament types. Second, the use of the term 'difficult' to describe one of the temperament types has been criticised for its negative con-notation, potentially leading to biased perceptions of children who display certain temperamental traits.

A later used framework by Rothbart (2019) conceptualised temperament as consist-ing of three dimensions, as shown in Table 8.3.

Table 8.3   Types of temperament according to Rothbart (2019)

Dimensions	Description	Example
Surgency/extraversion	High activity levels, impulsivity and a tendency towards positive emotions	A child high in surgency may eagerly approach new people and situations, showing enthusiasm and energy
Negative affectivity	Sensitivity to frustration, fear and discomfort	A child who becomes easily upset by changes or loud noises may score high in this trait
Effortful control	The ability to focus attention, inhibit impulses and regulate behaviour	A child who can wait their turn or persist with a challenging task demonstrates strong effortful control

Unlike Thomas and Chess's model, Rothbart's model emphasises individual differences along continuous dimensions, reflecting the intensity or tendency of specific traits. This dimensional approach allows for a more nuanced understanding of temperament, recognising that children vary in degree rather than fitting neatly into fixed categories. These traits significantly influence how children adapt to their environments. Children with high levels of effortful control, for example, are often better equipped to succeed academically and socially as they can regulate their emotions and behaviours in structured settings. In contrast, children who score high in negative affectivity may be more sensitive to stress and vulnerable to anxiety or mood disorders, particularly in unpredictable or unsupportive environments.

Shifting from co-regulation to self-regulation

This section explores how children develop emotion regulation skills and their progression from reliance on caregivers to managing their own emotions through self-regulation.

What is emotion regulation?

Emotion regulation (ER) is a fundamental aspect of self-regulation, which is the broader capacity to manage one's emotions, attention, behaviour and cognitions in pursuit of long-term goals (Gagne et al., 2021) and refers to the ability to control emotional experiences and expressions in ways that are adaptive and socially appropriate (Sanchis-Sanchis et al., 2020; Siegler et al., 2019). It includes adjusting the intensity, duration or expression of emotions like frustration, excitement or anxiety (Riediger & Bellingtier, 2022). Children who develop effective ER skills are better equipped to thrive in both everyday situations and long-term developmental challenges. ER is a cornerstone of healthy child development, influencing a wide range of outcomes across academic, social and emotional domains (Daniel et al., 2020; Sanchis-Sanchis et al., 2020). For the links between emotional regulation and the brain, see Chapter 6.

Greater academic success and resilience

Emotion regulation is closely tied to executive functions like attention control, working memory and cognitive flexibility, which are critical for academic success, school readiness and academic performance (Daniel et al., 2020). Children who can manage frustration or boredom are more likely to stay focused and persist through challenges. On the contrary, children who struggle with ER may be more prone to procrastination, frustration and disengagement in learning environments (see Chapter 4).

Stronger social relationships and empathy

Emotion regulation supports the ability to understand and respond appropriately to others' emotions, which is essential for building and maintaining friendships, resolving conflicts, communicating effectively and demonstrating empathy (Ritgens et al., 2024). By managing their own emotional responses, individuals are better equipped to interpret social cues and engage in positive social interactions. This capacity plays a foundational role in developing emotional intelligence and fostering meaningful interpersonal relationships.

Enhanced wellbeing, improved emotional and reduced risk-taking

As children grow into adolescence, ER becomes increasingly important for mental health and decision-making. Children who can manage their emotions are less likely to experience internalising problems (e.g., anxiety or depression) and externalising behaviours (e.g., aggression or defiance) (Lin et al., 2024; Vecchio et al., 2023). On the contrary, poor regulation is linked to impulsive or risky behaviours, while strong ER acts as a buffer against these risks and promotes healthier coping strategies.

In sum, ER is not just a skill, it is a developmental asset that shapes how children think, relate and grow. Supporting its development lays the foundation for lifelong wellbeing and success. On the contrary, the inability to recognise and regulate emotions in early life is a common origin for a wide range of physical and mental health problems in later life phases (Crowell et al., 2015).

Development of emotion regulation during childhood

Emotional regulation evolves significantly from infancy to adolescence, and is marked by a gradual transition from reliance on external support from parents and caregivers to children's increasing use of strategies (behavioural and cognitive) to regulate emotions.

Infancy to young childhood: Interpersonal

In early infancy, ER is primarily managed through co-regulation, where caregivers help infants to soothe distress through comforting actions like rocking, holding or speaking gently. Infants rely on these external strategies to manage emotions such as frustration or fear. A parent might calm a crying baby, for instance, by humming softly while rocking them. This process not only reduces distress but also models emotional support. According to Siegler et al. (2019), this stage is defined by external regulation, with caregivers playing a key role in helping infants to manage emotional states, laying the foundation for later self-regulation.

As infants grow, they begin to show self-regulation strategies as they gain control over their bodies and awareness of their surroundings. By around 5 months, behaviours like thumb-sucking, hand-rubbing or clinging to a blanket offer physical comfort and help to reduce arousal (Planalp & Braungart-Rieker, 2015). Infants also begin using self-distraction, such as looking away from distressing stimuli, to manage emotions (Ekas et al., 2013). Over the first year, there is a shift from self-comforting to more frequent use of self-distraction, reflecting cognitive and neurological development (Planalp & Braungart-Rieker, 2015). These changes are closely tied to the maturation of the frontal lobe, which supports attention control and behavioural inhibition, enabling infants to gradually manage their emotional responses more independently.

By 9 to 12 months, infants begin to show awareness of adult expectations and adjust their behaviour accordingly (Kopp, 1989). For example, a 10-month-old who bumps their knee may look to a caregiver before reacting. If the caregiver responds calmly, the infant may resume play without distress. This shift reflects early internalised regulation, where emotional responses are influenced by caregiver feedback. It also marks the beginning of socialisation, as infants start to align their behaviour with external emotional cues.

As children grow, they become increasingly capable of managing their own distress, such as engaging in solitary play (see Chapter 13), to distract themselves from upsetting situations, and gradually become less reliant on caregivers for comfort (Siegler et al., 2019). As language skills emerge (see Chapter 12), children express themselves verbally to manage emotions. Instead of crying or throwing tantrums, they may express their feelings or negotiate with caregivers. A toddler might say, for example, 'I'm sad', or ask for a hug when they are upset, instead of engaging in an emotional outburst.

Middle childhood to adolescence: Intrapersonal

As children grow, their ability to regulate emotion undergoes significant development. In early childhood, ER is largely behavioural, with infants and young children often relying on strategies such as self-soothing, distraction or seeking comfort from caregivers. As children enter middle childhood, however, they begin to adopt more sophisticated cognitive and problem-solving strategies to manage emotional challenges (Willner et al., 2022).

A key example is cognitive reappraisal – the process of changing one's perception of a situation to change its emotional impact (Gross, 2015). When teased by peers, for instance, a child may minimise the significance of the teasing rather than respond in a way that can escalate it (Siegler et al., 2019). Research shows that with adult guidance, children as young as 3 years can begin to use cognitive reappraisal, and by age 5 many can apply it independently (Willner et al., 2022).

During adolescence, ER becomes increasingly integrated with cognitive self-regulation, supporting better decision-making, social interactions and academic persistence (Sanchis-Sanchis et al., 2020). A teenager who can manage test anxiety, for instance, is more likely to try a different approach and seek help when needed, rather than shutting down or acting out.

Emotion regulation across contexts

Thus, ER is not only a marker of socio-emotional competence, it is itself a developmental process. Its expression and effectiveness varies across age groups and individuals, and is shaped by both biological maturation and environmental influences (Riediger & Bellingtier, 2022).

Cultural contexts play a crucial role in shaping the development of ER across communities. Children raised in individualistic Western cultures, which emphasise independence and personal autonomy, tend to regulate their emotions in ways that support self-expression and individual goals. In contrast, children from collectivist Asian cultures, where interdependence and social harmony are prioritised, are more likely to regulate their emotions in ways that preserve group cohesion. For example, individuals in Western societies may openly express negative emotions, such as frustration or anger, when faced with obstacles or unfair treatment. However, such expressions are often discouraged in many Asian cultures, where emotional restraint is seen as essential to maintaining social harmony (Trommsdorff, 2012). In fact, López-Pérez and Pacella (2021) argue that culture not only provides meaning to emotional experiences but also reinforces culturally specific ways of responding to and regulating emotions. In collectivist cultures, emotional suppression is often associated with greater social harmony and higher individual wellbeing (Matsumoto, 2006), whereas in individualistic cultures, higher levels of emotional suppression are typically linked to lower individual wellbeing (Soto et al., 2011).

Unreflective to reflective emotions: The development of emotional intelligence in childhood and adolescence

The following section discusses the how emotional intelligence develops during childhood and adolescence.

What is emotional intelligence?

Emotional intelligence (EI) is the capacity to perceive, understand and manage emotion. It emerges gradually across childhood, evolving from instinctive emotional reactions in infancy to deliberate, reflective emotional strategies in adolescence. This developmental trajectory reflects increasing cognitive maturity, social awareness and self-regulatory capacity. Goleman et al. (2002) conceptualised EI as comprising four core domains (see Table 8.4).

Table 8.4   Core domains of emotional intelligence

Domain	Description	Example in children	Example in adolescents
Intrapersonal			
Self-awareness	Recognising one's own emotions and their impact	A child notices that they feel nervous before a test and tells the teacher they are anxious	A teen reflects on feeling overwhelmed and realises it is due to academic pressure
Self-management	Managing emotions in healthy ways and adapting to changing circumstances	A child calms themselves by taking deep breaths after losing a game	A teen resists the urge to argue during a disagreement with a friend
Interpersonal			
Social awareness	Understanding others' emotions and showing empathy	A child notices a classmate is sad and offers to play with them	A teen recognises a peer is stressed and offers support or space
Relationship management	Building and maintaining healthy relationships through communication and conflict resolution	A child shares toys and takes turns during group play	A teen resolves a conflict with a friend by discussing the issue calmly and respectfully

Why emotional intelligence matters in childhood

Emotional intelligence is essential for children's mental health, relationships, academic achievement and long-term success (Brackett & Cipriano, 2020; Gonzales, 2022; MacCann et al., 2020). It plays a vital role in fostering healthy relationships by enhancing one's ability to understand others' emotions and manage their own. Higher EI is linked to greater empathy and stronger connections with family, peers, colleagues and partners throughout life (Brackett & Cipriano, 2020). From adolescence onward, EI serves as both a protective and a predictive role in mental health, correlating with lower levels of depression and reduced risk of suicidal behaviour (Soto-Sanz et al., 2024).

Emotional intelligence and emotion regulation are deeply interconnected in child development: EI provides the foundation for recognising and understanding emotions, while ER involves managing those emotions effectively. As children develop EI, they become better equipped to use strategies like cognitive reappraisal or problem-solving to navigate emotional experiences. Thus, ER is both a skill within and an outcome of growing EI.

Development of emotional intelligence

Emotional intelligence develops in infancy through interactions with caregivers and continues as children interact with parents, peers and teachers (Brackett & Cipriano, 2020). It is acquired through informal life experiences (e.g., observing how parents, peers, teachers and TV characters talk about and manage emotions) and formal instruction (e.g., direct instruction to build emotion vocabulary and learn helpful emotion regulation strategies). Table 8.5 summarises the milestones of emotional development from infancy to adolescence.

A strengths-based approach to emotional development

Emotion regulation is a foundational skill in childhood that supports mental health, wellbeing and adaptive functioning across diverse learning needs, and is closely linked to EI, which enables children to recognise, understand and manage their emotions effectively. Rather than being a fixed trait, ER is a developmental capacity that can be nurtured through inclusive, strengths-based approaches, helping children to build the emotional awareness and interpersonal skills that are essential for lifelong learning and relationships. This perspective views emotional challenges in children with Social Emotional Needs as meaningful opportunities to cultivate resilience, deepen self-awareness and develop adaptive coping strategies. It emphasises the developmental nature of emotional skills and highlights the critical role of supportive, responsive environments in nurturing these capacities. Two key strengths-based approaches that support emotion regulation in children with social emotional needs and Positive Psychology Interventions.

Social and emotional learning

Social and Emotional Learning (SEL) provides a structured framework for fostering five core emotional competences: (1) self-awareness, (2) self-management, (3) social awareness, (4) relationship skills, and (5) responsible decision making (CASEL, 2025). These competencies are essential for navigating emotional experiences and building positive relationships. Research shows that SEL interventions enhance emotional wellbeing, reduce psychological distress and improve academic engagement across varied educational settings (Hassani & Schwab, 2021; Hosokawa et al., 2024; Kim et al., 2024). For example, teaching self-management strategies can help a child with ADHD to regulate impulses during group activities, while fostering social awareness can support autistic learners in understanding peer perspectives.

Positive psychology intervention – character strengths

Positive psychology (see Chapter 1) complements SEL by focusing on character strengths, such as perseverance, empathy, curiosity and self-regulation, as tools for emotional growth. These strengths are not fixed traits but capacities that can be identified, nurtured and applied to help children to navigate emotional experiences with confidence and resilience. Perseverance, for instance, helps children to manage frustration during challenging tasks, while empathy supports social connection and conflict resolution. In children with SEN, recognising and applying these strengths can reduce feelings of helplessness and promote a sense of competence and belonging (Bressoud & Shankland, 2018; Vuorinen et al., 2019).

Integrating character strengths into SEL practices creates emotionally supportive environments where emotional expression is validated, reflection is encouraged and progress is celebrated. This approach helps children to recognise their inner resources and apply them in emotionally demanding situations, fostering agency and self-worth.

Building emotionally attuned environments

Emotion regulation is co-developed through relationships. Children thrive when educators and caregivers respond with empathy, consistency and encouragement. For children with social emotional needs, emotionally attuned environments honour diverse ways of expressing and managing feelings, and provide the scaffolding needed for emotional growth.

By integrating SEL and positive psychology, educators can support all children, not by correcting what is 'wrong', but by amplifying what is strong. This inclusive approach to mental health nurtures emotional intelligence, builds resilience and celebrates each child's unique developmental journey. The following table provides an overview of key emotional development milestones from infancy through adolescence, offering a concise reference for educators.

Table 8.5 A summary of milestones of emotional development from infancy to adolescence

Stages	Milestones of emotional development	Examples
Infancy	**Emotional expression and co-regulation with caregivers** • Emotional responses are largely automatic, expressing basic emotions, such as distress or joy, without conscious control • Caregivers play a central role in co-regulation (e.g., soothing the infant) • These early interactions lay the groundwork for emotional attunement, where infants begin to associate emotional states with social cues	A baby who is comforted when crying learns to associate a caregiver's presence with emotional relief, forming the basis of trust and emotional security

Stages	Milestones of emotional development	Examples
Toddlerhood to early childhood	**Emotional awareness and expression** • Emerging self-awareness and basic empathy, although emotional responses remain impulsive and often require adult support • Children using simple strategies, such as distraction or seeking comfort, are early signs of internal emotional management • Labelling emotions and recognising them in others	A 3-year-old may say 'I'm sad' when a toy breaks, but still need help calming down. They might also offer a toy to a crying peer, showing early signs of empathy
Middle childhood	**Strategic emotional thinking** • Emergence of self-conscious and moral emotions • Using cognitive strategies (e.g., cognitive reappraisal) to manage their emotions by reframing a situation to alter its emotional impact • ToM, perspective-taking, language skills and emotional vocabulary enable children to navigate social situations with greater nuance	A child excluded from a game may tell themselves, 'They just want to play something different', rather than feeling rejected
Adolescence	**Reflective emotional intelligence** • Increasing integration of abstract reasoning, emotional and cognitive processes • Capability of reflective emotional processing, such as analysing their feelings and motivations	A teenager experiencing anxiety before an exam may use breathing techniques, positive self-talk or seek support, demonstrating reflective emotional management

From reaction to reflection: A developmental curve

The journey from unreflective to reflective emotions is not linear but shaped by individual temperament, social environment and cognitive development. Emotional intelligence is both a product and a driver of socio-emotional competence, influencing academic success, mental health and interpersonal relationships.

Case study 8.1: Moving to another country

Yuki, a 3-year-old girl, has recently moved from Japan to the UK with her family due to her parents' job relocation. It is her third week attending a nursery setting. Yuki is quiet and reserved – she rarely speaks unless prompted, tends to avoid eye contact with practitioners and often looks down when they talk to her. Despite her quiet demeanour, she follows routines well, tidies up carefully and shows an early interest in books, often pointing to pictures and listening attentively during story time.

(Continued)

During group activities, Yuki typically sits slightly apart from the other children, watching rather than joining in. When encouraged to participate, she speaks softly and hesitantly, sometimes glancing at her peers before responding. Her key person, Mr Thompson, wonders whether Yuki might be feeling overwhelmed or emotionally unsettled, but he is also aware that her behaviour might reflect cultural norms rather than emotional distress.

At home, Yuki's parents describe her as lively and expressive in Japanese. They explain that in Japan, young children are often taught to listen attentively and show respect through quietness and restraint, especially in formal settings. Public displays of emotion may be discouraged, as they can be perceived as disruptive or attention-seeking.

Being critical

- In what ways can emotional expression, such as tone of voice, facial expression and eye contact, be interpreted differently across cultures?
- How might these cultural interpretations affect how a child is perceived in a new environment?

Reflection points

- How can understanding a child's temperament guide personalised emotional support strategies in educational settings?
- Emotion regulation evolves from co-regulation in infancy to self-regulation in adolescence. Reflect on how this progression supports resilience, academic success and mental health.
- What practices can educators adopt to scaffold ER skills at different developmental stages?
- Emotional intelligence is not fixed but develops through social interaction and intentional teaching. Reflect on how strengths-based approaches like SEL and positive psychology can support children with SEN.

Chapter summary

This chapter explored emotional development from childhood to adolescence, covering:

- Conceptualisation of emotions: It explored how children recognise, experience and express emotions.
- Temperament and individual differences: It examined how temperament influences emotional development and interacts with other emotional processes.
- Development of emotion regulation: It traced the progression from co-regulation with caregivers in early childhood to self-regulation in later stages.

- Strengths-based approach to SEN and mental health: It applied a strengths-based lens to understand ER and mental health in children with SEN, highlighting the role of supportive environments.
- Emotional intelligence milestones: It outlined key developmental milestones in emotional intelligence from early childhood to adolescence.

Further reading

British Psychological Society. (2020, October 15). A new take on the marshmallow test: Children wait longer for a treat when their reputation is at stake. *Research Digest*. BPS. www.bps.org.uk/research-digest/new-take-marshmallow-test

Kammermeier, M., & Paulus, M. (2023). Infants' responses to masked and unmasked smiling faces: A longitudinal investigation of social interaction during Covid-19. *Infant Behavior and Development, 73*, 101873.

Stahl, A., & Feigenson, L. (2015). Observing the unexpected enhances infants' learning and exploration. *Science, 348*(6230), 91–94.

Useful websites

Social and Emotional Learning: https://casel.org/fundamentals-of-sel/what-is-the-casel-framework/

This webpage offers a comprehensive overview of Social and Emotional Learning (SEL) and outlines practical strategies for implementing it to create supportive environments that nurture students' emotional competence.

Paul Ekman Emotion Psychologist: www.paulekman.com/about/paul-ekman/

Paul Ekman is a psychologist who pioneered research on facial expressions, emotion and deception, co-developing the Facial Action Coding System.

References

Baron-Cohen, S. (1991). Precursors to a theory of mind: Understanding attention in others. In A. Whiten (Ed.), *Natural Theories of Mind: Evolution, Development and Simulation of Everyday Mindreading* (pp. 233–251). Basil Blackwell.

Barrett, L. F. (2017). How emotions are made: The secret life of the brain. In L. F. Barrett, *How Emotions are Made: The Secret Life of the Brain*. Houghton Mifflin Harcourt.

Bastin, M., Bijttebier, P., Raes, F., & Vasey, M. (2014). Brooding and reflecting in an interpersonal context. *Personality and Individual Differences, 63*. https://doi.org/10.1016/j.paid.2014.01.062

Bennett, D., Bendersky, M., & Lewis, M. (2002). Facial expressivity at 4 months: A context by expression analysis. *Infancy, 3*(1). https://doi.org/10.1207/S15327078IN0301_5

Blair, C., & Raver, C. C. (2015). School Readiness and Self-Regulation: A Developmental Psychobiological Approach. *Annual review of psychology, 66*(Volume 66, 2015), 711–731. https://doi.org/https://doi.org/10.1146/annurev-psych-010814-015221

Brackett, M., & Cipriano, C. (2020, 1 July). Emotional intelligence comes of age. *Cerebrum*.

Bressoud, N., & Shankland, R. (2018, November). Character strengths and children with special needs: A way to promote wellbeing all together! *Well-Being in Education Systems*, *255*. https://www.researchgate.net/publication/317970856_Character_strengths_and_children_with_special_needs_A_way_to_promote_well-being_all_together

CASEL (2025). *What is the CASEL framework?* Collaborative for Academic, Social, and Emotional Learning. https://casel.org/fundamentals-of-sel/what-is-the-casel-framework/

Collaborative for Academic, Social, and Emotional Learning. (2025). *What is the CASEL framework?* CASEL. https://casel.org/fundamentals-of-sel/what-is-the-casel-framework/

Chess, S., & Thomas, A. (1996). *Temperament: Theory and Practice*. Brunner/Mazel.

Crowell, S., Puzia, M., & Yaptangco, M. (2015). The ontogeny of chronic distress: Emotion dysregulation across the life span and its implications for psychological and physical health. *Current Opinion in Psychology*, *3*, 91–99. https://doi.org/10.1016/j.copsyc.2015.03.023

Daniel, S., Abdel-Baki, R., & Hall, G. (2020). The protective effect of emotion regulation on child and adolescent wellbeing. *Journal of Child and Family Studies*, *29*(7), 2010–2027. https://doi.org/10.1007/s10826-020-01731-3

Eisenberg, N., & Miller, P. (1987). The relation of empathy to prosocial and related behaviors. *Psychological Bulletin*, *101*(1). https://doi.org/10.1037/0033-2909.101.1.91

Ekas, N., Lickenbrock, D., & Braungart-Rieker, J. (2013). Developmental trajectories of emotion regulation across infancy: Do age and the social partner influence temporal patterns? *Infancy*, *18*(5), 729–754. https://doi.org/10.1111/infa.12003

Ekman, P. (1992). An argument for basic emotions. *Cognition and Emotion*, *6*(3–4). https://doi.org/10.1080/02699939208411068

Frijda, N. (2017 [2007]). *The Laws of Emotion* (eBook). Psychology Press. https://doi.org/10.4324/9781315086071

Gagne, J., Liew, J., & Nwadinobi, O. (2021). How does the broader construct of self-regulation relate to emotion regulation in young children? *Developmental Review*, *60*. https://doi.org/10.1016/j.dr.2021.100965

Goleman, D., Boyatzia, R., & McKee, A. (2002). *Primal Leadership: Realizing the Power of Emotional Intelligence*. Harvard Business School Press.

Gonzales, M. (2022). *Emotional Intelligence for Students, Parents, Teachers and School Leaders: A Handbook for the Whole School Community*. Springer Nature. https://doi.org/10.1007/978-981-19-0324-3

Gross, J. (2015). Emotion regulation: Current status and future prospects. *Psychological Inquiry*, *26*(1), 1–26. https://doi.org/10.1080/1047840X.2014.940781

Hassani, S., & Schwab, S. (2021). Social-emotional learning interventions for students with special educational needs: A systematic literature review. *Frontiers in Education*, *6*. https://doi.org/10.3389/feduc.2021.808566

Hosokawa, R., Matsumoto, Y., Nishida, C., Funato, K., & Mitani, A. (2024). Enhancing social-emotional skills in early childhood: Intervention study on the effectiveness of social and emotional learning. *BMC Psychology*, *12*(1). https://doi.org/10.1186/s40359-024-02280-w

Izard, C. (2013). *Human Emotions*. Springer Science & Business Media.

Kim, E., Allen, J., & Jimerson, S. (2024). Supporting student social emotional learning and development. *School Psychology Review, 53*(3), 201–207. https://doi.org/10.1080/2 372966x.2024.2346443

Kopp, C. (1989). Regulation of distress and negative emotions: A developmental view. *Developmental Psychology, 25*(3), 343–354. https://doi.org/10.1037/0012-1649.25.3.343

Kulke, L., Atkinson, J., & Braddick, O. (2017). Neural mechanisms of attention become more specialised during infancy: Insights from combined eye tracking and EEG. *Developmental Psychobiology, 59*(2). https://doi.org/10.1002/dev.21494

Lagattuta, K., & Thompson, R. (2007). The development of self-conscious emotion: Cognitive processes and social influences. In J. L. Tracy, R. W. Robins, & J. P. Tangney (Eds.), *Self-Conscious Emotions: Theory and Research*. Guilford Press.

Lin, S. C., Kehoe, C., Pozzi, E., Liontos, D., & Whittle, S. (2024). Research Review: Child emotion regulation mediates the association between family factors and internalizing symptoms in children and adolescents – a meta-analysis. *Journal of Child Psychology and Psychiatry, 65*(3), 260–274. https://doi.org/10.1111/jcpp.13894

López-Pérez, B., & Pacella, D. (2021). Interpersonal emotion regulation in children: Age, gender, and cross-cultural differences using a serious game. *Emotion, 21*(1), 17–27. https://doi.org/10.1037/emo0000690

MacCann, C., Jiang, Y., Brown, L., Double, K., Bucich, M., & Minbashian, A. (2020). Emotional intelligence predicts academic performance: A meta-analysis. *Psychological Bulletin, 146*(2), 150–186. https://doi.org/10.1037/bul0000219.supp

Matsumoto, D. (2006). Culture and nonverbal behavior. In V. Manusov, M. L. Patterson (Eds.) *Culture and nonverbal behavior* (pp. 219–236). SAGE Publications, Inc., https://doi.org/10.4135/9781412976152.n12

Messinger, D. S. (2002). Positive and negative: Infant facial expressions and emotions. *Current Directions in Psychological Science, 11*(1). https://doi.org/10.1111/1467-8721.00156

Nikolić, M., Brummelman, E., de Castro, B., Jorgensen, T., & Colonnesi, C. (2023). Parental socialization of guilt and shame in early childhood. *Scientific Reports, 13*(1). https://doi.org/10.1038/s41598-023-38502-1

Planalp, E., & Braungart-Rieker, J. (2015). Trajectories of regulatory behaviors in early infancy: Determinants of infant self-distraction and self-comforting. *Infancy, 20*(2), 129–159. https://doi.org/10.1111/infa.12068

Riediger, M., & Bellingtier, J. (2022). Emotion regulation across the life span. In D. Dukes, A. Samson, & E. Walle (Eds.), *The Oxford Handbook of Emotional Development* (pp. 93–103). Oxford University Press. https://doi.org/10.1093/oxfordhb/978019

Ritgens, C., Bondü, R., & Warschburger, P. (2024). Links between self-regulation patterns and prosocial behavior trajectories from middle childhood to early adolescence: a longitudinal study [Original Research]. *Frontiers in Psychology, Volume 15 - 2024*. https://doi.org/10.3389/fpsyg.2024.1480046

Rothbart, M. K. (2019). Early temperament and psychosocial development. In R. E. Tremblay, M. Boivin, & R. DeV. Peters (Eds.), *Encyclopedia on Early Childhood Development*. Retrieved from: www.child-encyclopedia.com/temperament/according-experts/early-temperament-and-psychosocial-development

Sanchis-Sanchis, A., Grau, M., Moliner, A., & Morales-Murillo, C. (2020). Effects of age and gender in emotion regulation of children and adolescents. *Frontiers in Psychology*, *11*. https://doi.org/10.3389/fpsyg.2020.00946

Shaul, S., & Schwartz, M.. (2014). The role of the executive functions in school readiness among preschool-age children. *Reading and Writing*, *27*(4), 749–768. https://doi.org/10.1007/s11145-013-9470-3

Shuman, V., & Scherer, K. R. (2014). Concepts and structures of emotions. In R. Pekrun & L. Linnenbrink-Garcia (Eds.), *International handbook of emotions in education* (pp. 13–35). London: Routledge.

Siegler, R., Saffran, J., Gershoff, E., & Eisenberg, N. (2019). *How Children Develop* (6th ed.). Macmillan International Higher Education.

Sorce, J., Emde, R., Campos, J., & Klinnert, M. (1985). Maternal emotional signaling: Its effect on the visual cliff behavior of 1-year-olds. *Developmental Psychology*, *21*(1). https://doi.org/10.1037/0012-1649.21.1.195

Soto, J., Perez, C., Kim, Y., Lee, E., & Minnick, M. (2011). Is expressive suppression always associated with poorer psychological functioning? A cross-cultural comparison between European Americans and Hong Kong Chinese. *Emotion*, *11*(6), 1450–1455. https://doi.org/10.1037/a0023340

Soto-Sanz, V., do Céu Salvador, M., & Piqueras, J. (2024). Social anxiety and depression in Portuguese and Spanish adolescents: The moderating role of emotional intelligence. *Child Psychiatry and Human Development*. Advance online publication. https://doi.org/10.1007/s10578-024-01795-y

Sullivan, M., & Lewis, M. (1989). Emotion and cognition in infancy: Facial expressions during contingency learning. *International Journal of Behavioral Development*, *12*(2). https://doi.org/10.1177/016502548901200206

Trommsdorff, G. (2012). Development of 'agentic' regulation in cultural context: The role of self and world views. *Child Development Perspectives*, *6*(1), 19–26. https://doi.org/10.1111/j.1750-8606.2011.00224.x

Vecchio, G. M., Zava, F., Cattelino, E., Zuffianò, A., & Pallini, S. (2023). Children's prosocial and aggressive behaviors: The role of emotion regulation and sympathy. *Journal of Applied Developmental Psychology*, *89*, 101598. https://doi.org/https://doi.org/10.1016/j.appdev.2023.101598

Vuorinen, K., Erikivi, A., & Uusitalo-Malmivaara, L. (2019). A character strength intervention in 11 inclusive Finnish classrooms to promote social participation of students with special educational needs. *Journal of Research in Special Educational Needs*, *19*(1), 45–57. https://doi.org/10.1111/1471-3802.12423

Walden, T., & Ogan, T. (1988). The development of social referencing. *Child Development*, *59*(5). https://doi.org/10.1111/j.1467-8624.1988.tb01492.x

Willner, C., Hoffmann, J., Bailey, C., Harrison, A., Garcia, B., Ng, Z., Cipriano, C., & Brackett, M. (2022). The development of cognitive reappraisal from early childhood through adolescence: A systematic review and methodological recommendations. *Frontiers in Psychology*, *13*. https://doi.org/10.3389/fpsyg.2022.875964

Yoo, H., & Smetana, J. (2022). Distinctions between moral and conventional judgments from early to middle childhood: A meta-analysis of social domain theory research. *Developmental Psychology*, *58*(5). https://doi.org/10.1037/dev0001330

9

Attachment and adverse childhood experiences

Olga Fotakopoulou and Ioanna Palaiologou

Chapter objectives

By the end of the chapter, you will:

- Understand the foundational attachment theories of Bowlby, Winnicott and Ainsworth.
- Consider ethical issues in attachment research with infants and vulnerable groups.
- Identify the outcomes of secure versus insecure attachments, including attachment disorders.
- Explore how adverse childhood experiences (ACEs) and early trauma affect attachment and long-term wellbeing.

Overview of the chapter

This chapter will explore the foundational attachment theories of John Bowlby, Donald Winnicott and Mary Ainsworth and their relevance to adverse childhood experiences (ACEs). Bowlby's ethological theory, Winnicott's 'good enough mother' concept and Ainsworth's 'Strange Situation' procedure provide a framework for understanding how early relational experiences shape development. The chapter will examine attachment development from infancy to early childhood, highlighting stages, patterns and measurement methods. Ethical considerations in attachment research will be discussed and the consequences of secure and insecure attachments on emotional regulation, relationships and mental health are addressed, including disorders such as Reactive Attachment Disorder (RAD) and Disinhibited Social Engagement Disorder (DSED). The chapter will define and contextualise ACEs within Attachment Theory, exploring how abuse, neglect and household dysfunction impair attachment and contribute to developmental challenges. Finally, the chapter will discuss the importance of early intervention and supportive caregiving.

Why should you read this chapter?

By exploring the theories of Bowlby, Winnicott and Ainsworth, you will gain a deeper understanding of how secure and insecure attachments form and their lasting impact on wellbeing. The chapter also connects these theories to the concept of adverse childhood experiences (ACEs), highlighting how early trauma can disrupt attachment and contribute to long-term challenges.

Introduction

Between 1930 and 1959 psychoanalyst René Spitz conducted a series of studies of how the lack of adequate caregiving affects development (Spitz, 1945, 1949). Spitz filmed infants residing in orphanages and, together with colleague Katherine Wolf, famously depicted neglected infants in a 1947 film titled *Grief: A Peril in Infancy*. This film showed young children in varying states of disarray due to suffering in different institutionalised settings. It was widely viewed by researchers and medical personnel around the world and continues to be referenced today. The infants shown serve as compelling evidence of the critical importance of human contact in the first months and years of life. This research demonstrated that emotional deprivation and lack of relationships with the caregivers in the first years of life hinder (optimal) social, emotional and cognitive development (Bick et al., 2012). The exact reasons why children and their parents develop this bond were, however, initially a matter of debate.

The origins of attachment: Psychoanalytic, behaviourist and ethological perspectives

Freud's psychoanalytic theory posits that infants become attached to their caregivers, usually the mother, due to their ability to satisfy the infant's instinctual needs. Freud stated, 'The reason why the infant in arms wants to perceive the presence of its mother is only because it already knows that she satisfies all its needs without delay' (Freud, 1926, p. 20). He described that love originates from attachment to the satisfied need for nourishment (Freud, 1940, p. 188), emphasising the importance of feeding habits.

Behaviourism argues that the bond between infants and their mothers is primarily based on the provision of food, such as breast milk. Through classical conditioning, infants learn to associate their mothers with the pleasure derived from food, which acts as the unconditioned stimulus that naturally elicits pleasure, while mothers become the conditioned stimulus (Dollard & Miller, 1950).

John Bowlby, a British child psychiatrist in the 1950s, proposed that human beings have a natural tendency to form strong, enduring, affectionate bonds with significant individuals. This behaviour has evolved biologically and is crucial for survival and adaptation. Bowlby developed his theoretical positions from various disciplines, including psychoanalytic theory, evolution and ethology. Psychoanalytic object-relations theories, which were proposed by Fairbairn (1952) and Winnicott (1965), were congenial to Bowlby but his thinking developed independently. Bowlby also relied on his own observations and clinical research, which particularly focused on individuals he believed had inadequate attachment with significant others/primary caregivers.

Bowlby (1951, 1953, 1997) defined this bond as catering not only to the physiological needs of a child, such as food, but also to psychological needs, such as comfort or the sense of a 'safe base'. While attachment provides a secure base for young children, they also possess a natural inclination to explore their surroundings. This exploratory behaviour is essential for their learning and development, which can only be achieved if they feel able to draw away from their safe base (Gillibrand et al., 2016). Attachment is defined as a strong, enduring, affectionate bond that an infant shares with a significant individual, usually the mother, who knows and responds well to the infant's needs. Infants can always return to their safe base when they wish or when they feel threatened or distressed.

Bowlby initially grounded his theory on contemporaneous scientific evidence, making considerable efforts to create bridges across disciplines. He borrowed fundamental ideas from the ethologist Konrad Lorenz – in particular, the theory of imprinting (Lorenz, 1935) – and successfully integrated them with psychoanalytic developmental theories of object relations. Lorenz showed that attachment was innate in young ducklings and, therefore, has a survival value.

Essentially, Bowlby posited that attachment behaviours are instinctive and are activated by any conditions that threaten the achievement of proximity, such as separation, insecurity and fear. Bowlby explained that the fear of strangers represents an important survival mechanism; babies are born with the tendency to display certain innate behaviours, called social releasers (e.g., crying, smiling, crawling), that help to ensure proximity and contact with the primary caregiver or mother figure. The specific onset and nature of these behaviours depend on the infant or child's age, cognitive development and physical growth. These behaviours include recognising the caregiver, distinguishing her from others and forming representations (and recollections) of objects (including the mother in her absence) (Piaget, 1954). Bowlby suggested that the nature of monotropy – defined as a crucial and exclusive bond with a single attachment figure – meant that a failure to initiate, or a breakdown of the maternal attachment, would lead to serious negative consequences, possibly including affectionless psychopathy. Bowlby's theory of monotropy led to the formulation of his maternal deprivation hypothesis. Through detailed examination of 44 cases at the London Child Guidance Clinic, Bowlby linked their symptoms to histories of maternal deprivation and separation. The maternal deprivation hypothesis posits that the absence of a stable and consistent attachment figure during early childhood can lead to significant negative outcomes later in life.

John Bowlby

John Bowlby's early writings on the emotional experiences of affectionless children caught the attention of Ronald Hargreaves at the World Health Organization (WHO). Hargreaves subsequently commissioned Bowlby to produce a report on the mental health of homeless children in post-war Europe. This project provided Bowlby with the opportunity to engage with a network of practitioners and researchers across Europe and the USA who were investigating the effects of maternal separation and deprivation on young children. Among these were Spitz (1945) and Goldfarb (1943, 1945), whose work significantly influenced the field. Bowlby completed the report within six months and it was later translated into 14 languages.

> If mental development is to proceed smoothly, it would appear to
> the necessary for the undifferentiated psyche to be exposed during certain
> critical periods to the influence of the psychic organiser – the mother.
> (Bowlby, 1951, p. 53)

Bowlby proposed that during infancy and early childhood the child is dependent on their mother performing the different functions for them. She orients them in space and time, provides their environment, permits the satisfaction of some impulses and restricts others. She is their ego and their super-ego. Gradually the infant inevitably learns these arts themselves and the skilled parent transfers the roles to them. This is a slow, subtle and continuous process, beginning when they first learn to walk and feed themself and not ending completely until maturity is reached (Bowlby, 1951).

Bowlby maintained that infants and children experience separation anxiety when a situation activates both escape and attachment behaviour but an attachment figure is not available. Attachment behaviour tends to become more pronounced when the person feels frightened, tired or unwell, and is typically alleviated when the attachment figure offers protection, support and comfort.

Separation protest is a concept in Bowlby's Attachment Theory that describes the distress and anxiety children experience when separated from their primary attachment figure, typically their mother. According to Bowlby, this reaction is a natural and adoptive response as the attachment figure provides safety and security. When separated, children may cry, cling or search for their caregiver, demonstrating their strong and emotional bond and reliance on the attachment figure for comfort and protection. When a child begins to show anxiety upon separation from their primary caregiver, they also develop a fear or anxiety towards unfamiliar people-strangers. The attachment system envisaged by Bowlby (see Table 9.1) does not become organised until sometime until the second half of the first year.

Table 9.1 Bowlby's attachment phases

Phase	Age	Characteristics	Examples for early childhood educators
Pre-attachment	Birth to 6 weeks	Infants show no particular attachment to a specific caregiver	Infants may be comforted by any person who holds them
Early attachment	6 weeks to 6–8 months	Infants begin to show preference for primary and secondary caregivers	Infants may smile more at familiar caregivers and be soothed more quickly by them
Separation protest	6–8 months to 18–24 months	Infants show strong attachment to one specific caregiver and distress upon separation	Infants may cry when their primary caregiver leaves the room and may seek comfort from them on their return
Goal-corrected	18–24 months and onwards	Children understand that caregivers have goals and plans that are different from their own	Children may be able to wait for a caregiver to return, understanding that they will come back after completing a task

Donald Winnicott

In 1953, Donald Winnicott, a British paediatrician and psychoanalyst, developed a conceptual model of the earliest emotional development of a child (see Table 9.2). In the early stages after birth, the baby cannot be considered as an independent subject, but only in the 'mother–child' dyad. Winnicott introduced the concepts of 'ideal' mother, 'bad' mother and 'good enough' mother. The 'good enough' mother starts off with an almost complete adaptation to her infant's needs and, as time proceeds, she adapts less and less completely, and gradually, according to the infant's growing ability to deal with her failure (Winnicott, 1953).

Table 9.2 Winnicott's developmental stages and examples of transitional objects

Stage	Development	Examples
Infancy	Infants begin to use transitional objects to bridge the gap between their internal and external worlds. These objects provide comfort and help to reduce anxiety during separation from the primary caregiver	Teddy bears, blankets, dolls
Early childhood	Transitional objects continue to play a crucial role in providing emotional security. Children use these objects to explore their environment while feeling safe	Stuffed animals, favourite toys

(Continued)

Table 9.2 (Continued)

Stage	Development	Examples
Middle childhood	The reliance on transitional objects may decrease as children develop other coping mechanisms. However, these objects can still be important during stressful times	Special pillows, cherished items
Adolescence	Transitional objects may take on symbolic significance, representing important relationships or memories. They can provide comfort during periods of change	Jewellery, photographs, keepsakes
Adulthood	Adults may use transitional objects to maintain connections with loved ones or to cope with loss. These objects can be deeply meaningful and provide emotional support	Heirlooms, personal mementos

Winnicott explained that the 'good enough' mother was one who tried to meet all her child's needs but frequently made mistakes, thus not quite meeting the needs of her child. Winnicott explained that it was these mistakes, those times when she apparently failed, that helped her child to grow, develop and ultimately become independent.

Mary Ainsworth

Mary Ainsworth (1964, 1969), a pioneering developmental psychologist, made significant contributions to our understanding of Attachment Theory. Building on John Bowlby's foundational work, Ainsworth conducted extensive observational studies that revealed the intricate dynamics between infants and their caregivers.

One of her most notable achievements was the development of the 'Strange Situation' assessment in the 1970s. This innovative procedure involved observing a child's behaviour during a series of brief separations and reunions with their caregiver in a controlled environment (Ainsworth et al., 1978). Through these observations, Ainsworth identified three primary attachment styles: secure, insecure-avoidant and insecure-ambivalent/resistant (see Table 9.3).

Children with secure attachment felt confident in their caregivers' availability and responsiveness, which fostered healthy emotional and social development. In contrast, those with insecure-avoidant attachment tended to avoid or ignore their caregivers, showing little emotion during separations and reunions. Meanwhile, children with insecure-ambivalent/resistant attachment exhibited anxiety and clinginess, and struggled to be comforted even when their caregivers returned.

Table 9.3 Ainsworth's attachment styles

Style	Characteristics	Behavioural indicators	Examples for early childhood educators
Secure	Child feels confident that the caregiver will meet their needs	Child shows distress when caregiver leaves but is happy on their return	Child may seek comfort from the caregiver when upset and is easily soothed. In a classroom, they may explore new activities but check in with the teacher periodically
Avoidant	Child is emotionally distant from the caregiver	Child shows little distress when caregiver leaves and avoids them on their return	Child may prefer to play alone and avoid interaction with the teacher. They may not seek help even when struggling with a task
Ambivalent	Child is anxious and unsure if the caregiver will meet their needs	Child shows extreme distress when caregiver leaves and is not easily comforted on their return	Child may cling to the teacher and show reluctance to engage in activities. They may be difficult to soothe and show signs of anxiety
Disorganised	Child shows inconsistent and confused behaviour towards the caregiver	Child displays a mix of avoidant and ambivalent behaviours, often appearing dazed or apprehensive	Child may show unpredictable behaviour, such as sudden outbursts or withdrawal. They may struggle to form relationships with peers and teachers

Case study 9.1: Attachment

Amie was born eight weeks early. She was very small and needed help to breathe, so she was placed in an incubator in the neonatal intensive care unit (NICU) at a hospital in England. The nurses and doctors worked hard to keep her safe and warm, but Amie could not be held by her parents very often because of all the tubes and machines.

One day, a nurse placed a small, soft, crocheted octopus next to Amie. It had bright colours and curly tentacles. Amie's tiny fingers wrapped around the tentacles right away.

'This little octopus is special', the nurse told Amie's parents. 'The tentacles feel like the umbilical cord, which babies are used to holding in the womb. It helps them feel calm and safe.'

Figure 9.1 Cuddling tiny octopi

(Continued)

Amie's parents noticed something amazing. When Amie held the octopus, her breathing became steadier and her heartbeat was more regular. She seemed more relaxed. The octopus also helped to keep her hands busy so he did not pull on her tubes.
Why this is good practice:

- It supports attachment: The octopus helps babies to feel secure, which is important for emotional development.
- It reduces stress: It calms the baby and may improve breathing and heart rate.
- It encourages bonding: Parents feel more connected when they see their baby comforted.
- It is safe and thoughtful: The toy is designed to be safe and is carefully checked before use.

Being critical

- How do tactile and sensory experiences in early life contribute to emotional regulation and attachment development in premature infants?
- Can inanimate objects serve as emotional bridges in the absence of primary caregivers, especially in clinical settings?
- What observable behaviours in premature infants may indicate the formation of early attachment patterns, even in the NICU?

Sources

BBC News. (2017, 18 July). Toy octopuses help premature babies in Frimley Hospital. *BBC News*. www.bbc.com/news/uk-england-surrey-40645466

Charity Commission for England and Wales. (n.d.). *Octopus for a Preemie UK – Charity 1180950*. CCEW. https://register-of-charities.charitycommission.gov.uk/en/charity-search/-/charity-details/5123480/charity-overview

Family Education. (2022, 1 December). Crocheted octopi may comfort preemie babies. *Family Education*. www.familyeducation.com/babies/growth-development/cro-cheted-octopi-may-comfort-preemie-babies

Farnham Herald. (2017, 8 August). Octopuses a welcome addition at Frimley Park neonatal unit. *Farnham Herald*. www.farnhamherald.com/news/octopuses-a-welcome-addition-at-frimley-park-neonatal-unit-184394

Infant Journal. (n.d.). Poole Hospital introduces tentacles for tinies. *Infant Journal*. www.infantjournal.co.uk/news_detail.html?id=98

PIX11 News. (2017, 27 February). Crocheted octopuses comfort preemies in hospital NICU. *PIX11 News*. https://pix11.com/news/crocheted-octopuses-comfort-preemies-in-hospital-nicu/

Today. (2017, 28 February). NICU babies: Hospital gives stuffed octopus toys to preemies. *Today*. www.today.com/parents/nicu-babies-hospital-gives-stuffed-octopus-toys-preemies-t107823

World Health Organization. (2023, 10 May). *Preterm Birth*. WHO. www.who.int/news-room/fact-sheets/detail/preterm-birth

Attachment research in the 21st century: Embracing cultural diversity

In the 21st century, Attachment Theory has undergone significant evolution, particularly in response to critiques of its Western-centric foundations. Originally developed by John Bowlby in the mid-20th century, Attachment Theory emphasised the biological and evolutionary basis of the infant–caregiver bond (see Chapter 6 for attachment and the brain). However, 21st-century scholars (e.g., Thompson, 2017; van Ijzendoorn & Sagi-Schwartz, 2008) have increasingly recognised the need to contextualise attachment within diverse cultural frameworks, acknowledging that caregiving practices and emotional bonds are deeply influenced by sociocultural norms.

One of the most prominent developments in modern attachment research is the emphasis on cross-cultural variability. While Bowlby posited that attachment behaviours are universal, studies in non-Western societies have revealed a broader spectrum of caregiving arrangements and attachment outcomes (Bakaraki et al., 2024). In many collectivist cultures, such as those in East Asia, Africa and Latin America, for instance, caregiving is often distributed among extended family members or community networks. This practice challenges the Western notion of monotropy – the idea that infants form a primary attachment to a single caregiver.

In sub-Saharan African communities, such as among the Efe people of the Democratic Republic of Congo, infants are cared for by multiple adults throughout the day. Despite this shared caregiving model, children still develop secure attachments, suggesting that sensitivity and responsiveness, rather than exclusivity, are the key determinants of attachment security. Similarly, in Japanese culture, the concept of *amae* – a form of emotional dependence and indulgence – shapes the parent–child relationship in different ways from Western ideals of independence and autonomy.

Non-Western philosophical traditions also offer alternative conceptualisations of attachment. In African Ubuntu philosophy, the self is understood in relation to others, and is encapsulated in the phrase '*I am because we are*'. This worldview supports a communal approach to caregiving, where emotional and physical support is shared across the community, reinforcing the idea that attachment security can be fostered through collective caregiving, rather than individualised parenting.

Moreover, researchers (e.g., Granqvist, 2021) have begun to critique and adapt traditional attachment assessment tools, such as the Strange Situation procedure, which may not accurately capture attachment behaviours in non-Western contexts. For example, in cultures where children are rarely separated from caregivers, the stress induced by the Strange Situation may not reflect typical experiences, leading to a misinterpretation of attachment styles. As a result, scholars advocate for ethnographically informed methodologies that respect local caregiving norms and values.

To summarise, 21st-century attachment research is increasingly characterised by a pluralistic and culturally sensitive approach. By integrating non-Western theories and practices, contemporary scholars are reshaping Attachment Theory into a more inclusive framework that reflects the diversity of human relationships across the globe.

Consider this 9.1

- What are the implications of these variations for the universality of Attachment Theory as originally proposed by Bowlby?
- How effective are traditional attachment assessment methods, such as the Strange Situation procedure, in non-Western contexts?

Re-evaluating attachment studies: Ethics, vulnerability and the WEIRD paradigm

Conducting attachment research with infants presents a set of ethical challenges, at the heart of which is the issue of consent. Infants, of course, cannot provide informed consent themselves, so researchers must rely on parents or guardians to make decisions on their behalf. It places a responsibility on researchers to ensure that their methods are not only scientifically sound but also emotionally safe. Studies like Ainsworth's Strange Situation, for instance, which involve brief separations from caregivers, must be carefully designed to avoid causing undue stress or long-term emotional disruption.

Beyond consent there is the question of cultural sensitivity. Much of what we know about attachment comes from studies conducted in WEIRD societies, where parenting norms often emphasise independence and emotional expressiveness (Waters et al., 2024). These values are not universal, however, and in many cultures, practices such as co-sleeping, constant physical closeness or communal caregiving are the norm and are associated with healthy child development. Applying Western attachment frameworks to these contexts can lead to misinterpretation and even the pathologising of culturally appropriate behaviours.

Finally, researchers must consider the long-term implications of their work. Labelling a child as 'insecurely attached' can carry unintended consequences, especially if such labels influence how caregivers, educators or clinicians treat the child. Ethical research must therefore prioritise confidentiality, avoid stigmatisation and ensure that findings are used to support families rather than judge them.

Ethical attachment research therefore requires a balance between scientific inquiry and compassionate, culturally aware practice. It challenges us to ask not only *what* we study, but *how* and *why* and *for whose benefit*.

Attachment disorders: Understanding disrupted bonds in early development

Attachment disorders are psychological conditions that arise when a child fails to form a secure emotional bond with a primary caregiver during early development. Rooted in Attachment Theory, these disorders reflect the profound impact of early relational experiences on emotional, cognitive and social development. Bowlby emphasised that a warm, intimate and continuous relationship with a mother (or permanent mother substitute) is essential for mental health. There are two primary types of attachment disorders recognised in clinical settings: Reactive Attachment Disorder (RAD) and Disinhibited Social Engagement Disorder (DSED). RAD is characterised by emotionally withdrawn behaviour towards adult caregivers, while DSED involves indiscriminate sociability and a lack of appropriate social boundaries. Both are typically associated with severe neglect, abuse or frequent changes in caregivers during the first years of life.

Mary Ainsworth's empirical work, particularly the Strange Situation procedure, provided a framework for identifying different attachment styles – secure, avoidant, ambivalent and disorganised. Children with disorganised attachment, which is often linked to frightening or inconsistent caregiving, are at higher risk of developing attachment disorders. These early patterns can persist into adolescence and adulthood, influencing interpersonal relationships, emotional regulation and even susceptibility to psychopathology.

From a developmental perspective, attachment disorders are not merely behavioural issues but reflect disruptions in the child's internal working models – mental representations of self and others. These models guide expectations in relationships and are shaped by early caregiving experiences. Children with attachment disorders often internalise beliefs that others are untrustworthy and that they themselves are unworthy of love.

Ethically, diagnosing and treating attachment disorders requires caution. Over-pathologising children from non-WEIRD cultures can lead to misdiagnosis. Communal caregiving or less overt emotional expression, for example, may be normative in some cultures but misinterpreted through a Western lens as signs of attachment disturbance. Thus, culturally sensitive assessment tools and practices are essential.

Intervention strategies often focus on enhancing caregiver sensitivity and responsiveness. Attachment-based therapies, such as Dyadic Developmental Psychotherapy (DDP) and Parent–Child Interaction Therapy (PCIT), aim to rebuild trust and foster secure attachment patterns. These approaches emphasise emotional attunement (see Chapter 8), consistency and the repair of relational ruptures.

Consider this 9.2

- How do early caregiving experiences shape emotional, cognitive and social development?
- What are the risks of misdiagnosis due to cultural differences in caregiving practices and emotional expression?
- Although the literature often refers to *attachment disorders*, how can we critique this deficit language and consider non-deficit alternatives

Adverse childhood experiences

Adverse childhood experiences (ACEs) represent a constellation of traumatic events that occur during a child's formative years, often leaving indelible marks on their psychological, emotional and physiological development (Garner et al., 2021). These experiences include direct forms of harm, such as physical, sexual and psychological abuse, as well as environmental stressors, such as domestic violence, parental substance misuse, mental illness, incarceration and family breakdown. While these events may differ in nature, they share a common thread: they disrupt the child's sense of safety, stability and attachment, which are foundational to healthy development.

The Early Intervention Foundation (2020) categorises ACEs into two broad domains: abuse and neglect and family dysfunction. Abuse and neglect encompass physical, verbal, sexual and psychological maltreatment, as well as physical and emotional neglect. Family dysfunction includes living with a caregiver who misuses substances, has a mental illness, has been incarcerated, or where there is parental separation due to conflict. Table 9.4 shows some typical examples of ACEs.

Table 9.4   Common ACEs

Category	ACE	Description
Abuse	Physical abuse	Experiencing physical harm or injury from a caregiver
Abuse	Emotional abuse	Being subjected to verbal abuse, threats or humiliation
Abuse	Sexual abuse	Experiencing any form of sexual contact or exploitation
Neglect	Physical neglect	Lack of basic physical needs, such as food, shelter and hygiene
Neglect	Emotional neglect	Lack of emotional support, love and affection
Household dysfunction	Domestic violence	Witnessing violence between caregivers
Household dysfunction	Substance abuse	Living with a caregiver who abuses drugs or alcohol
Household dysfunction	Mental illness	Living with a caregiver who has a mental illness
Household dysfunction	Parental separation or divorce	Experiencing the separation or divorce of parents
Household dysfunction	Incarceration of a household member	Having a household member who is incarcerated

The psychological impact of ACEs is complex and far-reaching. Children exposed to chronic trauma may experience nightmares, intrusive thoughts and re-enact distressing events through play. They may lose interest in activities, express hopelessness about the future and suffer from psychosomatic symptoms like headaches or stomach aches. These behaviours reflect dysregulation in the stress response system. Prolonged exposure to cortisol can disrupt brain development, particularly in areas linked to emotion, memory and executive function, such as the amygdala, hippocampus and prefrontal cortex.

Research shows that ACEs can lead to long-term issues, including depression, anxiety, substance misuse and physical health problems like cardiovascular and autoimmune diseases. Despite growing awareness, gaps remain in understanding the overlap and context of adversities. The Early Intervention Foundation (2020) urges a more nuanced approach, considering the intensity and duration of trauma. Trauma-informed practices across education, healthcare and social services are essential for early identification and support. Understanding how early trauma affects development is vital for psychology and education professionals, alongside advocating for evidence-based, preventative interventions.

Integrating aces and attachment theory into trauma-informed practices

Understanding trauma involves recognising its deep and lasting effects on emotional, psychological and physical wellbeing. Trauma can present in various ways and supporting those affected requires insight into the mechanisms behind these responses. A trauma-informed approach is essential when working with individuals who have experienced trauma. It involves recognising the signs, understanding the impact and integrating this knowledge into practice. Creating a safe and supportive environment – both physically and emotionally – is crucial. Practitioners must be mindful of potential triggers and ensure individuals feel respected and secure.

Building trust is fundamental. Consistency, reliability and transparency help to establish a sense of safety. Active listening and validating experiences without judgement foster supportive relationships. Empowering individuals by offering choices and encouraging autonomy helps to restore a sense of control that is often lost through trauma. Collaboration in decision-making promotes respect and partnership. Cultural sensitivity is also vital, as trauma is experienced and expressed differently across cultures.

Knowing what supports healing and what may hinder it is key. Practices such as active listening, validation and patience can aid recovery. Conversely, actions that may trigger memories, impose solutions or ignore boundaries should be avoided to prevent re-traumatisation.

In education, trauma-informed practice involves embedding an understanding of trauma into teaching and policy. This approach aims to create inclusive, supportive learning environments. Educators should be trained to recognise trauma's impact on behaviour and learning. Providing a predictable and safe classroom, building strong relationships and adapting teaching methods are essential to meet diverse needs. Collaboration with mental health professionals further enhances support.

ACEs and Attachment Theory are closely linked to trauma but include events such as abuse, neglect and household dysfunction. These experiences can disrupt development and increase the risk of trauma-related disorders. A high number of ACEs is associated with greater vulnerability to mental health issues, risky behaviours and chronic illness.

Attachment Theory highlights the importance of early relationships between children and caregivers. Secure attachment supports healthy emotional and social development. Trauma can disrupt these bonds, leading to insecure or disorganised attachment styles, which may affect emotional regulation and the ability to form healthy relationships later in life. Secure attachment fosters trust and safety, which are qualities that trauma can undermine.

Integrating knowledge of ACEs and attachment into trauma-informed practice enhances support. Screening for ACEs helps professionals to understand an individual's background. Promoting secure attachment through consistent support and safe environments is especially important for children and adolescents. Therapeutic interventions that build emotional regulation skills and supportive relationships are also key. By understanding the interconnectedness of trauma, ACEs and attachment, professionals can provide more holistic and effective support. This approach fosters resilience and promotes positive outcomes for individuals on their healing journey.

Case study 9.2: ACE

Anna, who is 5 years old, and 7-year-old Jo had a childhood of which others could only dream. They were cherished and well-looked after by their loving parents, who ensured that their home was always filled with warmth and laughter. The siblings attended a prestigious independent school, known for its excellent facilities and nurturing environment. There they forged strong friendships and thrived academically and socially. Their family adventures took them around the world, exploring different cultures and creating memories that would last a lifetime. Whether they were snorkelling in the Great Barrier Reef or wandering the streets of Paris, the bond between the siblings grew stronger with each new experience.

Their idyllic life came to an abrupt halt, however, when their father was arrested for storing drugs in his warehouse. The news shattered their once-perfect world and the only connection they now had with their father was a brief five-minute phone call each evening from prison. Their mother, who was devastated by the scandal, struggled to keep the family afloat. As the news spread, she quickly lost her job and their once-stable life descended into chaos. The family home, once a sanctuary, now echoed with uncertainty and fear about the future.

As the months passed, the weight of the scandal proved too much for Maya. The constant judgement from the community, the financial strain and the emotional toll of raising two young children alone while grappling with her own heartbreak left her feeling hopeless. Despite her best efforts, she could not find stable work and the family was eventually evicted from their home.

They moved into temporary accommodation provided by social services – a cramped, cold flat in a rough part of town. The once-bright spark in Jo's eyes began to fade. He struggled to adjust to the new school, where he was bullied for his father's crimes. Anna, still too young to understand the full scope of what had happened, clung to her mother constantly, sensing the fear and sadness that now filled their days. Maya, overwhelmed and isolated, began to suffer from severe depression. She stopped attending the support group and withdrew from the few friends who had remained.

Being critical

- Consider how the sudden trauma of a parent's arrest may affect the emotional development of young children.
- Explore how social stigma and instability can disrupt a child's educational journey and peer relationships.
- Examine the complex nature of resilience, and how it can be nurtured or hindered by circumstances.

Chapter summary

This chapter explored the foundational attachment theories of Bowlby, Winnicott and Ainsworth, and their relevance to adverse childhood experiences (ACEs). The chapter discussed:

- Foundational theories:
    - Overview of attachment theories.
    - Bowlby's ethological theory emphasises the evolutionary basis of the child–caregiver bond.
    - Winnicott's concept of the 'good enough mother'.
    - Ainsworth's 'Strange Situation' procedure for identifying attachment styles.
- Consequences of attachment styles:
    - Impact of secure and insecure attachments on emotional regulation, relationships and mental health.
- Adverse childhood experiences (ACEs):
    - Definition and contextualisation within Attachment Theory.
    - Exploration of how ACEs (e.g., abuse, neglect, household dysfunction) impair attachment.
    - Developmental and psychological challenges resulting from ACEs.
- Cultural diversity in attachment:
    - Emphasis on cross-cultural variability in caregiving and attachment.
    - Critique of traditional attachment assessment tools in non-Western contexts.
    - Integration of non-Western theories and practices into attachment research.

- Ethical considerations:
  - o   Challenges in conducting attachment research with infants.
  - o   Importance of culturally sensitive assessment tools.
  - o   Avoiding misdiagnosis and stigmatisation.

Further reading

Geddes, H., & Bevington, D. (2021). *Nurturing Natures: Attachment and Children's Emotional, Sociocultural and Brain Development* (2nd ed.). Routledge.

Whitters, H. (2020). *Adverse Childhood Experiences, Attachment, and the Early Years Learning Environment: Research and Inclusive Practice*. Routledge.

Useful websites

Complex PTSD (post-traumatic stress disorder) – NHS: www.nhs.uk/mental-health/conditions/post-traumatic-stress-disorder-ptsd/complex/

This NHS webpage explains that Complex PTSD (C-PTSD) is a condition that arises from prolonged or repeated trauma, often occurring during childhood.

Mind: What is complex PTSD?: www.mind.org.uk/information-support/types-of-mental-health-problems/post-traumatic-stress-disorder-ptsd-and-complex-ptsd/complex-ptsd/

Mind's resource provides a detailed overview of C-PTSD, highlighting symptoms such as emotional numbness, dissociation and chronic feelings of emptiness or worthlessness.

References

Ainsworth, M. (1964). Patterns of attachment behavior shown by the infant in interaction with his mother. *Merrill-Palmer Quarterly of Behavior and Development, 10*(1), 51–58.

Ainsworth, M. (1969). Object relations, dependency, and attachment: A theoretical review of the infant–mother relationship. *Child Development, 40*(4), 969–1025. https://doi.org/10.2307/1127008

Ainsworth, M., Blehar, M., Waters, E., & Wall, S. (1978). *Patterns of Attachment: A Psychological Study of the Strange Situation*. Lawrence Erlbaum Associates.

Bakaraki, M., Dourbois, T., & Kosiva, A. (2024). Attachment theory across cultures: An examination of cross-cultural perspectives and alloparenting practices (Mini-Review). *Brazilian Journal of Science, 3*(8), 36–42. https://doi.org/10.14295/bjs.v3i8.616

Bick, J., Dozier, M., & Perkins, E. (2012). Convergence between attachment classifications and natural reunion behavior among children and parents in a child care setting. *Attachment & Human Development, 14*(1), 1–10.

Bowlby, J. (1951). *Maternal Care and Mental Health*. (WHO Monograph Series No. 2). World Health Organization.

Bowlby, J. (1953). *Child Care and the Growth of Love*. Penguin Books.

Bowlby, J. (1997). *Attachment. Vol. 1: Attachment and Loss Trilogy*. Pimlico.

Dollard, J., & Miller, N. (1950). *Personality and Psychotherapy: An Analysis in Terms of Learning, Thinking, and Culture*. McGraw-Hill.

Early Intervention Foundation. (2020). *Adverse Childhood Experiences: What We Know, What We Don't Know and What Should Happen Next*. EIF. www.eif.org.uk/report/adverse-childhood-experiences-what-we-know-what-we-dont-know-and-what-should-happen-next

Fairbairn, W. (1952). *Psychoanalytic Studies of the Personality*. Routledge & Kegan Paul.

Freud, S. (1926). Inhibitions, symptoms and anxiety. In J. Strachey (Ed.), *The Standard Edition of the Complete Psychological Works of Sigmund Freud* (pp. 77–175). The Hogarth Press.

Freud, S. (1940). *An Outline of Psychoanalysis*. W. W. Norton & Company.

Garner, A., Yogman, M., & Committee on Psychosocial Aspects of Child and Family Health. (2021). Preventing childhood toxic stress: Partnering with families and communities to promote relational health. *Pediatrics, 148*(2), e2021052582. https://doi.org/10.1542/peds.2021-052582

Gillibrand, R., Lam, V., & Donnell, V. (2016). *Developmental Psychology* (2nd ed.). Pearson.

Goldfarb, W. (1943). The effects of early institutional care on adolescent personality. *Journal of Experimental Education, 12*(2), 106–129. https://doi.org/10.1080/00220973.1943.11010296

Goldfarb, W. (1945). Psychological privation in infancy and subsequent adjustment. *American Journal of Orthopsychiatry, 15*(3), 247–255. https://doi.org/10.1111/j.1939-0025.1945.tb04623.x

Granqvist, P. (2021). Attachment, culture, and gene-culture co-evolution: Expanding the evolutionary toolbox of attachment theory. *Attachment & Human Development, 23*(1), 90–113.

Lorenz, K. (1935). The companion in the bird's world: The fellow-member of the species as releasing factor of social behavior. *Journal of Ornithology. Supplement (Leipzig), 83*, 137–213. https://doi.org/10.1007/BF01905355

Piaget, J. (1954). *The Construction of Reality in the Child* (Trans. M. Cook). Basic Books. https://doi.org/10.1037/11168-000

Spitz, R. (1945). Hospitalism: An inquiry into the genesis of psychiatric conditions in early childhood. *Psychoanalytic Study of the Child, 1*, 53–74.

Spitz, R. (1949). The role of ecological factors in emotional development in infancy. *Child Development, 20*, 145–155.

Thompson, R. (2017). Twenty-first century attachment theory: Challenges and opportunities. In H. Keller & K. Bard (Eds.), *The Cultural Nature of Attachment: Contextualizing Relationships and Development*. MIT Press. https://doi.org/10.7551/mitpress/9780262036900.003.0013

van Ijzendoorn, M., & Sagi-Schwartz, A. (2008). Cross-cultural patterns of attachment: Universal and contextual dimensions. In J. Cassidy & P. Shaver (Eds.), *Handbook of Attachment: Theory, Research, and Clinical Applications* (2nd ed., pp. 880–905). Guilford Press.

Waters, S., Richardson, M., Mills, S., Marris, A., Harris, F., & Parker, M. (2024). Beyond
    attachment theory: Indigenous perspectives on the child–caregiver bond from a
    northwest tribal community. *Child Development*, *95*(6), 1829–1844. https://doi.
    org/10.1111/cdev.14127

Winnicott, D. W. (1953). Transitional objects and transitional phenomena. *International
    Journal of Psycho-Analysis*, *34*, 89–97.

Winnicott, D. W. (1965). *The maturational processes and the facilitating environment:
    Studies in the theory of emotional development*. International Universities Press.

10

Social development

Fidelia Law and Shazza Ali

Chapter objectives

By the end of the chapter, you will gain an understanding of:

- The key theories related to social development across childhood.
- Early social interactions from infancy to late childhood.
- The development of social identity and perceived group membership.
- Intergroup relations, focusing on the social categories of gender, race and ethnicity.
- The application of group preferences in early childhood through a case study.

Chapter overview

This chapter examines the critical process of social development across early childhood, middle and late childhood, with a focus on social identity in relation to gender, race and ethnicity. It explains the formation of self-concept and the development of perceived group memberships while exploring the role of social comparison and intergroup dynamics, in terms of in-group and out-group distinctions. The chapter explores the influence from family, peers, teachers, society, and the media on social identity development, along with the importance of intersectional identities. The chapter emphasises the complexities of navigating social identity throughout different developmental stages. To illustrate these concepts, a case study is presented to enhance understanding of the practical application of theoretical concepts. Overall, this chapter provides a comprehensive understanding of social identity development across early developmental stages.

Why should you read this chapter?

Children's relationships with caregivers, peers and broader social groups play a pivotal role in shaping their emerging sense of self and social identity. This chapter provides a comprehensive examination of social development from infancy to late childhood, drawing on both classical psychological theories as well as more recent contemporary research in the field. By reading this chapter, you will gain an understanding of children's development of self-concept and social identities.

Introduction to social development

Social development is an area of developmental psychology that is concerned with how children learn to understand, interact and behave around others. Social development encompasses individuals' understanding of themselves, the development of relationships with others and an understanding of wider societal norms. As mentioned in other chapters, there are various theories that relate to social development, such as Piaget's stages of cognitive development, Vygotsky's Zone of Proximal Development (see Chapters 1 and 2) and the Attachment Theory developed by Bowlby and Ainsworth (see Chapter 9). This chapter will start by exploring additional theories that relate to social development and social identity specifically.

Social Learning Theory (SLT) (Bandura, 1977) and Social Cognitive Theory (SCT) (Locke & Bandura, 1987) are two closely related theories that suggest that people learn by observing others. SLT, initially developed by Rotter in the 1950s (see Rotter, 1982) and expanded by Bandura, emphasises the importance of imitation, modelling and reinforcement in the learning process. Observational learning refers to learning new behaviours, attitudes and emotional reactions by observing others. Bandura's classical experiment explored this with a series of Bobo doll studies (Bandura, 1961), in which children aged 3–6 years old watched adults interacting with an inflatable Bobo (clown) doll. One group viewed a model acting aggressively, one group viewed a model acting non-aggressively and the third group did not see a model. The results showed that children who observed a model behaving aggressively towards the doll were more likely to engage in aggressive behaviour themselves, compared to children who had not observed this behaviour. Additional Bobo doll studies showed that children were more likely to model observed behaviour that had been rewarded (vicarious reinforcement) rather than punished (vicarious punishment) (Bandura, 1965). Direct instruction increased the likelihood of children engaging in behaviour.

This chapter provides a developmental perspective of how key socialisers play a role in children's social development. In younger children, parents, caregivers and family members, such as siblings, are core models of behaviour, but as children spend more time at school, peers and teachers often fill these roles. Children may also model behaviours from others encountered through the media, such as characters in books, TV shows or online. In the digital age, children are exposed to a wide range of models who behave in both socially desirable and socially undesirable ways. Although some models can promote prosocial behaviours (behaviours that are intended to help others), exposure to risky, aggressive or violent behaviours can contribute to undesirable attitudes and behaviours. A Canadian study, for example, found that 10- to 17-year-olds preference for violent video games was significantly related to engaging in bullying or cyberbullying behaviour (Dittrick et al., 2013). Factors such as similarity to the model (e.g., age, gender), the status of the model and like/dislike towards the model can affect the likelihood of modelling the attitudes and behaviours that have been seen. In Bandura's Bobo doll studies, for example, boys were more likely to model male models than girls.

Social Cognitive Theory (see Table 10.1) emphasises the importance of cognitive processes such as attention, memory (see Chapter 11), action and motivation in learning behaviour and change. It emphasises that learning occurs within a social context via an interaction between the person, the behaviour and the environment. SCT has been applied in various fields, especially in education. According to SCT, a child may learn how to solve a mathematical problem, for example, by watching a peer solve it confidently. If they believe that they can solve it too (self-efficacy) by emulating the behaviour and receiving support from their peers/teachers (environment), they will be more likely to attempt the problem and succeed.

Table 10.1   Key cognitions in Social Cognitive Theory

Cognition	Description
Self-efficacy	The belief that one can achieve a goal
Reciprocal determinism	The interaction between personal cognitive processes, the behaviour and the environment
Outcome expectations	Beliefs about the consequences of actions
Self-regulation	Goal setting and self-monitoring

Social identity theory

Social identity refers to how one identifies with others and views oneself as part of a larger social group or environment (Tajfel & Turner, 1986). Social groups can be based on a number of factors, such as gender, age, ethnicity, religion and social class, as well as more arbitrary categories such as musical taste. These social groups hold emotional significance for their members, forming part of their self-concept, which influences how they feel about themselves and relate to others (Cvencek et al., 2016).

Social Identity Theory (SIT) (Tajfel & Turner, 1986) explains how social identity and group membership have an impact on attitudes and behaviours. Humans have an innate desire to belong and to feel good about themselves (Baumeister & Leary, 1995). As such, group membership is incorporated into an individuals' self-concept (i.e., beliefs, thoughts and feelings that people hold about themselves). People also seek to enhance their self-esteem (perceived competence) by identifying with members of their group (ingroup members) and differentiating themselves from those who belong to different groups (outgroup members). This distinction affects how they view themselves and how they interact with others. For example, people hold more positive views about ingroup members compared to outgroup members.

One of the first steps in the development of social identity and perceived group membership is categorisation. Humans tend to categorise objects based on similarities. At 3–4 months old, infants recognise similarities between objects (Quinn et al., 2002; Spelke et al., 1996). Shortly after this age, infants begin to group objects according to certain characteristics. At a few months old, infants can distinguish between male and female faces, and at around 9 months old, most infants prefer and pay more attention to same-race faces (Pauker et al., 2016). Preschool children are generally able to categorise objects along one dimension, such as colour, and in middle childhood, they are able to categorise objects along multiple dimensions, such as colour and size at the same time (Bigler & Liben, 1992). At around 4–5 years old, children engage in self/other evaluations and social comparisons based on personal and social categories (Yee & Brown, 1992).

Social Identity Development Theory (SIDT) builds on some of the tenets of SIT and incorporates key developmental milestones in children's social development to explain children's involvement in groups (Nesdale, 1999). SIDT focuses on the development of children's intra- and intergroup attitudes, cognitions and behaviours, especially in relation to gender, race and ethnicity. It suggests that it is children's desire for belonging and acceptance that drives their social interactions and motivates them to form friendships (see Table 10.2). This theory also recognises when children become aware of group differences (e.g., between low-status and high-status groups) and when/how certain group memberships can impact their self-esteem.

Table 10.2 The four key developmental phases of Social Identity Development Theory

Phase	Age	Key characteristics
Foundations of social group relations	0 to 2 years	Increased engagement in social observation and interactions, respond to others, play, problem-solve
Social group awareness	Preschool	Acknowledge social categories in the environment (such as gender), differentiate between others based on these categories
Ingroup preference stage	School age	Form groups, usually based on gender and ethnicity, form friendships based on similarity, ingroup preference and perceived outgroup homogeneity
Outgroup negativity	7 years upwards	Dislike outgroup members

Consider this 10.1

1   How does Social Identity Theory account for individual differences in the strength of group identification, and what implications does this have for understanding prejudice and intergroup conflict?

2   To what extent does Social Identity Development Theory adequately explain the role of early cognitive categorisation in shaping later social attitudes, and how might environmental factors (e.g., family, media) interact with these developmental processes?

The developing self in a social world through a development perspective

The following section explores the developing self in a social world from birth to late childhood.

Early years (0–3 years)

Infants begin to show awareness of others from an early age. By around 2 months, they hold gazes with other infants (Rubin et al., 1998), and by 6 months, they engage through vocalisations and smiling (Rubin & Coplan, 1992). By the end of the first year, infants display intentional social gestures such as smiles and frowns. Despite limited motor and linguistic skills, 1-year-olds can mimic and respond to others' behaviours.

Socialisation with significant adults plays a vital role in shaping children's interactions. Sensitive adult engagement supports the development of social skills with peers. A global review across 33 countries found that early parental involvement is crucial for positive social-emotional development (Jeong et al., 2021).

Between 18 and 24 months, children begin to develop a sense of self. This was demonstrated in the Rouge test (Amsterdam, 1972), where children's reactions to seeing a mark on their face in a mirror indicated self-recognition. By 20 months, most children recognise themselves, marking a key milestone in self-awareness and the emergence of Theory of Mind – the ability to understand others' perspectives (Keenan et al., 2003).

By age 2, children's social interactions become more complex due to advances in physical, emotional and cognitive development. They begin using simple language and engage in longer, reciprocal exchanges with peers and adults. Pretend play becomes prominent, helping children to learn social rules such as imitation and turn-taking (Eckerman, 1993; Rubin & Coplan, 1992). At this stage, children can also consistently identify their gender, which marks an early form of social categorisation (Leinbach & Fagot, 1986; Zosuls et al., 2009).

In summary, infants develop social awareness early, responding to cues like gaze and emotion. The sense of self emerges in toddlerhood and play becomes central to learning social norms. Adult interactions and environmental influences are key to supporting this development.

Early childhood (3–5 years)

Children begin to become group-minded and are affected by social and cultural norms (Tomasello, 2019). Studies show that prosocial behaviours, such as helping others, start to develop around that time (Radke-Yarrow et al., 1983). Children also begin to assign pretend and imagined roles in their social play (see Chapter 13), which are crucial developmental milestones (Astington & Jenkins, 1995; Howes, 1987; Lillard et al., 2013). A recent meta-analysis found that pretend play is related to the development of social competence in young children (Smits-van der Nat et al., 2024). This evidence also suggests that the development of the Theory of Mind starts from a young age (Astington

& Jenkins, 1995; Wellman et al., 1990). Through play, children begin friendship formation and are likely to encounter social conflict through positive and negative
interactions with peers (Hartup, 2021). Experiences with peers further develop key
social skills, such as empathy and perspective-taking, and also a sense of identity and
belonging. Parents and caregivers also play an important role as children learn how to
behave in their social context through modelling and observational learning from significant others (Bandura, 1977). Caregivers can stimulate both positive and negative
behaviours and facilitate the development of self.

Since gender is one of the first social identities developed by young children, gender
segregation among peers becomes apparent early. Evidence suggests that at around 4.5
years old, children spend nearly three times as much time playing with same-sex peers
compared to other-sex peers. At around 6.5 years, children's playmate preference for
same-sex peers increases to being 10 times more likely (Maccoby & Jacklin, 1987).
Children perceive more similarity with people of the same gender (Martin et al., 2017)
and express a preference for people who are similar to them (see the discussion on SIDT
above). Besides gender, children can also accurately apply racial labels from a young age,
and this is even more prominent for children from racial-ethnic minority groups (Rogers
& Meltzoff, 2017). Young children also acquire knowledge about characteristics and
behaviour associated with specific race and gender groups (e.g., boys like blue and play
with trucks). They will also assign more positive attributes to their own groups and more
negative attributes to other groups (Cvencek, Greenwald, & Meltzoff, 2016; Cvencek,
Meltzoff, & Greenwald, 2011).

Endorsement of gender stereotypes about toys, activities and roles is also apparent
in early childhood (Zosuls et al., 2009). Children around the age of 5 begin to develop
a sense of gender constancy in that they associate gender identity with stability. This
gender stability promotes the understanding that gender is stable across time and situations (Martin et al., 2002; Ruble et al., 2007). As a result, children show preferences
for toys and activities stereotypically associated with their gender relative to those
associated with the other gender (Shutts et al., 2010). The development of gender stereotypes emerges early and is reflected in learning and engagement throughout
childhood.

Another important development related to social interactions is the emergence of the
observance of social dominance hierarchies (Rubin & Coplan, 1992). Social dominance
hierarchies refer to the ranking of individuals that children interact with in terms of their
exerted dominance within a social group. It can include characteristics or abilities that are
important to the group, such as talkativeness. The more dominant children have a greater
ability to elicit conforming behaviours among peer-group children (Rubin et al., 2006).

In summary, during early childhood, children develop important socialisation skills
through interaction with others. With the facilitation of linguistic, locomotor and cognitive development, they can better coordinate play and socialise with their peers.
Notably, the role of significant adults and the environment in which children are nurtured also play an important role in their social development. Children begin to exhibit

clear distinctions with attributes that are associated with gender and ethnicity and the emergence of stereotypical beliefs starts to become apparent.

Middle to late childhood (5–12 years)

During middle childhood, children's interactions with peers increase significantly, rising from around 10% at age 2 to 30% (Ellis et al., 1981). They show a strong preference for same-sex peers, finding them more compatible with their play style – a trend that intensifies throughout the school years (Maccoby, 1990). These interactions reinforce gender identity and shape children's understanding of social norms and group membership. By age 6, children begin to endorse gender stereotypes, particularly favouring boys in STEM (Science, Technology, Engineering and Mathematics) subjects such as mathematics and computing (Cvencek et al., 2011; Kessels, 2005). Middle childhood is marked by rigid gender stereotypes, with boys more often being selected for STEM tasks (McGuire et al., 2022). These perceptions influence children's emerging self-concept, especially among girls in relation to STEM.

Despite increased peer interaction, parents remain key socialisers. Research shows that parents often perceive boys as more capable in mathematics and science, attributing boys' success to talent and girls' success to effort (Andre et al., 1999; Yee & Eccles, 1988). Boys report more encouragement in science, while girls receive more unsolicited help (Bhanot & Jovanovic, 2005). These parental expectations shape children's self-perceptions and attitudes towards learning (Gunderson et al., 2012).

Teachers also play a vital role. Children report differential treatment in classrooms, with boys often being disciplined more strictly, and perceiving this as unfair (Myhill & Jones, 2006). Repeated messages from adults influence academic self-concept and further engagement in learning. Furthermore, a study found that boys and girls interacted differently with informal STEM educators of different genders, with girls engaging in more verbal interaction, such as asking more questions and discussing more STEM concepts with male educators compared to female educators (Law et al., 2022). These educator–child social dynamics can shape the development of self.

Peer relationships play a crucial role in children's emotional and social development. When children experience positive interactions with peers – such as feeling accepted, included, and supported – they tend to develop higher levels of happiness and self-esteem. These positive relationships help children feel valued and confident, which contributes to overall wellbeing. However, when children face peer rejection or exclusion, they may experience feelings of loneliness or inadequacy. Over time, this can lead to internalising problems, such as anxiety or depression, because the lack of social support undermines their sense of belonging and security. (Ladd & Troop-Gordon, 2003; Yoo et al., 2015).

Different media also contribute to social development, often lacking diversity and reinforcing stereotypes (Evans & Davies, 2000). Thus, it is essential that careful attention is paid to the media content that children are consuming.

Social identity and group memberships focusing on ingroup preference and outgroup derogation

As mentioned above, children become aware of others early and start to identify with others based on social group membership, especially in terms of gender and race/ethnicity. Between the ages of 2 and 4 years children share toys equally with same and other race children and show no preference when choosing a playmate (Anzures et al., 2013). In line with research on gender, by 4–6 years old children show a preference to play with children of their own race. At this stage, however, ingroup preference does not necessarily equate to outgroup dislike.

The minimal group paradigm shows that when people are assigned to groups based on a single criterion (e.g., favourite colour), members show favouritism towards other ingroup members. This paradigm has been investigated with children aged 6–9 years old (e.g., Bigler et al., 1997), with findings showing that children who were randomly assigned to a colour group showed ingroup favouritism. Children aged 7–11 years old also allocated rewards in favour of the ingroup and sought to maximise differences between the ingroup and outgroup (Vaughan et al., 1981).

During middle childhood some children begin to show outgroup dislike. This typically emerges after age 7, as it requires an understanding of social context and group status (Nesdale, 2012). While similarity often drives group membership, Social Identity Theory suggests that perceived status and power also influence group preference. For example, children assigned to a high-status group (e.g., 'excellent drawing team') showed stronger ingroup favouritism than those in a lower-status group (Nesdale & Flesser, 2001).

Children also show preferences based on social class. Horwitz et al. (2014) found that 4-5-year-olds preferred wealthy groups, especially when they themselves belonged to such a group. This suggests that children prioritise belonging and acceptance, with status considerations developing later.

Ingroup bias is shaped by social comparisons and competitiveness (Yee & Brown, 1992). When social categories are linked to societal experiences, children may favour certain outgroups. Research on race and ethnicity shows that children from advantaged groups tend to favour their own, while those from disadvantaged groups often prefer higher-status groups. Hispanic and Asian children, for instance, have shown preference for White peers over Black peers (Kowalski & Lo, 2001). Research in South Africa showed that children favoured their own gender but not their race, with all groups showing preference for White individuals (Shutts et al., 2011).

These findings suggest that children from lower-status groups may show less ingroup favouritism due to awareness of their group's social standing. Studies confirm that Black children who value wealth are more likely to favour White individuals (Newheiser

& Olson, 2012). Educators must consider these nuances when addressing intergroup relations, as early experiences with group membership and perceived status shape children's social development.

Consider this 10.2

1   How do early ingroup preferences (based on race, gender, or social class) influence children's later attitudes toward diversity and inclusion, and what strategies can educators use to mitigate potential biases?
2   In what ways might ingroup favouritism and awareness of social status affect children's emotional wellbeing, particularly for those in lower-status groups?

Intersectional identities

Intersectional identities refer to the notion that individuals hold more than one important and overlapping social identity. We have thus far discussed a wide range of social identities, including gender, race, ethnicity, nationality and social class. These interact in complex ways to shape an individual's experiences. As we understand that children develop an awareness of social categories from an early age and can categorise themselves into multiple social categories, it is imperative to consider the intersection of these identities in social contexts. As discussed, social categories are constructed through personal, contextual and situational cues, and these identities do not exist in isolation. Thus, through interactions with the social world, importance may be placed on different social identities. For instance, children in general reported gender as a more important social identity compared to race; however, children of colour evaluate race as more important than White children (Rogers & Meltzoff, 2017). Furthermore, girls reported gender identity as more important to them compared to boys (Cvencek et al., 2016; Turner & Brown, 2007). It implies that the value a person places on their social identity, or how central it is to the overall self, varies across groups and settings. In particular, this pattern reflects the tendency for social identities to become salient when they are a source of disadvantage or discrimination. In other words, when the identity category is tied to unequal treatment, they are more likely to become a meaningful and active part of a person's self-concept. While social developmental research has long explored how social identities emerge over time, less work has adopted an explicit intersectionality approach with children. Integrating this perspective is essential for producing more inclusive and representative research that reflects the experiences of diverse young lives. The incorporation, therefore, of intersectional perspectives, which acknowledge that identities are multifaceted and meaningful to individuals, better reflects the diversity of experiences across communities and contexts, especially those who are marginalised and underrepresented.

Case study 10.1: Leo – exploring group preferences in early childhood

Leo is a 4-year-old boy attending a multicultural preschool. His class includes children from various ethnic backgrounds and both genders. Leo is sociable and enjoys group play, particularly with children he perceives as similar to himself.

Observations of ingroup preference

Leo consistently chooses to play with other boys and often gravitates towards peers who share his interests in building blocks and superhero games. His teachers note that he spends significantly more time with same-gender peers, aligning with research that shows gender segregation emerges early, with children around 4.5 years old playing three times more with same-gender peers.

Leo also shows a preference for children who speak English fluently, like himself, and tends to avoid children who speak other languages or have different accents. This behaviour reflects early signs of ingroup preference based on perceived similarity and familiarity.

During a group activity, Leo refused to share toys with a new classmate, Amir, who recently moved to the UK from abroad and speaks limited English. Leo commented, 'He's not in our group', and encouraged others to exclude Amir from the game. This incident illustrates the early stages of outgroup derogation, where children begin to show negative attitudes or exclusionary behaviours towards those perceived as different.

While Leo's behaviour may not stem from overt prejudice, it reflects the minimal group paradigm, where even arbitrary distinctions (e.g., language or accent) can lead to ingroup favouritism and outgroup exclusion.

Teacher intervention and reflection

Leo's teacher used the incident as a learning opportunity, introducing inclusive play activities and reading storybooks that celebrate diversity. Over time, Leo began to include Amir in play, especially after discovering they both liked dinosaurs. This shift highlights the importance of adult modelling and environmental influence in shaping children's social attitudes.

Being critical

- How does Leo's awareness of group membership and perceived status reflect the principles of Social Identity Development Theory and what strategies can teachers use to foster inclusive group dynamics in the classroom?
- In what ways can Leo's modelling of peer and media behaviours be shaped by Social Learning Theory and how can teachers critically curate classroom and media environments to support prosocial development?
- How can teachers support the development of Leo's self-concept and academic identity in light of Social Cognitive Theory, particularly in relation to self-efficacy and outcome expectations?

Reflection points

- Reflect on how children, even in infancy, begin to learn social behaviours through observation of caregivers, peers and the media. Consider how Bandura's Social Learning Theory explains the development of both prosocial and aggressive behaviours, and how the theory can influence early childhood education practices.
- Explore how children begin to categorise themselves and others based on social identities such as gender, race and ethnicity. Reflect on the implications of Social Identity Theory (SIT) and Social Identity Development Theory (SIDT) for understanding how children form ingroup preferences and how they can evolve into outgroup biases.
- Consider the impact of parental modelling, teacher interactions and media exposure on the development of a child's self-concept and social identity. Reflect on how these influences can either reinforce or challenge stereotypes and how practitioners can create environments that promote inclusive identity development.
- Reflect on the concept of intersectional identities – how children navigate multiple overlapping social categories (e.g., gender and race) and how these identities shape their experiences. Consider how an awareness of intersectionality can inform more equitable and representative approaches in research, policy and practice.

Chapter summary

This chapter explored social development in childhood, covering:

- Key theories of social development
  - Social Learning Theory and Social Cognitive Theory focus on learning by observation.
  - Social Identity Theory and Social Identity Development Theory focus on how children learn about social categories, how these social categories are incorporated into self-concept and how this understanding impacts attitudes and behaviours towards others.
- Key social developments from infancy to late childhood
  - From early interactions in infancy to group formation in later childhood.
- The development of social identity and group membership
  - Gender and race/ethnicity are salient social categories that children use to navigate social interactions and situations.
- Intergroup dynamics
  - Children show ingroup preference early on. Sometimes this evolves into outgroup dislike.

Further reading

Aboud, F. (2003). The formation of in-group favoritism and out-group prejudice in young children. *Developmental Psychology, 39*(1), 48–60.

Useful websites

First Discovers: Social and Emotional Development: www.firstdiscoverers.co.uk/the-science-of-childcare-social-emotional-development/

This website explains key theories, such as those of Bowlby, Vygotsky and Bandura, in child social-emotional development.

Buckinghamshire Early Years Web Personal, Social and Emotional Development: https://earlyyearsweb.buckinghamshire.gov.uk/eyfs/early-years-foundation-stage/personal-social-and-emotional-development/

This website provides EYFS-aligned guidance and tools for supporting children's personal, social and emotional development.

References

Amsterdam, B. (1972). Mirror self-image reactions before age two. *Developmental Psychobiology: The Journal of the International Society for Developmental Psychobiology, 5*(4), 297–305.

Andre, T., Whigham, M., Hendrickson, A., & Chambers, S. (1999). Competency beliefs, positive affect, and gender stereotypes of elementary students and their parents about science versus other school subjects. *Journal of Research in Science Teaching, 36*(6), 719–747.

Anzures, G., Quinn, P., Pascalis, O., Slater, A., Tanaka, J., & Lee, K. (2013). Developmental origins of the other-race effect. *Current Directions in Psychological Science, 22*(3). https://doi.org/10.1177/0963721412474459

Astington, J., & Jenkins, J. (1995). Theory of mind development and social understanding. *Cognition & Emotion, 9*(2–3), 151–165.

Bandura, A. (1965). Influence of model's reinforcement contingencies on the acquisition of imitative responses. *Journal of Personality and Social Psychology, 1*, 589–595.

Bandura, A. (1977). *Social Learning Theory*. Prentice Hall.

Bandura, A., Ross, D., & Ross, S. (1961). Transmission of aggression through the imitation of aggressive models. *Journal of Abnormal and Social Psychology, 63*(3), 575–582. https://doi.org/10.1037/h0045925

Baumeister, R. F., & Leary, M. R. (1995). The need to belong: Desire for interpersonal attachments as a fundamental human motivation. *Psychological Bulletin, 117*(3), 497–529. https://doi.org/10.1037/0033-2909.117.3.497

Bhanot, R., & Jovanovic, J. (2005). Do parents' academic gender stereotypes influence whether they intrude on their children's homework? *Sex Roles, 52*(9–10), 597–607.

Bigler, R. S., Jones, L. C., & Lobliner, D. B. (1997). Social categorization and the formation of intergroup attitudes in children. *Child Development, 68*(3), 530–543.

Bigler, R. S., & Liben, L. S. (1992). Cognitive mechanisms in children's gender stereotyping: Theoretical and educational implications of a cognitive-based intervention. *Child Development*, *63*(6), 1351–1363. https://doi.org/10.2307/1131561

Cvencek, D., Greenwald, A. & Meltzoff, A. (2016). Implicit measures for preschool children confirm self-esteem's role in maintaining a balanced identity. *Journal of Experimental Social Psychology*, *62*, 50–57. http://dx.doi.org/10.1016/j.jesp.2015.09.015

Cvencek, D., Meltzoff, A., & Greenwald, A. (2011). Math–gender stereotypes in elementary school children. *Child Development*, *82*(3), 766–779. http://dx.doi.org/10.1111/j.1467-8624.2010.01529.x

Dittrick, C. J., Beran, T., Mishna, F., Hetherington, R., & Shariff, S. (2013). Do children who bully their peers also play violent video games? A Canadian national study. *Journal of School Violence*, *12*(4), 297–318. https://doi.org/10.1080/15388220.2013.803244

Eckerman, C. (1993). Toddlers' achievement of coordinated action with conspecifics: A dynamic systems perspective. In L. Smith & E. Thelen (Eds.), *A Dynamic Systems Approach to Development: Applications* (pp. 333–357). The MIT Press.

Ellis, S., Rogoff, B., & Cromer, C. (1981). Age segregation in children's social interactions. *Developmental Psychology*, *17*(4), 399.

Evans, L., & Davies, K. (2000). No sissy boys here: A content analysis of the representation of masculinity in elementary school reading textbooks. *Sex Roles*, *42*(3), 255–270.

Gunderson, E., Ramirez, G., Levine, S., & Beilock, S. (2012). The role of parents and teachers in the development of gender-related math attitudes. *Sex Roles*, *66*(3–4), 153–166.

Hartup, W. W. (1998). The company they keep: Friendships and their developmental significance. In *The Social Child* (1st ed., p. 143–163). Psychology Press.

Horwitz, S., Shutts, K., & Olson, K. (2014). Social class differences produce social group preferences. *Developmental Science*, *17*(6). https://doi.org/10.1111/desc.12181

Howes, C. (1987). Social competence with peers in young children: Developmental sequences. *Developmental Review*, *7*(3), 252–272.

Jeong, J., Franchett, E., Ramos de Oliveira, C., Rehmani, K., & Yousafzai, A. (2021). Parenting interventions to promote early child development in the first three years of life: A global systematic review and meta-analysis. *PLoS Medicine*, *18*(5), e1003602.

Keenan, J., Wheeler, M., & Ewers, M. (2003). The neural correlates of self-awareness and self-recognition. *The Self in Neuroscience and Psychiatry*, *166*, 79.

Kessels, U. (2005). Fitting into the stereotype: How gender-stereotyped perceptions of prototypic peers relate to liking for school subjects. *European Journal of Psychology of Education*, *20*(3), 309–323. https://doi.org/10.1007/BF03173559

Kowalski, K., & Lo, Y. (2001). The influence of perceptual features, ethnic labels, and sociocultural information on the development of ethnic/racial bias in young children. *Journal of Cross-Cultural Psychology*, *32*(4). https://doi.org/10.1177/0022022101032004005

Ladd, G., & Troop-Gordon, W. (2003). The role of chronic peer difficulties in the development of children's psychological adjustment problems. *Child Development*, *74*(5), 1344–1367.

Law, F., Joy, A., McGuire, L., Winterbottom, M., Hoffman, A. J., Mathews, C. J., Mulvey, K. L., Hartstone-Rose, A., & Rutland, A. (2022). Children's engagement with parents and educators at informal STEM learning sites: The role of gender. *American Education Research Association Online Paper Repository*. https://doi.org/10.3102/1888918

Leinbach, M. D., & Fagot, B. I. (1986), Acquisition of gender labels: A test for toddlers. *Sex Roles, 15*, 655–666. https://doi.org/10.1007/BF00288221

Lillard, A., Lerner, M., Hopkins, E., Dore, R., Smith, E., & Palmquist, C. (2013). The impact of pretend play on children's development: A review of the evidence. *Psychological Bulletin, 139*(1), 1.

Locke, E., & Bandura, A. (1987). Social foundations of thought and action: A social-cognitive view. *The Academy of Management Review, 12*(1). https://doi.org/10.2307/258004

Maccoby, E. (1990). Gender and relationships: A developmental account. *American Psychologist, 45*(4), 513.

Maccoby, E., & Jacklin, C. (1987). Gender segregation in childhood. In H. Reese (Ed.), *Advances in Child Development and Behavior* (Vol. *20*, pp. 239–288). Academic Press.

Martin, C. L., Ruble, D. N., & Szkrybalo, J. (2002). Cognitive theories of early gender development. *Psychological Bulletin, 128*(6), 903.

Martin, C.L., Andrews, N.C., England, D.E., Zosuls, K. & Ruble, D.N. (2017) A Dual Identity Approach for Conceptualizing and Measuring Children's Gender Identity. Child Dev. 2017 Jan;88(1):167–182. doi: 10.1111/cdev.12568. Epub 2016 Jun 1. PMID: 27246654.

McGuire, L., Hoffman, A., Mulvey, K., Hartstone-Rose, A., Winterbottom, M., Joy, A., & Rutland, A. (2022). Gender stereotypes and peer selection in STEM domains among children and adolescents. *Sex Roles, 87*(9), 455–470.

Myhill, D., & Jones, S. (2006). 'She doesn't shout at no girls': Pupils' perceptions of gender equity in the classroom. *Cambridge Journal of Education, 36*(1), 99–113. https://doi.org/10.1080/03057640500491054

Nesdale, D. (1999). Developmental changes in children's ethnic preferences and social cognitions. *Journal of Applied Developmental Psychology, 20*, 501–519. doi: 10.1016/S0193-3973(99)00012-X

Nesdale, D. (2012). The development of children's ethnic prejudice: The critical influence of social identity, social group norms, and social acumen. In D. W. Russell & C. A. Russell (Eds.), *The Psychology of Prejudice: Interdisciplinary Perspectives on Contemporary Issues* (pp. 51–76). Nova Science Publishers.

Nesdale, D., & Flesser, D. (2001). Social identity and the development of children's group attitudes. *Child Development, 72*(2). https://doi.org/10.1111/1467-8624.00293

Newheiser, A., & Olson, K. (2012). White and Black American children's implicit intergroup bias. *Journal of Experimental Social Psychology, 48*(1). https://doi.org/10.1016/j.jesp.2011.08.011

Pauker, K., Williams, A., & Steele, J. (2016). Children's racial categorization in context. *Child Development Perspectives, 10*(1). https://doi.org/10.1111/cdep.12155

Quinn, P. C., Yahr, J., Kuhn, A., Slater, A. M., & Pascalis, O. (2002). Representation of the gender of human faces by infants: A preference for female. *Perception, 31*(9). https://doi.org/10.1068/p3331

Radke-Yarrow, M., Zahn-Waxler, C., & Chapman, M. (1983). Children's prosocial dispositions and behavior. *Handbook of Child Psychology, 4*, 469–545.

Rogers, L. O., & Meltzoff, A. N. (2017). Is gender more important and meaningful than race? An analysis of racial and gender identity among Black, White, and mixed-race children. *Cultural Diversity & Ethnic Minority Psychology*, *23*(3), 323–334. https://doi.org/10.1037/cdp0000125

Rotter, J. B. (1982). *The Development and Applications of Social Learning Theory*. Praeger

Rubin, K. H., & Coplan, R. J. (1992). Peer relationships in childhood. In M. H. Bornstein & M. E. Lamb (Eds.), *Developmental Psychology: An Advanced Textbook* (pp. 519–578). Lawrence Erlbaum.

Rubin, K. H., Hastings, P., Chen, X., Stewart, S., & McNichol, K. (1998). Intrapersonal and maternal correlates of aggression, conflict, and externalizing problems in toddlers. *Child Development*, *69*(6), 1614–1629.

Rubin, K. H., Wojslawowicz, J. C., Rose-Krasnor, L., Booth-LaForce, C., & Burgess, K. B. (2006). The best friendships of shy/withdrawn children: Prevalence, stability, and relationship quality. *Journal of Abnormal Child Psychology*, *34*, 139–153. https://doi.org/10.1007/s10802-005-9017-4

Ruble, D. N., Martin, C. L., & Berenbaum, S. A. (2007). *Gender development*. In N. Eisenberg (Ed.), Handbook of child psychology: Vol. 3. Social, emotional, and personality development (6th ed., pp. 858–932). Wiley

Shutts, K., Banaji, M.R. & Spelke, E.S. (2010). Social categories guide young children's preferences for novel objects. Dev Sci. 2010 Jul;13(4):599–610. doi: 10.1111/j.1467-7687.2009.00913.x. PMID: 20590724; PMCID: PMC2898520.

Smits-van der Nat, M., van der Wilt, F., Meeter, M., & van der Veen, C. (2024). The value of pretend play for social competence in early childhood: A meta-analysis. *Educational Psychology Review*, *36*(2), 46.

Spelke, E. S., Phillips, A., & Woodward, A. L. (1996). Infants' knowledge of object motion and human action. In *Causal Cognition*. https://www.semanticscholar.org/paper/Infants%27-knowledge-of-object-motion-and-human-Spelke-Phillips/cb789407a5e4cf1f0fcee50f64ab275d65e2ecca

Tajfel, H., & Turner, J. C. (1986). The social identity theory of intergroup behaviour. In S. Worchel & W. G. Austin (Eds.), *Psychology of Intergroup Relations* (pp. 7–24). Nelson-Hall.

Tomasello, M. (2019). *Becoming Human: A Theory of Ontogeny*. Belknap Press.\

Turner, K. L., & Brown, C. S. (2007). The centrality of gender and ethnic identities across individuals and contexts. *Social Development*, *16*(4), 700–719.

Vaughan, G. M., Tajfel, H., & Williams, J. (1981). Bias in reward allocation in an intergroup and an interpersonal context. *Social Psychology Quarterly*, *44*(1). https://doi.org/10.2307/3033861

Wellman, H. M., Carey, S., Gleitman, L., Newport, E. L., & Spelke, E. S. (1990). *The Child's Theory of Mind*. The MIT Press.

Yee, D. K., & Eccles, J. S. (1988). Parent perceptions and attributions for children's math achievement. *Sex Roles*, *19*(5–6), 317–333. https://doi.org/10.1007/BF00289840

Yee, M. D., & Brown, R. (1992). Self-evaluations and intergroup attitudes in children aged three to nine. *Child Development*, *63*(3). https://doi.org/10.1111/j.1467-8624.1992.tb01650.x

Yoo, S., Park, B., & Doh, H. S. (2015). Pathways from peer relationships to subjective well-being through self-esteem in late childhood. *Korean Journal of Child Studies*, *36*(2), 55–74

Zosuls, K. M., Ruble, D. N., Tamis-LeMonda, C. S., Shrout, P. E., Bornstein, M. H., & Greulich, F. K. (2009). The acquisition of gender labels in infancy: Implications for gender-typed play. *Developmental Psychology*, *45*(3), 688.

11

Memory, attention and perception

Monica Cheng

Chapter objectives

By the end of the chapter, you will gain:

- A theoretical understanding of memory, attention and perception in cognitive development.
- An understanding of practical strategies for supporting learning using cognitive principles.
- An awareness of sociocultural influences on cognition.
- Knowledge of inclusive approaches that promote cognitive diversity and wellbeing.

Overview of the chapter

This chapter will explore the cognitive foundations of learning, focusing on memory, attention and perception. It will introduce the key theories of cognitive processing, including the Multi-Store and Working Memory Models, long-term memory systems and major theories of attention. It will also explore ecological and constructivist perspectives on perception and explain how these functions develop and interact across childhood. The chapter will highlight the importance of sociocultural context, critically examining the limitations of the dominant psychological models that emerge from WEIRD societies. It will also discuss the role of language, cultural practices and environmental factors in shaping cognitive development. A strengths-based and inclusive lens will be used to explore trauma, mental health and neurodiversity, emphasising how emotional and social experiences shape memory and attention.

Why should you read this chapter?

By reading this chapter, you will gain insights on how children acquire, process and retain information, thus equipping with the knowledge and tools to support diverse cognitive needs in inclusive educational environments.

What is memory, attention and perception?

As mentioned elsewhere, cognitive development underpins how children learn, process information and engage with the world. Among core cognitive functions, memory, attention and perception form the foundation of most learning. These are deeply inter-woven systems that co-develop from infancy to adolescence.

To define these functions concisely: *memory* enables the encoding, storage and retrieval of information; *attention* allocates cognitive resources to determine what is pro-cessed; and *perception* allows individuals to interpret and make sense of sensory input.

Memory and learning

The following section explores memory and learning.

The multi-store model of memory

Memory underpins all learning by enabling the encoding, storage and retrieval of infor-mation. One of the most enduring frameworks in cognitive psychology is the Multi-Store Model of Memory (MSM), proposed by Atkinson and Shiffrin (1968). This model con-ceptualises memory as a linear system with three distinct stores: sensory memory, short-term memory (STM) and long-term memory (LTM). Each store is characterised by unique features in terms of capacity, duration and processing function. Movement between these stores is governed by attentional control and rehearsal processes.

The three stages of memory processing:

*   *Sensory memory.* This is the briefest stage. It holds raw input from the environment, such as visual, auditory or tactile data, for milliseconds. Most sensory information is lost unless it is selected for further processing by attention. As Broadbent (1958) proposed, attention acts as a cognitive bottleneck, filtering stimuli based on relevance and familiarity, and determining what proceeds to STM.
*   *Short-term memory (STM).* Information that passes through the attentional filter enters STM, where it is held temporarily for active processing. Most people can hold a short string of around 7–9 digits or items in mind, such as a phone number, for approximately 15–30 seconds without rehearsal (Peterson & Peterson, 1959). This limited capacity is why we often forget instructions or facts if they are not repeated or connected to prior knowledge.
*   More recent research suggests an even lower capacity of around 4–5 items when the influence of LTM is controlled for (Cowan, 2001). While maintenance

rehearsal can temporarily preserve this information, elaborative encoding, where new information is meaningfully linked to what we already know, is more effective for transferring it into long-term storage.

- *Long-term memory (LTM)*. When information is rehearsed and meaningfully encoded, it can be transferred to LTM, which has theoretically unlimited capacity and duration. However, LTM is not a static repository. Successful retention depends on consolidation, a neurocognitive process involving synaptic strengthening and structural changes in neural circuits, which is often supported by repeated retrieval and sleep-dependent processes (Dudai, 2004). Retrieval – the process of accessing stored information for use – is not always straightforward; it is an active, reconstructive process, subject to distortion, interference and decay (Schacter, 1999). Emotional salience and contextual cues play a vital role in enhancing both encoding and retrieving memories efficiently.
- A learner may struggle to recall a newly introduced phone number, for example, but easily remember the number of their childhood home. This contrast reflects how emotionally significant or frequently rehearsed experiences are more effectively encoded into LTM.

Working memory model

Although the Multi-Store Model of Memory offers a foundational framework, it has been critiqued for its oversimplified view of STM as passive and linear. In real-life scenarios individuals often manipulate, update and integrate information across multiple domains simultaneously rather than merely storing it. This raises an important question: How do we actively hold and manage multiple pieces of information at once when reasoning, problem-solving or following complex instructions?

To address this question, Baddeley and Hitch (1974) proposed the Working Memory Model (WMM), which reconceptualises STM as a dynamic, multi-component system. According to the WMM, working memory consists of specialised **subsystems** that process different modalities of information concurrently, while being coordinated by a central executive. See Figure 11.1 for a visual summary of how the WMM operates across its four key subsystems.

To operationalise the concept of active processing, Baddeley and Hitch (1974) proposed a framework comprising the following four subsystems. Each plays a distinct role in processing different types of information:

- *The central executive*. The central executive is the system's control centre, and is responsible for directing attention, managing cognitive tasks and integrating information from subsidiary systems. It has no storage capacity of its own, but plays a key role in cognitive flexibility, inhibition and updating working goals. Developmentally, this component overlaps with executive functions (see Chapter 6), such as planning, shifting and self-regulation.

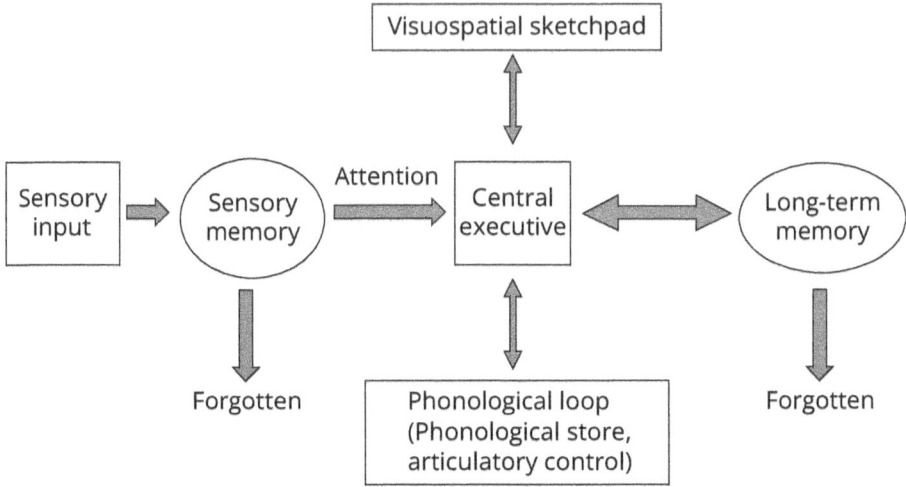

Figure 11.1 Working Memory Model, showing the four main components and their interactions with long-term memory (adapted from Baddeley, 2000; Baddeley & Hitch, 1974)

- *The phonological loop.* The phonological loop is specialised for processing verbal and auditory material. It comprises:
    - o The phonological store, which holds auditory information briefly (1–2 seconds), and
    - o The articulatory rehearsal process, which refreshes this information through subvocal repetition.
- This phonological loop is fundamental in language acquisition and early literacy development (see Chapter 12), helping children to retain phonemes, vocabulary and verbal instructions.
- *The visuospatial sketchpad.* Responsible for the temporary storage and manipulation of visual and spatial information, the visuospatial sketchpad enables learners to visualise diagrams, track spatial orientation and mentally rotate objects. It is especially important in mathematics, geometry, handwriting and problem-solving, and has been linked to spatial reasoning and STEM achievement.
- *The episodic buffer* (Baddeley, 2000). Added to the model later, the episodic buffer functions as an integrative platform, combining information from the phonological loop, visuospatial sketchpad and LTM into a coherent, multidimensional representation. It supports tasks such as recalling narrative sequences, drawing on personal experience and constructing meaning across domains.

Specific Learning Difficulties (SpLD), such as ADHD or dyslexia, have been associated with differences in working memory. For example, some learners may process verbal or auditory information differently due to variation in phonological loop capacity or may require additional support with attentional control and cognitive coordination associated with the central executive. These individual profiles underline the importance of responsive, strengths-based teaching strategies that build on children's cognitive assets while providing appropriate scaffolding.

Consider this 11.1

- Drawing on the Working Memory Model, how might you engage the phonological loop, visuospatial sketchpad and episodic buffer in practice, without overloading the central executive?
- How might these strategies support children with varied working memory strengths and challenges?

Long-term memory systems: Explicit and implicit processes

While working memory is responsible for the temporary processing and manipulation of information, long-term memory serves as the system for durable storage and retrieval of knowledge and experiences. Once information is encoded meaningfully and rehearsed, it may be consolidated into LTM, where it can be retained for days, years or even a lifetime. Unlike the capacity-limited and time-bound nature of working memory, LTM is thought to have a theoretically unlimited capacity and indefinite duration.

Critically, LTM is not a unitary system. It consists of multiple subsystems that differ in function and developmental pathways and the degree to which they are accessible to conscious awareness. Most commonly, researchers distinguish between explicit (declarative) and implicit (non-declarative) memory. This distinction is essential to understanding how different kinds of learning are stored, retrieved and supported through educational practices.

Explicit (declarative) memory

Explicit memory refers to knowledge that can be consciously recalled and verbally articulated, such as facts, events or definitions. It is typically divided into two subtypes: semantic memory and episodic memory:

- *Semantic memory*. Semantic memory involves memory for general knowledge, concepts and meanings that are not tied to specific personal experiences, for example, knowing that Paris is the capital of France or that mammals are warm-blooded. Semantic memory supports the acquisition of academic content and vocabulary and plays a central role in curriculum-based learning. As children grow, their semantic networks become richer and more interconnected, which enhances comprehension, inference-making and critical thinking.

- *Episodic memory.* Episodic memory refers to memory for personally experienced events situated in time and context, such as remembering what happened during a school trip or a class discussion. These memories are closely tied to emotional salience, context and perspective, and they are often reinforced when learning is meaningful, active or situated in real-life contexts. Episodic memory support learning by providing scaffolds for schema development and knowledge integration, particularly when instruction is meaningful and situated in real-life contexts.

Implicit (non-declarative) memory

Implicit memory refers to unconscious or automatic processes that influence behaviour without requiring deliberate recall. These types of memory are typically acquired through repetition and practice. Two key forms of implicit memory are procedural memory and conditioned associations:

- *Procedural memory.* Procedural memory involves memory for learned routines and motor skills, such as typing, riding a bike or decoding words. Procedural memory develops through consistent practice and becomes automatic over time, freeing up working memory for higher-level thinking. In the classroom, procedural memory underpins automaticity in foundational tasks, such as reading, writing and basic numeracy.
- *Conditioned associations.* Based on classical and operant conditioning, learners form associations between stimuli and responses through repeated experience. A child may feel anxious during mathematics lessons due to previous stressful experiences, for example, even if they cannot consciously recall or explain why.

Attention: The gateway to cognitive engagement

While previous sections have explored how information is stored and retrieved, attention determines what is processed in the first place. It acts as the cognitive gatekeeper, selecting which sensory inputs are prioritised for deeper encoding. Without attention, perception lacks coherence and memory formation becomes unreliable. In any learning context children must attend to relevant stimuli before they can encode, interpret or respond effectively. This section outlines the foundational models of attention, developmental changes across childhood, and strategies for supporting attentional control in diverse educational settings.

Selective attention and bottleneck theories

Broadbent's Filter Model (1958) was one of the earliest frameworks to conceptualise attention as a bottleneck, filtering sensory input based on physical characteristics such as pitch or location. According to this model, only one channel of input is selected for higher-level processing, while unattended information is blocked early in the stream. While this model explains basic filtering, it struggles to account for phenomena like the 'cocktail party effect', where salient unattended inputs, such as hearing one's name, break though.

To address such limitations, Treisman (1964) proposed the Attenuation Model (see Figure 11.2), which suggests that unattended inputs are not blocked entirely but are turned down. It allows personally relevant information to be processed even if it is not initially in focus. These foundational models helped to shift attention research towards more dynamic and flexible conceptions of attentional control.

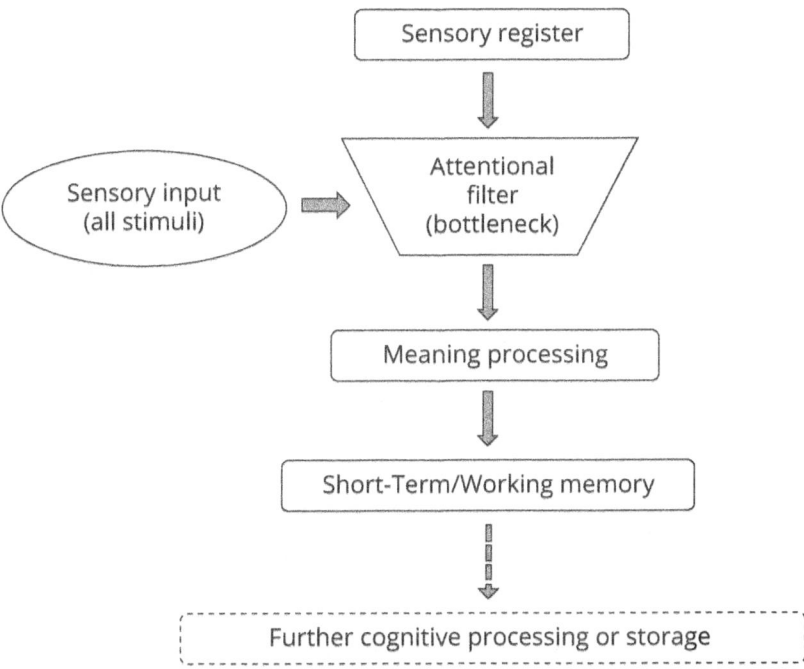

Figure 11.2 Bottleneck model of selective attention (inspired by Broadbent, 1958; Treisman, 1964)

Feature integration theory and attentional control

Treisman and Gelade's (1980) Feature Integration Theory (FIT) proposed that attention is essential for integrating distinct perceptual features, such as colour, shape and orientation, into coherent objects. While individual features are registered automatically during pre-attention processing, focused attention is required to bind them accurately. It explains why learners may misperceive information in cluttered or overstimulating environments where attentional resources are overtaxed.

Contemporary models build on FIT by conceptualising attention as part of a broader executive control system, encompassing the capacity to shift focus, sustain attention and inhibit distractions in response to task demands (Petersen & Posner, 2012). These functions, often described collectively as executive functions, support goal-directed behaviour and cognitive flexibility, both of which are crucial for learning in complex or multi-step tasks (Diamond, 2013). These control processes are particularly important in classroom settings, where learners must manage competing sources of information and sustain focus over time. These functions will be explored in further developmental detail in the following section.

Developmental changes in attention and executive function

Attention develops significantly across childhood and adolescence. Infants begin with reactive, stimulus-driven attention, gradually acquiring the capacity for sustained, voluntary control as the prefrontal cortex matures. By the early primary years, children begin to demonstrate greater flexibility in shifting focus, inhibiting distractions and managing multi-step tasks. These changes reflect the developmental maturation of attentional control and executive processes over time.

Individual variation in attentional development is substantial. Children with ADHD (see Chapter 5), for example, may show differences in sustaining attention, impulse inhibition and shifting flexibly between tasks. Likewise, children from linguistically or culturally diverse backgrounds may exhibit attentional style shaped by their home environments, which may not always align with classroom expectations. Recognising these differences is essential for fostering inclusive practices that support diverse cognitive profiles.

Perception: Constructing meaning from sensory experience

Perception is another cognitive process by which individuals interpret and make sense of the sensory information they receive from their environment. While sensation refers to the raw input received through the senses, such as light, sound or touch, perception involves the organisation, identification and interpretation of those inputs to form a meaningful experience. Perception is therefore not passive; it is active, constructive and influenced by prior knowledge, expectations and context.

Perception plays a foundational role in how children engage with the world, including how they recognise patterns, interpret instructions, read social cues, and develop spatial and motor coordination. From infancy, perceptual processes are active when a baby is tracking a caregiver's face, reaching for objects or responding to familiar voices. These early abilities allow children to make sense of complex sensory inputs and orient towards socially meaningful stimuli, such as faces or voices (Farroni et al., 2005), which supports early bonding and learning.

Perceptual development lay the groundwork for later cognitive functions, including language acquisition, problem-solving and emotional regulation. Importantly, perception bridges sensation and cognition: what is not perceived cannot be attended to, remembered or learned. Understanding perceptual development offers insights into how children construct representations of their environment and why certain learning tasks may be more challenging for some learners than others.

Perception frameworks: Ecological and constructivist perspectives

Two influential theories offer contrasting but complementary views on perceptual development: Gibson's ecological theory and Piaget's constructivist approach (see Chapters 1 and 2). Both explain how children make sense of their world through sensory engagement but differ in how they conceptualise the relationship between perception, action and learning.

Gibsons' ecological approach to perception

Eleanor Gibson (1969) and James Gibson (1979) proposed that perception is a direct, adaptive process rooted in environment affordances, which they defined as the action possibilities an object or situation offers. Rather than relying on internal representations or prior knowledge, the Gibsons argued that organisms detect information directly through active exploration. In this view, perception is not constructed internally, but emerges through engagement with the physical environment. A chair affords sitting due to its structure, for example, and a set of stairs affords climbing. It is not because a child has learned their labels, but because these affordances are perceived directly. Perceptual development thus involves becoming attuned to increasingly complex affordances as children interact with varied environments.

Developmental and cognitive constructivist perspectives

In contrast, Piaget's constructivist theory (1952) conceptualises perceptual development as a staged process of cognitive construction. Infants are not passive recipients of stimuli, but active organisers of knowledge. Unlike the ecological view, however, Piaget emphasised that perception is contingent on the internal development of cognitive schemas. A child's capacity to perceive depends on what they already know and can assimilate. A young child who sees a bicycle, for instance, may not yet perceive it as a vehicle for travel unless they have already developed the spatial and motor schemas necessary to understand balance and movement. As children progress through Piaget's stages, from sensorimotor to pre-operational and beyond, their perceptual understanding becomes increasingly differentiated and objective.

This view has direct implications for curriculum sequencing and scaffolding. Educators must align perceptual demands with a child's developmental readiness, introducing complex visual or spatial tasks only when cognitive coordination allows. It supports the use of manipulatives and discovery-based learning, where perception and reasoning involve guided interaction.

While Gibson highlighted the richness of the environment and Piaget the structure of cognition, they both agree that perception is active, embodied and shaped through development. Crucially, they underscore that perception is neither fixed nor uniform and varies across children based on experience and context. An integrative approach can therefore inform the design of learning environments that are both affordance-rich and developmentally appropriate and that promote perceptual growth through a balance of open-ended exploration and structured support.

Perceptual development in infancy

Perception begins to develop rapidly from the earliest days of life, forming the basis for how infants come to know and interact with the world. Although newborns arrive with functioning sensory systems, these systems undergo substantial refinement during the first months of life. Research in developmental psychology and cognitive neuroscience suggests that infants are not passive recipients of sensory input but active explorers who gradually learn to coordinate vision, hearing, touch and movement in order to perceive meaningful patterns and relationships in their environment (Adolph & Kretch, 2015; Gibson, 1988).

One of the most widely studied domains in early perceptual development is depth perception – the ability to judge the distance of objects in space. This skill is essential for motor planning, object avoidance and safe navigation. The classic visual cliff experiment by Gibson and Walk (1960) remains one of the most influential demonstrations of early depth perception. In this study, infants were placed on a glass-covered platform that created the illusion of a drop. Although there was no real danger, most infants around 6 months old refused to crawl across the apparent 'cliff', indicating that they could perceive depth and assess the risk.

These findings suggest that depth perception is not learned but emerges from an interaction between innate sensitivities and sensorimotor experience. Infants who had begun crawling were more likely to avoid the drop, reinforcing Gibsons' ecological theory that perceptual systems are calibrated through active engagement with the environment, especially through movement.

At the same time, constructivist interpretations aligned with Piaget's theory highlight how perceptual abilities become integrated into increasingly complex cognitive schemas. From this perspective, depth perception reflects not only sensory maturation, but also the development of internal cognitive representations of space and causality. An infant may initially reach for a distant object, for example, without adjusting for depth, but through repeated interactions and sensorimotor feedback learns to judge distances more accurately and adapt their actions accordingly.

Other studies, particularly those employing preferential looking and habituation paradigms, have revealed early competencies in face perception and categorical discrimination (e.g., Pascalis et al., 2002). Newborns rapidly learn to differentiate between familiar and unfamiliar faces, recognise emotional expressions, and even distinguish speech sounds across languages (Nelson, 2001). These findings suggest an early biological readiness for social perception, which is further shaped by environmental input and interaction.

Together, this body of research shows that perceptual development in infancy is multifaceted: it is driven by neural maturation, enriched by experience and highly sensitive to opportunities for action. These early perceptual capacities provide the foundations for later cognitive functions, including memory, attention, problem-solving and social understanding.

Neisser's perceptual cycle: A cognitive constructivist perspective

Ulric Neisser (1976) offered a perspective focused on the real-time process. Neisser's perceptual cycle theory conceptualises perception as a continuous loop between what the perceiver knows, what they expect to find and how they explore their environment. In this model, perception is shaped by schemas, which are internal cognitive structures that guide attention, direct exploration and influence interpretation. When a toddler sees an unfamiliar animal at the zoo, for instance, they might initially interpret it as a dog based on familiar categories. Through observing its movement, sound and reactions from adults, they may revise their understanding and form a new schema for a goat. This updated schema will then guide future encounters, shaping what the children notices and how they respond.

Neisser's model introduces a dynamic, moment-to-moment dimension to perception. Unlike Piaget, who focused on stage-wise changes in representational capacity, Neisser illustrated how perception is continuously constructed and updated in response to both prior knowledge and environmental feedback. Both perspectives converge, however, on the understanding that perception is not passive reception but an active, adaptive process. Neisser's contribution is particularly relevant for explaining individual variation in perception and the role of prior experience in shaping what learners attend to and how they interpret sensory information. Table 11.1 provides a triadic comparison of the theories of perceptual development.

Table 11.1 A triadic comparison of the key theories of perceptual development

	Gibson E (1969) & Gibson J (1988)	Piaget (1952)	Neisser (1976)
Theoretical position	Ecological (direct perception)	Developmental constructivism	Cognitive constructivism (with ecological influence)
Nature of perception	Perception is direct and based on affordances in the environment	Perception is constructed through sensorimotor interaction and cognitive stages	Perception is schema-driven and cyclical, involving sampling and interpretation
Temporal focus	Real-time and continuous	Developmental progression across stages	Real-time, moment-to-moment interaction
Role of schema	Not central; perception relies on detecting invariants and affordances	Central to structuring perception through assimilation and accommodation	Central; schemas guide exploration and interpretation

Multisensory integration in perceptual development

Perception rarely occurs through a single sensory modality. From early infancy, children encounter the world through concurrent visual, auditory, tactile and proprioceptive stimuli. Multisensory integration refers to the developmental process by which the brain combines inputs from different sensory channels into a coherent and unified perceptual experience.

Rather than functioning independently, the senses interact in systemic ways. When a caregiver speaks while smiling and gesturing, for example, an infant processes the synchronised visual (facial expression), auditory (voice) and tactile (warmth or touch) signals together. Research by Bahrick and Lickliter (2000) suggests that intersensory redundancy, which is the simultaneous presentation of similar information across multiple modalities, enhances early learning by directing infants' attention to salient patterns.

This capacity for multisensory integration is fundamental for navigating social environments, learning language and developing causal understanding. When singing a nursery rhyme, for instance, children coordinate rhythmic auditory input with visual and motor cues such as clapping or bouncing. Over time, with increased experience and neurological maturation, children become more adept at filtering incongruent sensory information (e.g., background noise) and selectively integrating those that are relevant to task demands.

In educational and caregiving contexts, materials and practices that engage multiple senses, such as tactile books, musical games or visual-tactile manipulatives, can enhance attention, engagement and comprehension. According to Shams and Seitz (2008), multisensory learning environments support more robust encoding and retrieval by activating parallel sensory pathways. Broadbent et al. (2018) and Denervaud et al. (2020) demonstrate that incidental learning in multisensory environments improves information retention across childhood, highlighting developmental benefits beyond intentional learning contexts. These strategies are especially beneficial for young children and neurodivergent learners, who may process information more effectively when multiple modalities are simultaneously activated. Poorly designed or overstimulating environments can overwhelm developing sensory systems, however, particularly in children with sensory processing differences (Staats et al., 2024), emphasising the need for thoughtful, developmentally appropriate multisensory design.

Sociocultural and cross-cultural consideration

Cognitive development is not solely a product of individual biology or universal mental architecture. It is deeply embedded in the cultural and linguistic environments in which children grow, interact and learn. Processes such as memory encoding, attentional focus and perceptual interpretation do not operate in a vacuum but are mediated by sociocultural norms, educational expectations and communicative practices. As highlighted in Chapter 1, many foundational theories in developmental psychology have historically emerged from WEIRD societies, raising critical questions about their cross-cultural applicability.

Research in cultural psychology and developmental science highlights how language and culture shape cognitive processing. The principle of *linguistic relativity* (Whorf et al., 1956) suggests that the structure and vocabulary of a language can influence cognitive habits (see Chapter 12). For example, foundational research (Levinson, 1997) has shown that speakers of languages that use absolute spatial terms (e.g., North and South), such as Guugu Yimithirr, exhibit more accurate spatial orientation and memory than relative ones (e.g., left and right). Similarly, learners in Confucian-influenced societies such as Hong Kong, mainland China or South Korea are often socialised into valuing sustained attention, repetition and memory accuracy. As Li (2012) observes, these expectations are embedded in highly structured classroom environments, where cognitive effort is associated with self-discipline and moral development. In contrast, many Western educational systems emphasise autonomy, open-ended inquiry and critical questioning. Such differing cultural orientations influence not only what is learned but how it is learned, including which cognitive strategies are cultivated, valued and rewarded.

These variations reflect not deficits but diverse cognitive adaptations to different cultural environments. It also reminds us that the development of cognitive processes cannot be meaningfully understood in isolation from the cultural and social contexts in which they unfold. Practices that appear as cognitive 'deficits', when judged against a narrow normative benchmark, may in fact reflect cultural adaptive strategies. For educators and practitioners, it underscores the importance of adopting inclusive, reflexive approaches that view cultural variation as a source of diversity, rather than as a deviation from developmental norms.

Applications to wellbeing, mental health and neurodivergence

In addition to biological maturation and sociocultural context, cognitive processes such as memory, attention and perception are also deeply influenced by emotional wellbeing, relational safety and lived experience. While culture and language mediate how cognition is formed and expressed, psychological factors such as trauma, stress and secure attachments play a crucial role in sustaining or disrupting these processes. Emotional stability, consistency and responsive support are essential for optimal cognitive functioning, whereas chronic stress or exclusion can interfere with key neural systems.

The impact of emotional wellbeing and stress on cognition

Stress and trauma activate the body's physiological stress systems, including the hypothalamic-pituitary-adrenal (HPA) axis (see also Chapters 6 and 9). This activation can impair the brain regions that are central to learning, particularly the hippocampus (memory), the prefrontal cortex (executive function) and the amygdala (emotional regulation). Chronic or toxic stress during sensitive periods of development may interfere with memory consolidation, reduce attentional flexibility and hinder goal-directed learning. Conversely, environments that are emotionally safe and predictably structured can buffer stress responses and promote neural integration. Relational factors such as attachment security, emotional attunement and affirmation play a crucial role in stabilising cognitive functions and building resilience. These insights are particularly relevant to trauma-informed education and school-based mental health practices.

Neurodiversity and strength-based support

As discussed in Chapter 5, neurodiversity provides a critical framework for rethinking how we approach cognitive variability in educational contexts. Conditions such as ADHD, autism and dyslexia are not defined by deficits but by differences in how cognition is structured and expressed. Strengths-based approaches involve identifying and amplifying cognitive assets while scaffolding challenges. Rather than remediating 'deficits', inclusive pedagogies create environments with multiple modes of engagement, flexible pacing and opportunities for learners to demonstrate understanding through their strengths.

Cognitive wellbeing: Supporting confidence, autonomy and engagement

Cognitive wellbeing refers to how individuals experience and evaluate their cognitive processes, including feelings of competence, agency and satisfaction in thinking and learning. In education, it is reflected in learners' motivation, self-efficacy (Bandura, 1997), metacognitive awareness, and belief in their capacity to learn (Dweck, 2016). Research shows that children with high cognitive wellbeing are more likely to persist through difficulty, use effective learning strategies and show resilience when learning (Putwain et al., 2013). Conversely, repeated failure can lead to internalised beliefs of being 'not good at learning', which may become a self-fulfilling barrier to engagement and achievement.

Educators and caregivers play a key role in fostering cognitive wellbeing. Psychologically safe environments that validate effort, scaffold success and promote metacognitive reflection build learners' confidence and curiosity. Practices such as strengths-based feedback, normalising cognitive diversity and explicitly teaching about brain plasticity – such as through a growth mindset approach (Dweck, 2016) – can transform children's relationship to learning from anxiety to a source of empowerment to experience learning as meaningful and rewarding.

Case study 11.1: Supporting thinking and learning in a nursery class

Ahmed is a nursery teacher working in a busy city school. His class includes:

- Children who learn in different ways (e.g., those with ADHD)
- Children who are learning English as an additional language
- Children from many different cultures and family backgrounds.

Ahmed notices that some children:

- Find it hard to follow more than one instruction at a time
- Forget new words quickly
- Get distracted during group activities.

He wants to make sure every child feels included and supported in their learning.

Helping children to remember and learn

Ahmed uses ideas from the Working Memory Model to help children to remember and understand better:

1 Listening and Speaking (Phonological Loop)
- He uses songs, rhymes and repetition to teach new words.
- Children repeat words together and sing songs that include key vocabulary.

2 Seeing and Doing (Visuospatial Sketchpad)
- Ahmed uses pictures, story maps and drawings to help children to understand stories and ideas.
- He encourages children to draw what they remember from a story or activity.

3 Connecting to Real Life (Episodic Buffer)
- He links learning to the children's own experiences.
- For example, when talking about places, he uses photos of local parks or shops the children know.

4 Managing Tasks (Central Executive)
- Ahmed gives one instruction at a time and uses picture cards to show what to do next.
- He uses visual timetables so children know what is happening during the day.
- He gives gentle reminders and uses gestures to help children to stay on track.

These strategies help children who find it hard to focus or remember things, especially those with ADHD.

Keeping children engaged with multisensory and inclusive activities

Ahmed makes learning fun and engaging by using different senses:

- In science, children touch, look and talk about materials during simple experiments.
- In the reading corner, he includes:
  - Audiobooks for children who like listening
  - Books with textures for children who enjoy touching
  - Quiet spaces for children who need calm to concentrate.

(Continued)

He also celebrates the different cultures in his class:

- He reads stories from around the world.
- He invites children to share songs or games from home.
- He encourages different ways of learning and paying attention.

These strategies help every child to feel welcome and excited to learn.

Supporting emotional and cognitive wellbeing

- He keeps routines predictable and checks in with children's feelings each day.
- He helps children to talk about how they learn best, using simple discussions or drawings.
- He supports children with tasks like looking at maps or pictures, giving extra help when needed.

What changed over time

- Children remembered more and finished tasks more often.
- Shy or distracted children became more confident.
- Children paid attention for longer periods.
- They worked together more and talked about how they learn.

Being critical

- Are there any challenges or limitations to using these methods in a busy nursery classroom?
- Why are predictable routines and emotional check-ins important for young children's learning?
- How can teachers balance emotional support with academic goals in early years settings?

Reflection points

- Reflect on how these cognitive functions are not isolated but interdependent. Consider how attention filters sensory input, perception constructs meaning from it, and memory encodes and retrieves it. How can understanding these interactions help educators to design more effective learning environments?
- Think about how cultural norms, language and educational expectations shape attentional styles, memory strategies and perceptual interpretations. How can educators move beyond WEIRD-centric models to embrace cognitive diversity and foster inclusive practices?

- Consider the impact of stress, trauma and relational safety on memory and attention. Reflect on how strengths-based approaches and trauma-informed practices can support neurodivergent learners and promote cognitive resilience and wellbeing.
- Drawing on models like the Working Memory Model and multisensory integration research, reflect on how educators can scaffold learning through visual, auditory and experiential methods. How can these strategies be adapted to meet the needs of learners with different strengths and challenges?

Chapter summary

This chapter explored the cognitive foundations of learning, focusing on:

- Core cognitive functions:
  - Overview of memory, attention and perception as interrelated processes in learning.
  - Introduction to key models, including the Multi-Store Model and Working Memory Model.
- Long-term memory systems
  - Distinction between explicit (semantic, episodic) and implicit (procedural, conditioned) memory.
- Attention and executive function
  - Review of selective attention theories and developmental changes in attentional control.
  - Educational strategies to support focus and reduce cognitive load.
- Perception and development
  - Comparison of ecological and constructivist theories of perception.
- Sociocultural and cross-cultural influences
  - Discussion of WEIRD bias and the impact of culture and language on cognition.
- Applications to wellbeing and neurodiversity
  - Impact of stress and trauma on cognitive function.
  - Strength-based approaches to support diverse learners and promote cognitive wellbeing.

Further reading

Baddeley, A., Eysenck, M., & Anderson, M. (2020). *Memory* (3rd ed.). Routledge.
Gibson, E., & Pick, A. (2000). *An Ecological Approach to Perceptual Learning and Development*. Oxford University Press. https://doi.org/10.1093/oso/9780195118254.001.0001

Useful websites

This site provides research-based insights and practical tools to improve early childhood development, focusing on brain science, resilience, and policy innovations to support children and families.

Centre on the Developing Child, Harvard University: https://developingchild.harvard.edu/

An online platform offering free, evidence-based training modules for professionals working with children and young people, aimed at improving understanding and support for mental health and well-being.

MindEd – Mental Health e-Learning for Professionals: www.minded.org.uk/

References

Adolph, K., & Kretch, K. (2015). Gibson's theory of perceptual learning. In J. D. Wright (Ed.), *International Encyclopedia of the Social & Behavioral Sciences* (2nd ed., pp. 127–134). Elsevier. https://doi.org/10.1016/B978-0-08-097086-8.23096-1

Atkinson, R., & Shiffrin, R. (1968). Human memory: A proposed system and its control processes. In K. W. Spence & J. T. Spence (Eds.). *Psychology of Learning and Motivation* (Vol. *2*, pp. 89–195). Elsevier. https://doi.org/10.1016/S0079-7421(08)60422-3

Baddeley, A. (2000). The episodic buffer: A new component of working memory? *Trends in Cognitive Sciences, 4*(11), 417–423. https://doi.org/10.1016/S1364-6613(00)01538-2

Baddeley, A., & Hitch, G. (1974). Working memory. In G. H. Bower (Ed.), *Psychology of Learning and Motivation* (Vol. 8, pp. 47–89). Elsevier. https://doi.org/10.1016/S0079-7421(08)60452-1

Bahrick, L., & Lickliter, R. (2000). Intersensory redundancy guides attentional selectivity and perceptual learning in infancy. *Developmental Psychology, 36*(2), 190–201. https://doi.org/10.1037/0012-1649.36.2.190

Bandura, A. (1997). *Self-efficacy: The Exercise of Control*. W. H. Freeman.

Broadbent, D. (1958). *Perception and Communication*. Pergamon Press. https://doi.org/10.1037/10037-000

Broadbent, H., White, H., Mareschal, D., & Kirkham, N. (2018). Incidental learning in a multisensory environment across childhood. *Developmental Science, 21*(2), e12554. https://doi.org/10.1111/desc.12554

Cowan, N. (2001). The magical number 4 in short-term memory: A reconsideration of mental storage capacity. *Behavioral and Brain Sciences, 24*(1), 87–114. https://doi.org/10.1017/S0140525X01003922

Denervaud, S., Gentaz, E., Matusz, P., & Murray, M. (2020). Multisensory gains in simple detection predict global cognition in schoolchildren. *Scientific Reports, 10*(1), 1394. https://doi.org/10.1038/s41598-020-58329-4

Diamond, A. (2013). Executive functions. *Annual Review of Psychology, 64*(1), 135–168. https://doi.org/10.1146/annurev-psych-113011-143750

Dudai, Y. (2004). The neurobiology of consolidations, or, how stable is the engram? *Annual Review of Psychology, 55*(1), 51–86. https://doi.org/10.1146/annurev. psych.55.090902.142050

Dweck, C. (2016). *Mindset: The New Psychology of Success: How We Can Learn to Fulfill Our Potential: Parenting, Business, School, Relationships* (Updated ed.). Random House.

Farroni, T., Johnson, M., Menon, E., Zulian, L., Faraguna, D., & Csibra, G. (2005). Newborns' preference for face-relevant stimuli: Effects of contrast polarity. *Proceedings of the National Academy of Sciences, 102*(47), 17245–17250. https://doi.org/10.1073/pnas.0502205102

Gibson, E. J. (1969). *Principles of perceptual learning and development.* New York, NY: Appleton-Century-Crofts.

Gibson, J. J. (1979). *The ecological approach to visual perception.* Boston, MA: Houghton Mifflin.

Gibson, E. (1988). Exploratory behavior in the development of perceiving, acting, and the acquiring of knowledge. *Annual Review of Psychology, 39*(1), 1–42. https://doi.org/10.1146/annurev.ps.39.020188.000245

Gibson, E., & Walk, R. (1960). The 'visual cliff'. *Scientific American, 202*(4), 64–71. https://doi.org/10.1038/scientificamerican0460-64

Levinson, S. (1997). Language and cognition: The cognitive consequences of spatial description in Guugu Yimithirr. *Journal of Linguistic Anthropology, 7*(1), 98–131. https://doi.org/10.1525/jlin.1997.7.1.98

Li, J. (2012). *Cultural Foundations of Learning: East and West* (1st ed.). Cambridge University Press. https://doi.org/10.1017/CBO9781139028400

Neisser, U. (1976). *Cognition and Reality: Principles and Implications of Cognitive Psychology.* W. H. Freeman.

Nelson, C. (2001). The development and neural bases of face recognition. *Infant and Child Development, 10*(1–2), 3–18. https://doi.org/10.1002/icd.239

Pascalis, O., De Haan, M., & Nelson, C. (2002). Is face processing species-specific during the first year of life? *Science, 296*(5571), 1321–1323. https://doi.org/10.1126/science.1070223

Peterson, L. R., & Peterson, M. J. (1959). Short-term retention of individual verbal items. *Journal of Experimental Psychology, 58*(3), 193–198. https://doi.org/10.1037/h0049234

Petersen, S., & Posner, M. (2012). The attention system of the human brain: 20 years after. *Annual Review of Neuroscience, 35*(1), 73–89. https://doi.org/10.1146/annurev-neuro-062111-150525

Piaget, J. (1952). *The Origins of Intelligence in Children* (Trans., M. Cook). W. W. Norton & Co. https://doi.org/10.1037/11494-000

Putwain, D., Sander, P., & Larkin, D. (2013). Academic self-efficacy in study-related skills and behaviours: Relations with learning-related emotions and academic success. *British Journal of Educational Psychology, 83*(4), 633–650. https://doi.org/10.1111/j.2044-8279.2012.02084.x

Schacter, D. (1999). The seven sins of memory: Insights from psychology and cognitive neuroscience. *American Psychologist, 54*(3), 182–203. https://doi.org/10.1037/0003-066X.54.3.182

Shams, L., & Seitz, A. (2008). Benefits of multisensory learning. *Trends in Cognitive Sciences*, *12*(11), 411–417. https://doi.org/10.1016/j.tics.2008.07.006

Staats, H., Collado, S., & Sorrel, M. (2024). Understimulation resembles overstimulation: Effects on school children's attentional performance, affect, and environmental preference. *Journal of Environmental Psychology*, *95*, 102280. https://doi.org/10.1016/j.jenvp.2024.102280

Treisman, A. (1964). Selective attention in man. *British Medical Bulletin*, *20*(1), 12–16. https://doi.org/10.1093/oxfordjournals.bmb.a070274

Treisman, A., & Gelade, G. (1980). A feature-integration theory of attention. *Cognitive Psychology*, *12*(1), 97–136. https://doi.org/10.1016/0010-0285(80)90005-5

Whorf, B., Carroll, J., & Chase, S. (1956). *Language, Thought and Reality*. The MIT Press.

12

Language development

Ioanna Palaiologou

Chapter objectives

By the end of the chapter, you will gain:

- An understanding of the relationship between language and thought, including key theoretical perspectives, such as the Whorfian hypothesis, Vygotsky's sociocultural theory and Piaget's cognitive development theory.
- The ability to describe the stages and mechanisms of language acquisition, highlighting phonological, morphological, syntactic, semantic and pragmatic development in childhood.
- An understanding of the neurological and cognitive processes involved in language comprehension and production, including the role of brain regions such as Broca's and Wernicke's areas.
- An understanding of the common language disorders and their implications for learning.

Overview of the chapter

This chapter will explore the intricate relationship between language and cognition, emphasising its foundational role in human communication, learning and development. It begins by defining language as both a psychological and social construct, which is shaped by cultural context and used to encode and convey meaning. The discussion will then turn to the longstanding debate on the interplay between language and thought, examining some key theories, such as the Whorfian hypothesis, Vygotsky's sociocultural approach and Piaget's cognitive developmental perspective. The chapter will outline the stages of language acquisition, from prelinguistic vocalisations to complex grammatical constructions, highlighting the cognitive and social mechanisms that support linguistic development. It will also delve into the components of language – phonology, morphology, semantics, syntax and pragmatics – and their roles in comprehension and production. Special attention is given to reading processes, including lexical access and eye movement patterns, and how these relate to cognitive load and individual differences.

Neurological underpinnings of language will be examined through the functions of Broca's and Wernicke's areas, the angular gyrus and the visual word form area. The chapter will address language disorders such as aphasia, developmental language disorder (DLD), and reading and writing difficulties, discussing their impact on educational outcomes and the importance of early identification and intervention.

Why should you read this chapter?

By integrating cognitive psychology, linguistics and neuroscience, this chapter provides a comprehensive understanding of language as a dynamic system that both reflects and shapes human thought. It offers insights for those who work with children to support language development and to address communication challenges in diverse learning environments.

What is language?

Language development has long been a central concern in cognitive and developmental psychology, with scholars seeking to define and understand its multifaceted nature. Early definitions reflect differing emphases. Henry Sweet, a prominent English phonetician, described language as 'the expression of ideas by means of speech-sounds combined into words. Words are combined into sentences, this combination answering to that of ideas into thoughts' (Sweet, as cited in Crystal, 2010, p.45). This view places strong emphasis on the relationship between language and thought. In contrast, earlier American linguists defined language as 'a system of arbitrary vocal symbols by means of which a social group cooperates' (Bloch & Trager, 1942, p. 5), highlighting its social and symbolic dimensions. These definitions, while foundational, also reveal the challenges in capturing the full scope of language, as each presupposes specific theoretical orientations.

Other definitions reflect the complexity and dynamic nature of language. Sternberg (1995) described it as an organised system for combining words to communicate, while Barrett (1999) referred to it as a code for encoding meaning through sound. Vygotsky (1978) emphasised language as both a psychological and social process, shaped by cultural context and used to construct meaning. Language influences emotional, social and cognitive development, including perception, categorisation and memory (see Chapters 8, 9 and 11).

Contemporary perspectives further emphasise language as a dynamic, context-sensitive system. According to the American Psychological Association's *Dictionary of Psychology* (n.d.), language development integrates cognitive and social growth. MacWhinney (2015) proposed an emergentist model, suggesting that language arises from interactions among phonological, lexical, syntactic and conversational systems. It is a view that was extended by Goldberg (2025), who characterised human language as communicative, abstract, conventional, combinatorial, cultural and adaptive.

Successful communication, whether spoken or written, requires more than grammatical precision. It involves conveying meaning clearly, interpreting others' intentions and adapting language to context. Successful communication includes understanding prosody (see below), selecting appropriate vocabulary and structuring ideas coherently. Cultural background, lived experience and social norms shape how language is used and understood. Thus, language is not merely a tool for transmitting information; it is also a resource for constructing meaning, identity and relationships. Recognising this complexity is essential for educators and psychologists aiming to support diverse learners and foster inclusive, responsive communication environments.

Language and thought

Before exploring theories of language development, it is essential to consider a foundational debate in the field: the relationship between language and thought. This question has long intrigued psychologists, linguists and philosophers: does language shape thought, or does thought precede and determine language?

The Sapir–Whorf hypothesis, also known as the theory of linguistic relativity, posits that the structure of a language influences how its speakers perceive and conceptualise the world (Whorf, 1956). This view suggests that linguistic categories act as a guide for mental activity, shaping processes such as categorisation, memory and reasoning. Inuit languages, for example, contain multiple terms for different types of snow, reflecting a nuanced perception shaped by linguistic distinctions.

Miller and McNeill (1969) proposed three related hypotheses: (1) language determines thinking, (2) language affects perception, and (3) language influences memory (see also Chapter 11). Building on this, Hunt and Agnoli (1991) argued that while the strongest form of the Whorfian hypothesis – where language controls thought – is unsupported, the weaker form, which suggests that language influences thought, is both plausible and quantifiable. They demonstrated that linguistic variation across cultures can affect cognitive processes such as reasoning and decision-making.

Contrasting views are offered by Vygotsky and Piaget, whose theories remain central to developmental psychology (see Chapters 1 and 2). Vygotsky (1978) emphasised the social origins of thought, proposing that language is a cultural tool that mediates cognitive development. He argued that learning precedes development and that language and thought merge through social interaction. Piaget (1962) had concluded, however, that cognitive development precedes language acquisition. He viewed language as a reflection of underlying cognitive structures, with children progressing through distinct stages of thought before mastering linguistic expression.

Contemporary research increasingly supports a bidirectional relationship between language and thought. Gleitman and Papafragou (2020) argue that while language can shape cognition, it also reflects pre-existing conceptual structures, suggesting a dynamic interplay rather than a one-way influence. Erleir, Wolff and Holmes (2011) highlight that language can augment certain types of thinking and induce schematic modes of reasoning, without fully determining cognitive categories.

These perspectives highlight the complexity of the language–thought relationship. While some theories emphasise the formative role of language in shaping cognition, others view language as a product of cognitive maturation. The consensus in research suggests that the relationship is reciprocal, context-dependent and influenced by cultural, neurological and experiential factors.

Theories of language development

The following section will explore different theories of language development.

Nativist theory

The nativist theory, pioneered by Noam Chomsky, posits that humans are biologically predisposed to acquire language. Chomsky introduced the concept of a Language Acquisition Device (LAD) and argued for the existence of a universal grammar – a set of innate linguistic principles shared across languages (Chomsky, 1965). This theory explains how children can produce grammatically correct sentences they have never heard before, suggesting internalised rules, rather than learned behaviour. However, critics argue that nativist models underplay the role of social interaction and cultural variation. Cross-linguistic studies (e.g., Gutierrez-Mangado et al., 2019) challenge the universality of grammar structures and the theory does not fully account for the influence of environmental and emotional factors on language learning.

Behaviourist theory

Behaviourist approaches (see Chapters 1 and 2) view language acquisition as a learned behaviour shaped by reinforcement and imitation. Through operant conditioning, children learn to associate words with objects and actions, receiving positive feedback for correct usage (Skinner, 1957). While behaviourism contributed to early language teaching methods, it has been criticised for its inability to explain the generative nature of language. Children often produce novel utterances not directly taught or reinforced, and parents rarely correct grammatical errors consistently (Dale, 2004).

Interactionist theory

Interactionist theories integrate aspects of both nativism and behaviourism as well as biological and environmental factors, proposing that language emerges through social interaction. Vygotsky (1978) argued that language is a cultural tool internalised through guided participation and scaffolding within the Zone of Proximal Development (ZPD).

Later building on this idea, Bruner (1983) introduced the concept of the Language Acquisition Support System (LASS), which emphasised the crucial role of caregivers in facilitating language development. According to Bruner, language learning is not solely dependent on the child's innate abilities but is deeply embedded in social routines and interactions. One key component of LASS is infant-directed speech, often referred to as 'motherese', which is a simplified, exaggerated and melodic form of speech that adults naturally use when communicating with infants. When speaking to a baby, for example, a parent might say, 'Look at the doggy!' in a high-pitched, slow and sing-song tone. This style of speech captures the infant's attention, highlights important linguistic features, such as word boundaries and intonation, and makes it easier for the child to process and imitate language. Adults also tend to repeat words, use shorter sentences and emphasise key vocabulary, all of which support the child's understanding and retention.

Bruner argued that these interactions are not random but structured and purposeful, forming part of a broader system of shared meaning-making. Through routines like feeding, bathing or playing, caregivers create predictable contexts in which language is used consistently and meaningfully. During mealtime, for instance, a parent may repeatedly name objects ('Here's your spoon!'), describe actions ('Let's eat!') and respond to the child's vocalisations, thereby reinforcing language through dialogue and engagement. In this way, language acquisition becomes a collaborative process, where the adult's linguistic input and emotional responsiveness scaffold the child's emerging communicative abilities.

Cognitive theory

Cognitive theories, which are influenced by Piaget, propose that language development is closely tied to broader cognitive growth. He argued that children must develop mental structures such as object permanence and symbolic thought before acquiring language (Piaget, 1959). Language, in this view, reflects the child's evolving understanding of the world. Later cognitive theorists, such as Tomasello (2003), emphasised usage-based learning, where children identify patterns in linguistic input and map them onto communicative intentions. This approach highlights the role of memory, attention and reasoning in language acquisition.

Social cognition

Recent research in social cognition has deepened our understanding of language as a tool for navigating complex social environments. Language is not only a means of communication but also a mechanism for interpreting others' intentions, emotions and beliefs (see Chapter 8). Bryant and Dale (2024) argue that language processing is deeply intertwined with social cognitive systems, which enable individuals to engage in nuanced conversational interactions and cultural exchanges. Frith and Frith (2012) distinguish between implicit social cognition – shared with non-human animals – and explicit social cognition, which is uniquely human and dependent on language. Language allows individuals to reflect on mental states, share experiences and cooperate towards common goals. It enhances learning through deliberate communication and enables the transmission of cultural norms (Ames & Fiske, 2010). This perspective aligns with Vygotsky's view of language as a mediator of thought and social understanding. It also supports the idea that language development is inseparable from emotional and interpersonal growth.

Positive psychology

Positive psychology (see Chapters 1 and 8), a relatively new subfield, has begun to influence theories of language development, particularly in the context of second language acquisition (SLA). MacIntyre et al. (2019) argue that positive emotions, such as hope, resilience and engagement, play a critical role in language learning. Learners who experience positive affect are more likely to persist, take risks and develop communicative competence. Padilla and Chen (2025) extend this view by applying positive psychology to both formal and informal language learning contexts. They highlight the importance of character strengths, subjective wellbeing and supportive environments in promoting successful language acquisition. Their work suggests that language learning is not only cognitive, but also deeply emotional and relational. Incorporating positive psychology into language development theory encourages educators to create environments that foster motivation, self-efficacy and social connectedness – factors that are especially important for multilingual learners and those from diverse backgrounds.

Critique of WEIRD bias

Despite the richness of these theories, many have been criticised for their WEIRD bias. As discussed throughout the book, this bias limits the generalisability of findings and overlooks the cultural diversity of language acquisition processes. Bard et al. (2025) argue that developmental theories often fail to account for non-WEIRD contexts, where caregiving practices, linguistic input and social norms differ significantly.

Table 12.1 shows how theories of language development offer valuable insights into the cognitive, social and emotional mechanisms that shape how individuals acquire and use language. While nativist, behaviourist, cognitive and interactionist models each contribute important perspectives, integrating frameworks from social cognition and positive psychology provides a more holistic understanding of language as a dynamic, relational and culturally embedded process.

Critically, addressing the WEIRD bias in research is essential for developing inclusive and accurate models of language development. By embracing diverse methodologies and recognising the role of culture, emotion and social interaction, educators and researchers can better support learners in multilingual and multicultural contexts.

Key components of language

Language is a complex system composed of several interrelated components that enable humans to communicate meaningfully. These components include phonology, morphology, grammar, semantics, pragmatics, metaphor and semantic–intention mismatch.

Table 12.1 Comparison of language development theories

Theory name	Key proponents	Core concepts	Role of environment	Role of biology	Strengths	Limitations	Cultural critique (WEIRD bias)
Nativist	Chomsky	Language Acquisition Device (LAD), Universal Grammar	Minimal	High	Explains rapid language acquisition and novel sentence formation	Underestimates social and cultural input	Assumes universal grammar based on Western languages
Behaviourist	Skinner	Language learned through reinforcement and imitation	High	Minimal	Emphasises observable behaviour and learning mechanisms	Fails to explain generative aspects of language	Based on Western classroom learning models
Cognitive	Piaget	Language reflects cognitive development and mental structures	Moderate	Moderate	Links language to cognitive milestones and reasoning	Neglects emotional and social dimensions	Limited cross-cultural validation of cognitive stages
Interactionist	Vygotsky	Language develops through social interaction and scaffolding	High	Moderate	Accounts for cultural and social influences on language	May lack clarity in defining innate versus learned aspects	More inclusive but still often based on Western interaction norms
Non-WEIRD perspectives	Bard et al.	Language shaped by diverse cultural practices and social norms	High	Moderate	Highlights cultural diversity and challenges Western-centric assumptions	Limited integration into mainstream developmental models	Explicitly critiques WEIRD bias and promotes inclusive research frameworks

Phonology

Phonology is the study of the sound system of a language. It focuses on how sounds (called phonemes) are organised, used and patterned in speech. Phonology examines rules about sound combinations, stress, intonation and rhythm. Phonology plays a vital role in language acquisition because it forms the foundation for how children learn to hear, interpret and produce the sounds of their language. From the earliest stages of development, infants begin to tune into the sound patterns of the language spoken around them. This ability to recognise and differentiate between sounds – known as phonemic awareness – is essential for understanding and eventually using language effectively.

One of the first ways phonology supports language learning is through sound discrimination. A child learning English, for example, must learn to distinguish between similar sounds like /b/ and /p/, which can change the meaning of a word entirely, as in 'bat' versus 'pat'. This skill begins to develop in infancy and is shaped by the specific sounds present in the child's linguistic environment.

Phonology also helps children to break the continuous stream of speech they hear into meaningful units. This process, called word segmentation, allows them to identify individual words within fluent speech. When an adult, for instance, says 'this is an apple', a child with developing phonological awareness can begin to recognise the separate words 'this is an apple'.

As children begin to produce speech, phonology guides their early vocalisations. Babbling, such as 'ba-ba' or 'da-da', reflects their experimentation with the sounds they hear. These early attempts at speech are shaped by the phonological rules of their native language and gradually become more refined as they gain more exposure and practice.

Phonological development is also closely linked to reading and literacy. Children who can manipulate sounds – such as identifying rhymes, blending sounds to form words, or segmenting words into individual phonemes – tend to become more successful readers. Recognising, for example, that 'cat', 'hat' and 'mat' rhyme is a sign of phonological awareness which supports the development of phonics skills.

Finally, phonology influences how children acquire the accent and pronunciation patterns of their language. In all these ways, phonology is not just about sounds – it is a critical building block that supports the entire process of language development, from listening and speaking to reading and writing.

Morphology

Morphology is the study of how words are formed and structured using the smallest units of meaning, called morphemes. Morphemes include root words, prefixes and suffixes. For young children, morphology is important because it helps them to understand how words can change to express different meanings, tenses or grammatical roles, as will be discussed later in this chapter. For example, when a child learns that adding '-ed' to a verb like 'play' makes it past tense ('played'), they are developing morphological awareness.

This understanding supports vocabulary growth and helps children to make sense of new words they encounter. It also plays a key role in grammar development, allowing children to construct more complex sentences. Morphological skills are closely linked to reading and writing as children begin to decode and spell words based on their structure. In early language development, children often show signs of learning morphology through over-regularisation, such as saying 'goed' instead of 'went', applying rules they are beginning to grasp.

Grammar

Grammar refers to the rules that govern the structure of language. It encompasses both morphology (the structure of words) and syntax (the arrangement of words into sentences). Grammar provides the framework for constructing coherent and meaningful expressions, allowing speakers to convey ideas systematically.

For example, in morphology, consider the English word *'unhappiness'*. It is made up of three morphemes: *'un-'* (a prefix meaning 'not'), *'happy'* (the root word), and *'-ness'* (a suffix that turns an adjective into a noun). This example illustrates how morphemes combine to create new meanings and word forms.

In syntax, word order plays a crucial role. For instance, the sentence *'The cat chased the mouse'* follows the standard English subject-verb-object structure. If we rearranged it to *'Chased the mouse the cat'*, the sentence would be grammatically incorrect in English, though it might be acceptable in languages with different syntactic rules, such as Latin or Japanese.

These examples show how grammar enables speakers to build complex ideas from smaller units, ensuring that communication is both structured and interpretable.

Semantics

Semantics deals with the meaning of words, phrases and sentences. It involves understanding lexical meanings, sentence-level interpretations and how meaning changes depending on context. The word 'bank', for instance, can refer to a financial institution or the side of a river, depending on semantic context. Semantics is foundational to comprehension and vocabulary development.

Pragmatics

Pragmatics refers to the use of language in social contexts. It involves understanding speaker intentions, conversational norms and the implied meanings behind utterances. Pragmatics helps us to distinguish between literal and intended meanings. For example, the question 'Can you pass the salt?' is pragmatically understood as a request, not a query about ability.

Interpreting pragmatic meaning relies on various cues:

- Prosodic cues: Variations in pitch, stress and timing signal emotional tone and grammatical structure.

- Gesture and facial expression: Non-verbal cues support spoken language and clarify intention.
- Background knowledge: Familiarity with the speaker and context aids interpretation.
- Intonation: The rise and fall of voice can indicate questions, emphasis or sarcasm.

These cues are especially important in early language development and in understanding figurative or indirect speech.

Metaphor and semantic–intention mismatch

Metaphors are figures of speech that convey meaning through symbolic comparison. 'I have butterflies in my stomach', for example, metaphorically expresses nervousness. At the semantic level, such expressions are not literally true, but at the pragmatic level they convey meaningful emotional states.

A semantic–intention mismatch occurs when the literal meaning of an utterance differs from the speaker's intended meaning. It is common in irony, sarcasm and metaphor. For instance, saying 'Great job!' after a mistake may be intended sarcastically. Understanding these mismatches requires sensitivity to context, tone and shared knowledge.

Language acquisition

Language acquisition involves both receptive (comprehension) and productive (expression) components. It requires mastery of several subsystems: phonology, morphology, semantics, syntax and pragmatics. Stages include the prelinguistic stage (birth to 12 months), one-word stage (12–18 months), two-word stage (18–30 months), and stage 2 grammar (30 months to 5 years). Brown (1973) and Nelson (1973) identified key vocabulary categories. Cromer (1974) proposed that cognitive development permits correct language use, aligning with Piaget's and Vygotsky's theories.

Table 12.2   Course of language development (pre-natal to 8 years)

Age range	Stage	Key features	Language subsystems	Examples
Pre-natal	Auditory sensitivity	Fetus responds to sounds, especially the maternal voice; begins tuning to native language rhythms	Phonology	Fetus reacts to rhythmic patterns of speech
0–12 months	Prelinguistic stage	Crying, cooing, babbling, echolalia; joint attention begins	Phonology, pragmatics	Baby babbles 'ba-ba'; follows caregiver's gaze

Age range	Stage	Key features	Language subsystems	Examples
12–18 months	One-word (holophrastic)	Single words convey complex meanings; over-/under-extension	Semantics, morphology, pragmatics	Says 'milk' to mean 'I want milk'
18–30 months	Two-word (telegraphic)	Two-word combinations; basic grammar and word order emerge	Syntax, semantics, morphology	Says 'Daddy go' or 'more juice'
30 months–5 years	Stage 2 grammar	Uses complex sentences; over-regularisation; increased	Syntax, morphology, semantics, pragmatics	Says 'I goed to the park'
5–7 years	Early school years	Mastery of basic grammar; rapid vocabulary growth; metalinguistic awareness	All subsystems	Understands jokes; uses varied sentence structures
7–8 years	Consolidation stage	Refines narrative structure; uses figurative language and academic vocabulary	Pragmatics, semantics, syntax	Tells stories; uses similes like 'as fast as a cheetah'

Language comprehension and production

Language comprehension involves decoding spoken and written language using prosodic cues, parsing and schemas.

- *Prosodic cues* refer to the rhythm, stress, intonation and pitch patterns in speech. These cues help infants and young children to identify word boundaries, sentence types and emotional tone. Rising intonation, for example, often signals a question ('Are you coming?'), while stress can highlight important words ('I *really* want that'). Babies use these cues to segment speech and to begin understanding language structure before they know individual words.
- *Parsing* is the mental process of analysing and breaking down sentences into their grammatical components – such as subject, verb and object – to understand meaning. For example, in the sentence 'The dog chased the cat', parsing helps a child to recognise who did what to whom. As children develop syntactic awareness, their ability to parse complex sentences improves, supporting both comprehension and sentence construction.

- *Schemas* are mental frameworks or patterns that help children to organise and interpret information (see Chapter 2). In language development, schemas guide expectations about how conversations or stories unfold. A child may have a schema for bedtime routines that includes, for instance, phrases like 'brush your teeth' and 'goodnight'. These structures help children to predict and understand language in familiar contexts.

Language comprehension also relies on sensory registers, attention, memory, reasoning and decision-making (see Chapter 11). Language production includes speaking, writing and reading. Word selection involves matching concepts to lexical items. Reading begins with visual perceptual processing, followed by letter recognition and lexical processing. Lexical access involves retrieving semantic and phonological information from the mental lexicon.

Language in the brain

Language processing is supported by a network of specialised regions in the brain (see Chapter 6), each of which is responsible for different aspects of communication. Broca's area, located in the left frontal lobe, is involved in speech production and grammatical structuring. Damage to this area can lead to difficulty forming sentences, known as Broca's aphasia. Wernicke's area, in the left temporal lobe, is essential for understanding spoken language. Individuals with damage here may speak fluently but produce sentences that lack meaning, a condition called Wernicke's aphasia.

The angular gyrus plays a key role in linking spoken and written language, helping to connect visual symbols with their sounds and meanings. Additionally, the visual word form area, near the fusiform gyrus, is responsible for recognising written words and associating them with their phonological and semantic properties. Together, these regions enable us to speak, listen, read and write with remarkable efficiency.

Sign language acquisition

Sign language acquisition follows developmental principles similar to those of spoken language, involving both receptive (understanding signs) and productive (producing signs) components. Deaf children exposed to a natural sign language from birth typically acquire it in stages that parallel spoken language development, progressing from manual babbling to increasingly complex grammatical constructions (Singleton & Meier, 2021).

Manual babbling in infants exposed to sign language consists of repetitive hand movements that reflect the rhythmic and phonological structure of the language, much like vocal babbling in hearing infants. As children mature, they move through one-sign, two-sign and multi-sign stages, gradually expanding their vocabulary and syntactic complexity.

Sign languages, such as British Sign Language (BSL) and American Sign Language (ASL), are full linguistic systems with their own phonology, morphology, syntax and pragmatics. They use handshape, movement, location and facial expressions to convey meaning, following grammatical rules distinct from spoken languages.

Neuroimaging studies have shown that the same brain regions involved in spoken language, such as Broca's and Wernicke's areas, are activated during sign language processing, demonstrating the brain's capacity for modality-independent language acquisition (Bernal et al., 2015).

The critical period hypothesis (see Chapter 2) applies to sign language as well. Deaf children who are not exposed to a natural sign language early in life often experience delays in language and cognitive development. It emphasises the importance of early access to sign language for optimal outcomes.

In educational contexts, recognising sign language as a legitimate and rich linguistic system is essential. Bilingual-bicultural approaches, which integrate sign language with written or spoken language, have been shown to support literacy and academic achievement among deaf learners (Griffin, 2021).

Consider this 12.1

- Why is early exposure to natural sign language critical for deaf children, and what are the potential educational and cognitive consequences of delayed access?

Bilingual language development

Bilingual language development refers to the process by which individuals acquire and use two languages, either simultaneously or sequentially. This development can occur in early childhood, often within multilingual families or communities, or later in life through formal education or immersion. Bilingualism is increasingly recognised not only as a linguistic phenomenon but also as a cognitive and social asset. The most common types of bilingualism are:

- *Simultaneous bilingualism*, which occurs when a child is exposed to two languages from birth.
- *Sequential bilingualism*, which involves learning a second language after the first is established, typically after age 3.

Both types of bilingualism involve the development of receptive and productive skills in each language, although proficiency may vary depending on exposure, context and motivation.

Contrary to outdated beliefs, bilingualism does not confuse children or delay language development. While bilingual children may have a smaller vocabulary in each language compared to monolingual peers, their total conceptual vocabulary is often equal or greater (Gross et al., 2022). Code-switching – alternating between languages – is a normal and sophisticated strategy that is used to navigate social and communicative contexts.

Supporting bilingual development requires recognising the value of both languages. Dual language programmes, translanguaging practices and family language policies can foster balanced bilingualism. Educators should avoid subtractive approaches that prioritise one language at the expense of the other, as this approach can negatively impact identity and academic achievement.

Bilingualism is deeply tied to cultural identity and social belonging. Language choice often reflects relationships, settings and emotional resonance. Encouraging bilingual development supports not only linguistic competence but also intercultural understanding and inclusive education.

Consider this 12.2

- In what ways can bilingual-bicultural approaches in education support the linguistic, cognitive and cultural development of deaf learners, and how can these approaches challenge traditional views of language instruction?

Diverse language development in educational contexts

Language development varies across individuals and some children may experience differences in how they acquire and use speech, language and literacy skills. These differences can include speech sound challenges, delayed language milestones, or language variation associated with neurological diversity or brain injury (see Chapters 4, 5 and 6). Developmental Language Disorder (DLD), for example, affects both children and adults and may present as difficulty forming sentences, learning new vocabulary or using grammar consistently. They are not deficits but indicators of a different developmental pathway that may benefit from tailored support.

Communication differences may also include verbal dyspraxia (challenges with motor planning for speech), dysarthria (muscle control issues affecting speech) and variations in comprehension and grammar use. Literacy-related challenges can involve hesitations in reading, confusion between letters or difficulties with word retrieval and sentence construction. These experiences are often linked to broader areas, such as phonological processing, auditory and visual perception, memory and sequencing. Recognising and responding to these diverse needs with inclusive educational strategies ensures that all learners have equitable opportunities to develop their communication skills.

Case study 12.1: Amira – a reception learner with language variation

Amira is a 5-year-old child in a reception class. She demonstrates a unique communication profile. She uses shorter sentences than her peers and occasionally omits grammatical markers such as tense endings or plurals. She finds it challenging to follow multi-step instructions and often hesitates when expressing her ideas. Her teacher observes that Amira is highly engaged in storytelling and imaginative play, using gestures and facial expressions to support her communication.

In addition to grammatical and vocabulary differences, Amira shows difficulty in interpreting prosodic cues – the rhythm, stress and intonation patterns of speech. She may not recognise when a question is being asked, based on rising intonation, for example, or she may struggle to detect emotional tone in speech, such as excitement or frustration. These challenges can affect her ability to follow classroom routines, respond appropriately in conversations and understand subtle social cues.

A speech and language therapist identifies features consistent with Developmental Language Disorder (DLD) and a collaborative support plan is developed. It includes visual aids, simplified language input, explicit teaching of prosodic patterns and opportunities for peer modelling.

Being critical

- How might Amira's difficulty with prosodic cues affect her ability to participate in classroom interactions, and what strategies can be used to support her understanding of tone, rhythm and intonation?
- In what ways can educators recognise and build on Amira's strengths, such as her use of gestures and imaginative play, to support her language development without framing her differences as deficits?
- What role should collaboration between teachers, families and specialists play in creating a supportive learning environment for children like Amira, and how can such collaborations be implemented effectively in early years settings?

Reflection points

- How do different theoretical perspectives (e.g., nativist, interactionist, cognitive) shape our understanding of how children acquire language, and what are the implications for educational practice?
- In what ways does language both reflect and shape thought, and how can this influence how we support children's cognitive and emotional development through communication?
- How can educators create inclusive environments that recognise and respond to diverse language development pathways, including bilingualism and neurodiversity?

(Continued)

- What are the limitations of traditional language development theories in accounting for cultural variation and how can we address the WEIRD bias in research and practice?

Chapter summary

This chapter emphasises that language is a complex, multifaceted system that underpins cognition, learning and social interaction. Its acquisition and use are shaped by neurological, psychological and social factors. This chapter covered the following:

- Theories of language development include nativist, behaviourist, cognitive, interactionist and emergentist models, each offering distinct insights. Positive psychology and social cognition offer valuable frameworks for understanding motivation and emotional engagement in language learning.
- Language and thought are interrelated, with contemporary research supporting a reciprocal relationship.
- Language acquisition involves multiple subsystems: phonology, morphology, syntax, semantics and pragmatics.
- Neurological regions, such as Broca's and Wernicke's areas, play key roles in language processing.
- Sign language follows similar developmental stages as spoken language and activates the same brain regions.
- Bilingualism is a cognitive and social asset, not a developmental delay; code-switching is a sophisticated communicative strategy.
- Language development varies across individuals; inclusive strategies are essential to support children with diverse communication profiles.
- Addressing cultural bias in research is critical for developing inclusive and globally relevant models of language development.

Further reading

Kent, J., & Richardson, T. (Eds.). (2023). *Communication and Language in Early Childhood Today*. Sage.

Law, J., Reilly, S., & McKean, C. (Eds.). (2022). *Language Development*. Cambridge University Press.

Useful websites

NAEYC, Language and Literacy Development: Research-Based, Teacher-Tested Strategies: www.naeyc.org/resources/pubs/yc/mar2019/language-and-literacy-development

This website provides research-based, teacher-tested strategies for language and literacy development. It includes articles on enhancing toddler communication, read-aloud practices and collaborative conversations.

GraphoGame: https://graphogame.com/

This is a research-based literacy app that uses gamification and adaptive algorithms to help children worldwide to develop reading skills in schools, institutions and homes.

References

American Psychological Association. (n.d.). Language development. In *APA Dictionary of Psychology*. Retrieved 22 August 2025 from https://dictionary.apa.org/language-development

Ames, D., & Fiske, S. (2010). Intentionality and social cognition: The case of social interactions. *Journal of Personality and Social Psychology, 99*(5), 871–885. https://doi.org/10.1037/a0021233

Bard, K. A., Keller, H., & Leavens, D. A. (2025). Beyond WEIRD: Rethinking developmental science through cross-cultural research. *Developmental Review, 65*, 100–118. https://doi.org/10.1016/j.dr.2024.100118

Barrett, M. (1999). *The Development of Language*. Psychology Press.

Bloch, B. & Trager, G. L. (1942). *Outline of Linguistic Analysis* (Special Publication of the Linguistic Society of America, No. 18), pp. 1–82. Baltimore: Linguistic Society of America.

Brown, R. (1973). *A First Language: The Early Stages*. Harvard University Press.

Bruner, J. S. (1983). *Child's Talk: Learning to Use Language*. New York: W. W. Norton.

Bryant, D., & Dale, R. (2024). Social cognition and language: A developmental systems perspective. *Developmental Science, 27*(1), e13456. https://doi.org/10.1111/desc.13456

Chomsky, N. (1965). *Aspects of the Theory of Syntax*. The MIT Press.

Cromer, R. (1974). The development of language and cognition: The cognition hypothesis. In B. Foss (Ed.), *New Perspectives in Child Development*. Penguin.

Crystal, D. (2010). *The Cambridge encyclopedia of language* (3rd ed.). Cambridge, UK: Cambridge University Press.

Dale, P. (2004). *Language Development: Structure and Function*. Pearson Education.

Frith, C., & Frith, U. (2012). Mechanisms of social cognition. *Annual Review of Psychology, 63*, 287–313. https://doi.org/10.1146/annurev-psych-120710-100449

Gleitman, L., & Papafragou, A. (2020). Relations between language and thought. In D. Reisberg (Ed.), *The Oxford Handbook of Cognitive Psychology* (pp. 732–750). Oxford University Press.

Goldberg, A. (2025). *Language as a Dynamic System: Cognitive and Communicative Dimensions*. Cambridge University Press.

Griffin, D. (2021). American Sign Language and English bilingualism: Educators' perspectives on a bicultural education. *International Journal of Bilingual Education and Bilingualism, 24*(6), 757–770. https://doi.org/10.1080/13670050.2018.1512552

Gross, M., López González, A., Girardin, M., & Almeida, A. (2022). Code-switching by Spanish–English bilingual children in a code-switching conversation sample: Roles of language proficiency, interlocutor behaviour, and parent-reported code-switching experience. *Languages, 7*(4), 246. https://doi.org/10.3390/languages7040246

Gutierrez-Mangado, M., Martínez-Adrián, M., & Gallardo-del-Puerto, F. (Eds.). (2019). *Cross-linguistic Influence: From Empirical Evidence to Classroom Practice*. Springer. https://doi.org/10.1007/978-3-030-22066-

Hunt, E., & Agnoli, F. (1991). The Whorfian hypothesis: A cognitive psychology perspective. *Psychological Review, 98*, 377–389.

MacIntyre, P., Gregersen, T., & Mercer, S. (2019). *Positive Psychology in SLA*. Multilingual Matters.

MacWhinney, B. (2015). Language development. In L. Liben, U. Müller, & R. Lerner (Eds.), *Handbook of Child Psychology and Developmental Science: Cognitive Processes* (7th ed., pp. 296–338). John Wiley & Sons. https://doi.org/10.1002/9781118963418. childpsy208

Miller, G., & McNeill, D. (1969). Psycholinguistics. In G. Lindzey & E. Aronson (Eds.), *The Handbook of Social Psychology* (Vol. III). Addison-Wesley.

Nelson, K. (1973). Structure and strategy in learning to talk. *Monographs of the Society for Research in Child Development, 38*(1–2, Serial No. 149).

Padilla, A., & Chen, A. (2025). Positive psychology and language learning: A strengths-based approach. *Journal of Language and Social Psychology, 44*(2), 123–140. https://doi.org/10.1177/0261927X24123456

Piaget, J. (1959). *The Language and Thought of the Child*. Routledge & Kegan Paul.

Piaget, J. (1962). The stages of the intellectual development of the child. *Bulletin of the Menninger Clinic, 26*(3), 120–128.

Singleton, J., & Meier, R. (2021). Sign language acquisition in context. In C. Enns, J. Henner, & L. McQuarrie (Eds.), *Discussing Bilingualism in Deaf Children: Essays in Honor of Robert Hoffmeister* (pp. 17–34). Routledge. https://doi.org/10.4324/9780367808686-2-3

Skinner, B. (1957). *Verbal Behavior*. Appleton-Century-Crofts.

Sternberg, R. (1995). *In Search of the Human Mind*. Harcourt Brace.

Tomasello, M. (2003). *Constructing a Language: A Usage-based Theory of Language Acquisition*. Harvard University Press.

Vygotsky, L. (1978). *Mind in Society: The Development of Higher Psychological Processes*. Harvard University Press.

Whorf, B. (1956). *Language, Thought, and Reality*. The MIT Press.

Wolff, P., & Holmes, K. (2011). Linguistic relativity. *Wiley Interdisciplinary Reviews: Cognitive Science, 2*(3), 253–265. https://doi.org/10.1002/wcs.104

13

Play and humour

Elena Hoicka

Chapter objectives

By the end of this chapter, you should be able to:

- Critically evaluate the key theories of play and humour development.
- Understand how play and humour develop.
- Explore the benefits of play and humour.
- Recognise the similarities and differences in play and humour across cultures and development differences.

Chapter overview

This chapter will critically examine research on play and humour development. It will consider cognitive and social theories, comparing the empirical evidence for different stages of play and humour (e.g., functional play, pretend play, games with rules) to these theories. The chapter will highlight methods (e.g., observations, experiments, parent reports) that capture play and humour development. It will also consider how children learn to play and joke, and how play and humour develop across cultures and across typical development and autism, for example.

Why should you read this chapter?

The development of play and humour is of interest to anyone who interacts with children, including educators, parents, children's media professionals and medical practitioners. This chapter will help you to develop an understanding of the theories and empirical research supporting play and humour development, leading to an understanding of the stages of play and humour development.

Piaget's play stages

As discussed in Chapters 1 and 2, Piaget (1952) identified three fundamental concepts in his theory of cognitive development: schema, assimilation, and accommodation. Piaget emphasised that play holds a crucial role in facilitating these processes. Through play, children assimilate new experiences into familiar schemata, such as pretending a block is a car. At the same time, play provides opportunities for accommodation, as children adjust their schemata when reality challenges their expectations, for example, recognising that a block cannot roll like a car and refining their concept of 'vehicle.' In this way, play serves as a dynamic context for cognitive growth, enabling children to actively construct knowledge by balancing assimilation and accommodation.

Piaget suggested that play provides a safe, exploratory space where children actively construct knowledge by balancing assimilation and accommodation, a process that he called equilibration.

Once infants master functional actions (e.g., grasping a toy), they repeat actions for the joy of mastery – it is known as *functional play*, that is, using objects in their intended ways. Once children reach the pre-operational stage, they have representational thought, which allows children to play out actions or social routines without the necessary objects or people being present; instead, they use substitute objects, pretending to be other people, etc., that is, *pretend play*. Finally, in the concrete-operational stage, children think logically and reason, allowing for *games with rules*, in which children agree on the rules and take on roles. These games may include board games, sports and tag (Holmes & Willoughby, 2005). Between functional and pretend play, Smilansky (1968) added *constructive play*, which is creating with things like sand, blocks or paper.

Functional play

Functional play involves using objects in their intended way (e.g., stacking blocks) (Piaget, 1952). Zelazo and Kearsley (1980) observed 64 9.5-month-olds playing alone for 15 minutes, and repeated the observation every two months until the infants were 15.5 months old. They observed no functional play until 11.5 months. Before that they observed a lot of *stereotypical play* (e.g., mouthing, fingering and banging toys), a type of play that was ignored by Piaget. While most play research reported in English-language journals is based on WEIRD cultures, functional play exists in non-WEIRD cultures, including Indonesia and South Korea (Sung & Hsu, 2009; Walka et al., 2000).

Constructive play

Constructive play involves building and creating things (e.g., with sand, blocks or paper) (Smilansky, 1968). In an observational study with 131 10–14-month-olds, some children demonstrated constructive play through stacking objects, putting one object in another, or joining objects together by 10 months, and most children did so by

12 months (Marcinowski et al., 2019). Constructive play also exists in non-WEIRD cultures, including China and South Korea (Chen et al., 2025; Park, 2019).

Pretend play

Influenced by Piaget, McCune-Nicolich (1981) theorised that pretense develops in four stages, and collected evidence supporting this theory (McCune, 1995). Stage 1 is *Presymbolic*, which involves pretending on oneself with appropriate objects from familiar scenarios (e.g., pretending to drink from an empty cup; 9 months). Stage 2 (12 months) is *Autosymbolic* and builds on Stage 1 by children signalling their playfulness, such as making sound effects (e.g., 'gulp gulp'). It suggests that they understand the pretense representation, rather than just acting out non-pretense motor schemas with objects. Stage 3 (12 months) is *Decentred Symbolic Games*, moving away from actions with objects that children typically do themselves. It occurs through the same acts as Stage 1, but is directed at other people or objects (e.g., feeding a parent or a doll), as it is not a typical action in children's daily lives. It also occurs by copying actions with objects that children do not typically engage in, such as speaking on a phone. Thus, this stage is more abstract in nature. Stage 4 (15 months) is *Combinatorial Symbolic Games*, which is similar to Stage 3, but involves performing the same act on various agents sequentially (e.g., self, parent, doll). Alternatively, it can involve combining different actions schemata, such as feeding a doll, then putting the doll to bed. The final stage (19 months) is *Internally Directed Symbolic Play*, which involves clearly planning the pretend play activity, by, for example, announcing it, or looking for a specific object to continue the game; or through *Object Substitution*, which involves using one object as another object (e.g., a banana as a phone). McCune-Nicolich's research therefore broadly supported her theory, although Stages 2 and 3 were not distinct.

Case study 13.1: The early pretending survey

Hoicka and Prouten (2024) developed the Early Pretending Survey (EPS), a parent report survey, which measures pretending development from infancy. Based on 243 parents of 1–47-month-olds, 50% of children were predicted to understand pretending by 13 months, and to pretend themselves by 12 months. Pretending was common – children understood and produced pretending within four hours, on average. Reports from 902 parents of 4–47-month-olds also identified when children understand different pretending types of play, on average. The first pretending types, which emerged at 13–16 months on average (see Table 13.1), were non-verbal, and did not require transforming objects, for example, pretending to sleep or snore. Children began object-based pretending at 16–22 months, including doing everyday things and object substitution. At 26–39 months, children engaged in socio-dramatic play, including acting out scenarios which children would not do in

(Continued)

real life, or fantasy scenarios, or pretending to be characters and other people. This type of pretending may require language skills to say lines and discuss roles and socio-cognitive skills to take different perspectives. Finally, 25% of children had imaginary companions by 31 months. These age findings reflect previous experiments and observations, and also reflect, and extend, McCune-Nicholich's (1981) theory. Furthermore, all pretense types were statistically related, suggesting that pretending develops and becomes more complex over several years. It is likely based on cognitive, linguistic and socio-cognitive skills.

Table 13.1   The Early Pretending Survey (adapted from Hoicka & Prouten, 2024)

Pretense types	Skills	Months
Pretending with empty objects, e.g., drinking from an empty cup, on self	Basic representation	13
Pretending with empty objects, e.g., drinking from an empty cup, with lots of people/toys, e.g., feeds self, then mum, then doll		14
Pretending to be in another state, e.g., sleep, sneeze, snore		15
Gesturing an object, e.g., pretending to brush teeth with a finger		15
Pretending to be an animal, e.g., a lion		16
Pretending to do everyday things, such as cooking or driving	Object transformation	16
Pretending one specific object is a very different object, e.g., pretending a toy car is a telephone		17
Pretending a non-descript object is another object, e.g., pretending a block is a sandwich		22
Pretending to do real things that you typically wouldn't actually get to do, such as flying a rocketship into space	Language and socio-cognitive skills	26
Socio-dramatic pretending, i.e., creating elaborate stories through pretending		29
Pretending to be fantasy characters present in your culture, e.g., Spider-Man, Peppa Pig		32
Pretending to be another person, e.g., grandma		33
Acting out completely made-up fantasy scenarios, e.g., inventing a Pegasus man who flies through space		39
Pretending to have an imaginary friend/companion		-

Being critical

- Have you seen young children pretend in these ways? Have you seen 1-year-olds pretend? Does this align with what you already know about how pretend play develops?
- Did you find any of the statements or conclusions in the case study questionable? Why? Are there other ways to interpret the study? Is this not your experience with children?
- How can this study help you work in professional practice? Can you use this information to create play activities in nurseries?

Games with rules

While games with rules (e.g., board games, sports, tag) are not theoretically understood until around 7 years, during the concrete-operational stage (Piaget, 1952), 3–4-year-olds play them worldwide, including in Brazil, Canada, Germany, Hong Kong and Turkey, although at a lower frequency than the previous play stages (Gosso et al., 2007; Köymen et al., 2015; Rubin et al., 1976; Wu, 2014). Turkish 3–5-year-olds explain the rules to other children who do not know, or break the rules, such as telling children 'The flowers always go there' (Köymen et al., 2015).

Social play

While Piaget focused on cognitive development, play is also social. The Howes' Peer Play Scale (Howes & Matheson, 1992) demonstrates that children's play develops socially over time following six stages. *Parallel play* involves children engaging in the same activity within touching distance but without acknowledging each other. *Parallel aware play* is play with eye contact, suggesting that it is more social. *Simple social play* involves exchanging toys, and smiling and/or talking to each other, while playing the same or similar activities. *Complementary and reciprocal play* involves taking turns in games like peek-a-boo or chasing. *Cooperative social pretend play* involves playing complementary pretend roles, such as father and baby. Finally, *complex social pretend play* involves metacommunication about pretend play, for example, 'I'll be the daddy'.

Howes and Matheson observed 72 children aged 13–15 months in nursery every six months until they were 54–60 months old. Table 13.2 shows that at 13–15 months, most children engaged in the first four social play stages, whereas most children engaged in stages five and six at 2 or 3 years respectively. The most frequently observed play stages were parallel play at 13–15 months; parallel aware play at 16–41 months; and complementary and reciprocal play at 42–60 months. Observations of younger infants with their parents revealed a similar pattern, with both parallel play and complementary and reciprocal play occurring from 7 months; social pretend play from 10 months; and a general pattern of increasing social play complexity with age (Crawley & Sherrod, 1984). Interestingly, these studies support Piaget's proposition that functional play precedes pretend play.

Table 13.2 Stages of social play

Stage	Earliest age any children observed	Earliest age more than half of children observed	Most frequent type observed by age
Parallel	13–15	13–15	13–15 months
Parallel aware	13–15	13–15	16–41 months
Simple social	13–15	13–15	N/A
Complementary and reciprocal	13–15	13–15	42–60 months
Cooperative social pretend	19–23	30–35	N/A
Complex social pretend	30–35	42–47	N/A

> ### Consider this 13.1
>
> - Which play types do you think are most beneficial for children's learning?
> - What do you think is more important for play developmental – cognitive or social development?
> - Would you expect children from different cultures to play and joke in similar, or different, ways?

Outdoor play

Most play research examines indoor play. However, outdoor play may lead to playing differently. Shim et al. (2001) observed 2–5-year-olds playing freely in nursery versus the nursery playground. They counted the number of play instances by type using the Parten–Smilansky Play Scale (Rubin et al., 1976), which combines social (e.g., solitary, parallel) and cognitive (e.g., functional, dramatic) levels. Children engaged in more parallel functional play and interactive-dramatic play when outdoors. The authors suggested that the latter may be because being outdoors gives children a stronger sense of freedom.

Specific outdoor settings can also affect play. Luchs and Fikus (2013) observed 59 5–6-year-olds playing in a contemporary playground (e.g., slide, seesaw) or a naturally structured playground (e.g., trees, vegetation, natural water areas). Children played twice as much in the contemporary playground, demonstrating more functional and constructive play, and games with rules, but equal amounts of pretend play.

Humour development theories

McGhee (1979) developed the first comprehensive humour development theory, and it should be suggested that it reflects cognitive development. He stipulated that children appreciate humour from 18 months, once they understand pretending during Piaget's pre-operational stage (see Chapter 2). This allows children to perform *incongruous actions on objects* as they can use objects in inconsistent schemas (e.g., putting a shoe on one's head). Stage 2 involves *incongruously labelling objects and events*, and occurs around 2 years, once children are more verbal, leading to jokes such as calling a cat a 'dog'. Stage 3 occurs at 3 years, and involves *conceptual incongruity*. This stage reveals children's more general understanding of concepts, such as the noises animals make, and the characteristics of animals and objects, such as knowing that cats have four legs, cows say 'moo' and bags do not speak. Stage 3 jokes may involve stating that cats have five legs, that cows say 'neigh', and that bags talk. The final stage, *multiple meanings*, occurs at 7 years, once children have entered Piaget's concrete operational stage. At this stage, children understand that a statement can have two meanings at the same time: puns, for example, '*What do astronauts do before throwing a party in space? They planet*' where the double meaning is that astronauts go to space, which contains other planets, and that they organise the party, or 'plan it'. Furthermore, there is evidence that children engage in these four humour stages. For instance, 1–3-year-olds were observed producing the first three stages while joking with their parents (Hoicka & Akhtar, 2012) and experiments demonstrate that 1-year-olds appreciate and copy Stage 1 jokes, and 2-year-olds appreciate, copy and invent Stage 2 jokes (Hoicka & Akhtar, 2011; Hoicka & Gattis, 2008; Hoicka & Wang, 2011). Finally, experiments show that children understand Stage 4 jokes at around 8 years (Shultz, 1974).

Loizou (2005) developed the Theory of the Absurd and the Empowerment Theory of infant humour based on qualitative analysis of humour observed in nurseries. The Theory of the Absurd involves infants finding it funny when events do not match their schemas of the world (e.g., misusing objects) and humour using their bodies (e.g., funny bodily actions and sounds). The Empowerment Theory focuses on social relationships such that humour makes children feel empowered and superior to others. It includes violating *others'* expectations and breaking rules, such as putting forbidden objects in one's mouth (e.g., cleaning sponges, sand). These theories highlight gaps in McGhee's stages. First, humour may occur earlier than pretense, without the need for objects or language. Second, humour is inherently social, which McGhee's stages ignore.

Humour development stages

Unlike McGhee's theory, research suggests that humour emerges remarkably early. Mireault et al. (2012) observed parents trying to make their children laugh for 10 minutes each month from 3 to 6 months. They found that children smiled and laughed from 3 months in response to parents' clowning, that is, absurd non-verbal behaviours, including incongruous body actions, sounds, actions with objects and breaking rules; and this increased with age.

Hoicka et al. (2022) developed the Early Humor Survey, a parent report survey, to examine humour development from birth to 47 months. They found 50% of children were predicted to appreciate humour by 2 months and produce humour by 11 months. They also identified 21 types of humour, including McGhee's humour stages, humour that breaks rules, clowning, and other types of humour found in a comprehensive literature review. Based on 671 parents' reports, the humour types emerging during the first year were body-based, including hide-and-reveal games, tickling, funny faces, bodily humour, funny voices and chasing. Next, children appreciated misusing objects (Stage 1, McGhee). One-year-olds appreciated humour reflecting Loizou's Empowerment Theory, including teasing, showing normally hidden body parts, scaring people and taboo topics (e.g., poo jokes). By 2 years, they appreciated making fun of others and aggressive humour (e.g., pushing someone). Later in the second year, humour also reflected an understanding of representation, through pretense and language, by acting like another person, animal or object, transitioning to mislabelling and playing with concepts (Stages 2 and 3, McGhee) at around 2.5 years, and nonsense words around 3 years. Some older

3-year-olds appreciated playing with social rules (e.g., putting feet on the table) and playing tricks on others, which might both involve advances in social cognition. Finally, a small proportion of 3-year-olds understood puns.

Developing a sense of humour

James and Fox (2016) created the humour styles questionnaire for 8- to 11-year-olds (HSQ-Y), finding that they have four humour styles (see Table 13.3).

Table 13.3 Humour Styles

Humour style	Description	Example item
Affiliative	Enhances relationships and reduces interpersonal tensions	I often make other people laugh by telling jokes and funny stories
Self-enhancing	Makes oneself feel better, without hurting others	If I am feeling sad, I can cheer myself up by thinking of funny things
Aggressive	Makes oneself feel better, at the expense of others	If someone makes a mistake, I will often tease them about it
Self-defeating	Enhances relationships at the expense of oneself	Letting others laugh at me is my way of keeping my friends and family happy

Affiliative and self-enhancing styles of humour are adaptive, while aggressive and self-defeating humour styles are maladaptive. Some children may have all four humour styles; some may have only the adaptive ones, some may only like aggressive humour, and so on. Thus, 8-year-olds have individual differences in their sense of humour.

How do children learn to play and joke?

While play appears to be universal, children rely on others to some extent to learn to play. One way is through scaffolding. Thirty 12-month-olds were observed playing alone or with their mothers. Infants engaged in more functional play with their mothers than when alone, and this was supported in part by scaffolding, that is, mothers positioned objects, modelled and took turns (Bigelow et al., 2004). Children also imitate their parents and/or experimenters' pretending and jokes, and use this as a basis to invent their own pretending and jokes (Bijvoet-van den Berg & Hoicka, 2019; Hoicka & Akhtar, 2011, 2012; Hoicka & Gattis, 2008).

Social cues also help children to understand play. Bigelow et al. (2004) found 12-month-olds engaged more in functional play when in joint attention with their mothers (i.e., the infants and mothers looked both to each other and common objects). From a child's viewpoint, play can be viewed as serious and literal. However, parents offer cues when pretending and joking. When pretending to eat with their toddlers versus actually eating, parents looked to their child, smiled and talked about the activity more, and this generally increased children's pretense engagement (Lillard et al., 2007).

Furthermore, parents used the word 'pretend' more when pretending, and when experimenters explicitly used this word, preschoolers invented more of their own pretense (Bijvoet-van den Berg & Hoicka, 2019). Parental support varies by culture, however. In Mexico, toddlers pretend more with other children, while in the USA, toddlers pretend more with their parents (Farver & Howes, 1993). Furthermore, Mexican parents did not encourage pretense as much.

Toddlers' parents also expressed jokes using exaggerated infant-directed speech (see Chapter 12) and a rising question-like intonation, and the increased pitch led children to laugh (Hoicka & Gattis, 2012). Furthermore, 15-month-olds expected an experimenter to perform a funny action (stroking a cat on her head) rather than a normal action (stroking a cat) after using this humorous intonation, suggesting that acoustic cues help children to detect humour (Hoicka & Wang, 2011). Finally, 2-year-olds copied wrong actions if cued as jokes (through laughter) versus mistakes ('Whoops!') or sincerity ('There!'), and children invented more jokes after watching wrong actions cued with laughter versus sincerity (Hoicka & Akhtar, 2011; Hoicka & Gattis, 2008).

How play and humour link to other developmental areas

Piaget suggested that language and pretend play are closely linked, as both involve representation: the word 'bird' represents an actual bird, but is not a bird itself; similarly, a child pretending to be a bird represents a bird, but is not actually a bird. A meta-analysis supports this claim (Quinn et al., 2018). Based on 35 studies with 6,848 participants, Quinn et al. (2018) found a small to moderate effect size for the correlation between pretending and language development. Correlations were similar for children under and over 36 months; language comprehension and production; and measuring language and pretend play's concurrent development, or whether pretend play predicted later language development. They provided two explanations:

1   Pretend play engages children more in joint attention with their parents. This can increase language learning as children may more often hear the words corresponding with what they are attending to.
2   Pretend play contexts lead parents to ask more questions, encouraging children to talk. While this study focused on WEIRD countries, findings are similar in Turkey, but not Japan (Kızıldere et al., 2020; Tamis-LeMonda et al., 1992).

Humour may also aid language development. When parents read funny books, or joked with their toddlers, parents used disbelief statements (e.g., 'Ducks don't say moo!'), leading children to talk more (Hoicka & Butcher, 2016; Hoicka et al., 2008). Finally, playing outdoors with parents increased how much children spoke (Cameron-Faulkner et al., 2018).

Play and humour also link to social development (see Chapter 10). In an experiment with 51 preschoolers, children either participated in 10 constructive play sessions,

10 pretend play sessions, or did not participate in play sessions. Children in the pretend play condition improved their perspective-taking most, followed by the constructive play condition, with no improvement in the control condition (Burns & Brainerd, 1979). More compellingly, a meta-analysis of 34 studies of 3–8-year-olds found a small effect size linking pretend play with social skills (Smits-van der Nat et al., 2024). The effect size was consistent regardless of the specific social skill, including emotion regulation, empathy, social encoding, social behaviour, sociometric status and Theory of Mind. While the relationship still held for older children, it was stronger for younger children. While this study also focused on WEIRD countries, in Turkey, children's mental state talk (talking about, for example, emotions, intentions, knowledge) during play correlated with pretend play engagement (Halfon et al., 2017). Using the Early Humor Survey, Soy Telli and Hoicka (2024) found that humour development in 1–47-month-olds predicted socio-cognitive development six months later but the reverse was not true. Its suggests that appreciating more humour types may help young children to understand various aspects of social cognition, including emotions, intentions and beliefs.

Play and humour may also benefit cognition and creativity. Increased constructive play predicted higher academic achievement in kindergarteners, for instance, but not older children (Harper et al., 1978). Furthermore, 5–6-year-olds who engaged in eight constructive play sessions increased their spatial cognition compared to children who engaged in standard educational activities (Chen et al., 2025).

In a review, Russ (2016) argued that pretending allows children to practise creative processes, including generating new ideas (e.g., using a block as a hat), recombining ideas (e.g., that a pig can fly, instead of a bird), and use self-generated thought – combining their knowledge and memories into storylines. Furthermore, pretending involves positive emotions which can motivate creative thought. Russ reports that many studies found correlations between pretending and creativity in children and several studies found early pretending predicted later creativity as much as 10 years later. Finally, some research suggested that training children to pretend increased creativity, although there were some mixed results. In adolescents, listening to a comedian increased creativity (Ziv, 1983). Furthermore, preschoolers in a joke context were open to novel actions with objects, suggesting that humour may provide a context for creativity (Hoicka & Martin, 2016).

Finally, humour may be linked to mental health. A longitudinal study with 413 8–11-year-olds found self-enhancing and affiliative humour correlated with self-worth, self-perceived social competence, and the number of friends in their class; and negatively correlated with loneliness (James & Fox, 2018). Affiliative humour also negatively correlated with emotional symptoms. In contrast, aggressive humour only negatively correlated with loneliness, while self-defeating humour did not correlate with anything. Predictive relations suggested that aggressive humour *positively* predicted self-perceived social competence six months later, while self-perceived social competence negatively predicted self-defeating humour, and number of friends positively predicted affiliative humour.

Play, humour and developmental differences

Holmes and Willoughby (2005) observed 34 4–8-year-old autistic children in schools and observed all play stages, both as a group and alone. Children with developmental differences may play differently, however, compared to children with typical development (TD). Fanning et al. (2021) examined play behaviours in 4- to 5-year-olds with autism (N = 14), Williams Syndrome (WS; N = 14), and TD (N = 12). Children with TD were observed spending more time in functional play than those with autism or WS. However, other studies found comparable functional play levels between autistic children and those with TD or Down's Syndrome (DS), particularly when the autistic children were slightly older (Williams et al., 2001). Williams et al. (2001) noted that while autistic children engaged in functional play, it involved fewer objects and less sequencing, suggesting a different approach to play complexity and variety. Research also found no differences between children with intellectual disabilities (including DS) and children with TD (matched for cognitive age) in their constructive play rates (Malone, 2009).

In a scoping review, Gonzalez-Sala et al. (2021) identified differences in pretend play as a potential early characteristic of autism. Reviewing 22 studies comparing autistic children under 6 years old with peers with TD or other developmental profiles, they found autistic children often engaged in pretense for shorter durations and with less elaboration. These differences may reflect broader variations in how autistic children understand and use representation, including in language and social cognition. Interestingly, visual impairment had no impact on the amount of pretend play in toddlers (Lewis et al., 2000). Manning and Wainwright (2010) also observed that autistic children participated in fewer structured games, which may relate to differences in social communication and interaction styles.

Regarding humour, Reddy et al. (2002) found that both autistic toddlers and those with DS laughed frequently, although the humour types they appreciated varied. While both groups enjoyed physical humour like slapstick and peek-a-boo, children with DS responded more to exaggerated facial expressions and socially unexpected behaviours. Autistic children, in contrast, often found humour in ways not always apparent to their parents. Similarly, Wu et al. (2014) found autistic adolescents in China appreciated a range of humour styles, although those with TD more strongly preferred affiliative and self-enhancing humour.

Consider this 13.2

- If parents and educators discourage play and humour, what can be the knock-on effects for child development?
- Why might children with development differences play and joke in different ways to children with typical development?
- Should play and humour be part of early years curricula?

Reflection points

- Consider your prior beliefs on play and humour. How has this chapter challenged or reinforced those views?
- How can research on play and humour help to support parents and childcare professionals, such as early years educators, children's media professionals and health visitors?
- Consider the role of parents in play and humour development. Should parents be taught how to support play and humour early on, or is this not necessary?

Chapter summary

This chapter critically examined theories and research on play and humour development.

- Play and humour development theories:
  - Piaget's play stages linked to his cognitive development stages: functional play, pretend play and games with rules; and Smilansky's additional stage: constructive play.
  - Howes theorised that play also develops socially, including solitary, parallel, social and social pretend play stages.
  - Pretend play includes several stages, including autosymbolic, object substitution and dramatic pretend play.
  - McGhee suggested four humour stages, based on Piaget's cognitive development stages: incongruous actions, incongruous labelling, conceptual incongruity and multiple meanings (puns).
  - Like Howes, Loizou demonstrated humour's social dimensions: violating *others'* expectations and breaking rules.
  - Empirical research supports McGhee's humour stages, but suggests that simpler forms exist earlier on (e.g., funny faces) and that a wider variety of social humour types exist (e.g., making fun of others).
- How children learn to play and joke:
  - Children learn to play and joke through social means, following parents' and other adults' cues (e.g., smiles, laughter) and imitating.
- Benefits of play and humour:
  - Play and humour have several benefits, including encouraging linguistic, social and cognitive development, and mental health.
- Cultural and developmental differences and similarities of play and humour:
  - Play and humour are fairly universal, although some cultural differences exist in the frequency and content of play types.
  - Children with developmental differences engage in play and humour, although sometimes differently to children with typical development (TD).

Further reading

Mireault, G., & Reddy, V. (2016). *Humor in Infants: Developmental and Psychological Perspectives*. Springer.

Smith, P., & Roopnarine, J. (Eds.). (2018). *The Cambridge Handbook of Play: Developmental and Disciplinary Perspectives*. Cambridge University Press.

Useful websites

CBeebies Parenting – How do children learn to play? Six styles of play in early childhood: www.bbc.co.uk/tiny-happy-people/articles/zsc9qyc

This BBC website explores six play stages. It provides information to parents about what to look for and how to encourage each play stage.

References

Bigelow, A., MacLean, K., & Proctor, J. (2004). The role of joint attention in the development of infants' play with objects. *Developmental Science*, *7*(5), 518–526. https://doi.org/10.1111/j.1467-7687.2004.00375.x

Bijvoet-van den Berg, S., & Hoicka, E. (2019). Preschoolers understand and generate pretend actions using object substitution. *Journal of Experimental Child Psychology*, *177*, 313–334. https://doi.org/10.1016/j.jecp.2018.08.008

Burns, S., & Brainerd, C. J. (1979). Effects of constructive and dramatic play on perspective taking in very young children. *Developmental Psychology*, *15*(5), 512–521. https://doi.org/10.1037/0012-1649.15.5.512

Cameron-Faulkner, T., Melville, J., & Gattis, M. (2018). Responding to nature: Natural environments improve parent–child communication. *Journal of Environmental Psychology*, *59*, 9–15. https://doi.org/10.1016/j.jenvp.2018.08.008

Chen, W., Zheng, X., Wu, X., Li, W., Cao, X., Su, Y., & Wang, Y. (2025). Exploring the development of spatial orientation and the cognitive levels of preschoolers during 'three-stage' constructive play. *International Journal of Early Childhood*, 1–30. https://doi.org/10.1007/s13158-025-00420-w

Crawley, S., & Sherrod, K. (1984). Parent–infant play during the first year of life. *Infant Behavior and Development*, *7*(1), 65–75. https://doi.org/10.1016/S0163-6383(84)80023-5

Fanning, P., Sparaci, L., Dissanayake, C., Hocking, D., & Vivanti, G. (2021). Functional play in young children with autism and Williams syndrome: A cross-syndrome comparison. *Child Neuropsychology*, *27*(1), 125–149. https://doi.org/10.1080/09297049.2020.1804846

Farver, J., & Howes, C. (1993). Cultural differences in American and Mexican mother–child pretend play. *Merrill-Palmer Quarterly*, *39*(3), 344–358.

Gonzalez-Sala, F., Gomez-Mari, I., Tarraga-Minguez, R., Vicente-Carvajal, A., & Pastor-Cerezuela, G. (2021). Symbolic play among children with autism spectrum disorder: A scoping review. *Children*, *8*(9), 801. https://doi.org/10.3390/children8090801

Gosso, Y., e Morais, M., & Otta, E. (2007). Pretend play of Brazilian children: A window into different cultural worlds. *Journal of Cross-Cultural Psychology*, *38*(5), 539–558. https://doi.org/10.1177/0022022107305237

Halfon, S., Bekar, Ö., Ababay, S., & Dorlach, G. Ç. (2017). Dyadic mental state talk and sophistication of symbolic play between parents and children with behavioral problems. *Journal of Infant, Child, and Adolescent Psychotherapy*, *16*(4), 291–307. https://doi.org/10.1080/15289168.2017.1370952

Harper, G., Guidubaldi, J., & Kehle, T. (1978). Is academic achievement related to classroom behavior? *The Elementary School Journal*, *78*(3), 202–207.

Hoicka, E., & Akhtar, N. (2011). Preschoolers joke with jokers, but correct foreigners. *Developmental Science*, *14*(4), 848–858. https://doi.org/10.1111/j.1467-7687.2010.01033.x

Hoicka, E., & Akhtar, N. (2012). Early humour production. *British Journal of Developmental Psychology*, *30*(4), 586–603. https://doi.org/10.1111/j.2044-835X.2011.02075.x

Hoicka, E., & Butcher, J. (2016). Parents produce explicit cues which help toddlers distinguish joking and pretending. *Cognitive Science*, *40*(4), 941–971. https://doi.org/10.1111/cogs.12264

Hoicka, E., & Gattis, M. (2008). Do the wrong thing: How toddlers tell a joke from a mistake. *Cognitive Development*, *23*(1), 180–190. https://doi.org/10.1016/j.cogdev.2007.06.001

Hoicka, E., & Gattis, M. (2012). Acoustic differences between humorous and sincere communicative intentions. *British Journal of Developmental Psychology*, *30*(4), 531–549. https://doi.org/10.1111/j.2044-835X.2011.02062.x

Hoicka, E., Jutsum, S., & Gattis, M. (2008). Humor, abstraction, and disbelief. *Cognitive Science*, *32*(6), 985–1002. https://doi.org/10.1080/03640210801981841

Hoicka, E., & Martin, C. (2016). Two-year-olds distinguish pretending and joking. *Child Development*, *87*(3), 916–928. https://doi.org/10.1111/cdev.12526

Hoicka, E., & Prouten, E. (2024). The Early Pretending Survey (EPS): A reliable parent-report measure of pretense type development for 4- to 47-month-olds. *Cognitive Development*, *71*, 101483. https://doi.org/10.1016/j.cogdev.2024.101483

Hoicka, E., Soy Telli, B., Prouten, E., Leckie, G., Browne, W., Mireault, G., & Fox, C. (2022). The Early Humor Survey (EHS): A reliable parent-report measure of humor development from 1 to 47 months. *Behavior Research Methods*, *54*, 1928–1953. https://doi.org/10.3758/s13428-021-01704-4

Hoicka, E., & Wang, S. (2011). Fifteen-month-old infants match vocal cues to intentional actions. *Journal of Cognition and Development*, *12*(3), 299–314. https://doi.org/10.1080/15248372.2010.542215

Holmes, E., & Willoughby, T. (2005). Play behaviour of children with autism spectrum disorders. *Journal of Intellectual and Developmental Disability*, *30*(3), 156–164. https://doi.org/,10.1080/13668250500204034

Howes, C., & Matheson, C. C. (1992). Sequences in the development of competent play with peers – social and social pretend play. *Developmental Psychology*, *28*(5), 961–974. https://doi.org/10.1037//0012-1649.28.5.961

James, L., & Fox, C. (2016). The development of a humor styles questionnaire for younger children. *Humor*, *29*(4), 555–582. https://doi.org/10.1515/humor-2016-0042

James, L., & Fox, C. (2018). Longitudinal associations between younger children's humour styles and psychosocial adjustment. *British Journal of Developmental Psychology*, *36*(4), 589–605. https://doi.org/10.1111/bjdp.12244

Kızıldere, E., Aktan-Erciyes, A., Tahiroğlu, D., & Göksun, T. (2020). A multidimensional investigation of pretend play and language competence: Concurrent and longitudinal relations in preschoolers. *Cognitive Development*, *54*, 100870. https://doi.org/10.1016/j.cogdev.2020.100870

Köymen, B., Schmidt, M., Rost, L., Lieven, E., & Tomasello, M. (2015). Teaching versus enforcing game rules in preschoolers' peer interactions. *Journal of Experimental Child Psychology*, *135*, 93–101. https://doi.org/10.1016/j.jecp.2015.02.005

Lewis, V., Norgate, S., Collis, G., & Reynolds, R. (2000). The consequences of visual impairment for children's symbolic and functional play. *British Journal of Developmental Psychology*, *18*(3), 449–464. https://doi.org/10.1348/026151000165797

Lillard, A., Nishida, T., Massaro, D., Vaish, A., Ma, L., & McRoberts, G. (2007). Signs of pretense across age and scenario. *Infancy*, *11*(1), 1–30. https://doi.org/10.1207/s15327078in1101_1

Loizou, E. (2005). Infant humor: The theory of the absurd and the empowerment theory. *International Journal of Early Years Education*, *13*(1), 43–53. https://doi.org/10.1080/09669760500048329

Luchs, A., & Fikus, M. (2013). A comparative study of active play on differently designed playgrounds. *Journal of Adventure Education & Outdoor Learning*, *13*(3), 206–222. https://doi.org/10.1080/14729679.2013.778784

Malone, M. (2009). Patterns of home- and classroom-based toy play of preschoolers with and without intellectual disabilities. *International Journal of Disability, Development and Education*, *56*(4), 333–347. https://doi.org/10.1080/10349120903306558

Manning, M., & Wainwright, L. (2010). The role of high level play as a predictor social functioning in autism. *Journal of Autism and Developmental Disorders*, *40*, 523–533. https://doi.org/10.1007/s10803-009-0899-9

Marcinowski, E., Nelson, E., Campbell, J., & Michel, G. (2019). The development of object construction from infancy through toddlerhood. *Infancy*, *24*(3), 368–391. https://doi.org/10.1111/infa.12284

McCune, L. (1995). A normative study of representational play in the transition to language. *Developmental Psychology*, *31*(2), 198–206. https://doi.org/10.1037/0012-1649.31.2.198

McCune-Nicolich, L. (1981). Toward symbolic functioning: Structure of early pretend games and potential parallels with language. *Child Development*, *52*(3), 785–797. https://doi.org/10.2307/1129078

McGhee, P. (1979). *Humor: Its Origin and Development*. W. H. Freeman.

Mireault, G., Poutre, M., Sargent-Hier, M., Dias, C., Perdue, B., & Myrick, A. (2012). Humour perception and creation between parents and 3- to 6-month-old infants. *Infant and Child Development*, *21*(4), 338–347. https://doi.org/10.1002/icd.757

Park, J. (2019). The qualities criteria of constructive play and the teacher's role. *TOJET: The Turkish Online Journal of Educational Technology*, *18*(1), 126–132.

Piaget, J. (1952). *Play, Dreams and Imitation in Childhood*. W. W. Norton & Co.

Quinn, S., Donnelly, S., & Kidd, E. (2018). The relationship between symbolic play and language acquisition: A meta-analytic review. *Developmental Review, 49*, 121–135. https://doi.org/10.1016/j.dr.2018.05.005

Reddy, V., Williams, E., & Vaughan, A. (2002). Sharing humour and laughter in autism and Down's syndrome. *British Journal of Psychology, 93*(2), 219–242. https://doi.org/10.1348/000712602162553

Rubin, K., Maioni, T., & Hornung, M. (1976). Free play behaviors in middle- and lower-class preschoolers: Parten and Piaget revisited. *Child Development, 47*(2), 414–419. https://doi.org/10.2307/1128796

Russ, S. (2016). Pretend play: Antecedent of adult creativity. *New Directions for Child and Adolescent Development, 151*, 21–32. https://doi.org/10.1002/cad. 20154

Shim, S., Herwig, J., & Shelley, M. (2001). Preschoolers' play behaviors with peers in classroom and playground settings. *Journal of Research in Childhood Education, 15*(2), 149–163. https://doi.org/10.1080/02568540109594956

Shultz, T. (1974). Development of the appreciation of riddles. *Child Development, 45*(1), 100–105. https://doi.org/10.2307/1127755

Smilansky, S. (1968). *The Effects of Sociodramatic Play on Disadvantaged Preschool Children.* Wiley.

Smits-van der Nat, M., van der Wilt, F., Meeter, M., & van der Veen, C. (2024). The value of pretend play for social competence in early childhood: A meta-analysis. *Educational Psychology Review, 36*, 46. https://doi.org/10.1007/s10648-024-09884-z

Soy Telli, B., & Hoicka, E. (2024). Testing the effectiveness of a social cognition training program on preschoolers' social cognition and humor understanding. *The American Journal of Psychology, 137*(4), 375–392. https://doi.org/10.5406/19398298.137.4.03

Sung, J., & Hsu, H. (2009). Korean mothers' attention regulation and referential speech: Associations with language and play in 1-year-olds. *International Journal of Behavioral Development, 33*(5), 430–439. https://doi.org/10.1177/0165025409338443

Tamis-LeMonda, C., Bornstein, M., Cyphers, L., Toda, S., & Ogino, M. (1992). Language and play at one year: A comparison of toddlers and mothers in the United States and Japan. *International Journal of Behavioral Development, 15*(1), 19–42. https://doi.org/10.1177/016502549201500102

Walka, H., Triana, N., Jahari, A., Husaini, M., & Pollitt, E. (2000). Effects of an energy and micronutrient supplement on play behavior in undernourished children in Indonesia. *European Journal of Clinical Nutrition, 54*(2), S91–S106. https://doi.org/10.1038/sj.ejcn.1601010

Williams, E., Reddy, V., & Costall, A. (2001). Taking a closer look at functional play in children with autism. *Journal of Autism and Developmental Disorders, 312*, 67–77. https://doi.org/10.1023/A:1005665714197

Wu, C., Tseng, L., An, C., Chen, H., Chan, Y., Shih, C., & Zhuo, S. (2014). Do individuals with autism lack a sense of humor? A study of humor comprehension, appreciation, and styles among high school students with autism. *Research in Autism Spectrum Disorders, 8*(10), 1386–1393. https://doi.org/10.1016/j.rasd.2014.07.006

Wu, S. (2014). Practical and conceptual aspects of children's play in Hong Kong and German kindergartens. *Early Years, 34*(1), 49–66. https://doi.org/10.1080/09575146.2013.818936

Zelazo, P., & Kearsley, R. (1980). The emergence of functional play in infants: Evidence for a major cognitive transition. *Journal of Applied Developmental Psychology,* *1*(2), 95–117. https://doi.org/10.1016/0193-3973(80)90002-7

Ziv, A. (1983). The influence of humorous atmosphere on divergent thinking. *Contemporary Educational Psychology, 8*(1), 68–75. https://doi.org/10.1016/0361-476x(83)90035-8

Index

Page numbers in *italics* refer to figures; page numbers in **bold** refer to tables.